Language in Time

OXFORD STUDIES IN SOCIOLINGUISTICS
Edward Finegan, *General Editor*

Editorial Advisory Board
Douglas Biber   Suzanne Romaine
Alessandro Duranti   Deborah Tannen
John R. Rickford

Locating Dialect in Discourse
The Language of Honest Men and Bonnie Lasses in Ayr
RONALD K. S. MACAULAY

English in Its Social Contexts
Essays in Historical Sociolinguistics
EDITED BY TIM W. MACHAN AND CHARLES T. SCOTT

Coherence in Psychotic Discourse
BRANCA TELLES RIBEIRO

Sociolinguistic Perspectives on Register
EDITED BY DOUGLAS BIBER AND EDWARD FINEGAN

Gender and Conversational Interaction
EDITED BY DEBORAH TANNEN

Therapeutic Ways with Words
KATHLEEN WARDEN FERRARA

Sociolinguistic Perspectives
Papers on Language in Society, 1959–1994
CHARLES FERGUSON
EDITED BY THOM HUEBNER

The Linguistic Individual
Self-Expression in Language and Linguistics
BARBARA JOHNSTONE

The Discourse of Classified Advertising
Exploring the Nature of Linguistic Simplicity
PAUL BRUTHIAUX

Queerly Phrased
Language, Gender, and Sexuality
EDITED BY ANNA LIVIA AND KIRA HALL

Claiming Power in Doctor-Patient Talk
NANCY AINSWORTH-VAUGHN

Kids Talk
Strategic Language Use in Later Childhood
EDITED BY SUSAN HOYLE AND CAROLYN ADGER

Talking about Treatment
Recommendations for Breast Cancer Adjuvant Treatment
FELICIA D. ROBERTS

Language in Time
The Rhythm and Tempo of Spoken Interaction
PETER AUER, ELIZABETH COUPER-KUHLEN AND FRANK MÜLLER

Language in Time

The Rhythm and Tempo of
Spoken Interaction

PETER AUER
ELIZABETH COUPER-KUHLEN
FRANK MÜLLER

New York   Oxford
Oxford University Press
1999

Oxford University Press

Oxford New York
Athens Auckland Bangkok Bogotá Buenos Aires Calcutta
Cape Town Chennai Dar es Salaam Delhi Florence Hong Kong Istanbul
Karachi Kuala Lumpur Madrid Melbourne Mexico City Mumbai
Nairobi Paris São Paulo Singapore Taipei Tokyo Toronto Warsaw

and associated companies in
Berlin Ibadan

Copyright © 1999 by Peter Auer, Elizabeth Couper-Kuhlen, Frank Müller

Published by Oxford University Press, Inc.
198 Madison Avenue, New York, New York 10016

Oxford is a registered trademark of Oxford University Press.

All rights reserved. No part of this publication may be reproduced,
stored in a retrieval system, or transmitted, in any form or by any means,
electronic, mechanical, photocopying, recording or otherwise,
without the prior permission of Oxford University Press.

Library of Congress Cataloging-in-Publication Data
Auer, J. C. P.
Language in time : the rhythm and tempo of spoken interaction /
Peter Auer, Elizabeth Couper-Kuhlen, Frank Müller.
    p. cm.—(Oxford studies in sociolinguistics)
Includes bibliographical references and index.
ISBN 0-19-510928-7
1. Language and languages—Rhythm.   2. Tempo (Phonetics)
3. Conversation analysis.   I. Couper-Kuhlen, Elizabeth.
II. Müller, Frank.   III. Title.   IV. Series.
P311.A9 1999
414'.6—dc21   98-20722

9 8 7 6 5 4 3 2 1

Printed in the United States of America
on acid-free paper

PREFACE

The research reported in this book was made possible by a grant to the first author and to Aldo di Luzio from the Deutsche Forschungsgemeinschaft (Au 72–3, 1987–1993), which we gratefully acknowledge. Our colleague Aldo di Luzio has contributed substantially to the success of the project, particularly its Italian parts, and we wish to express our gratitude to him here.

We would also like to thank Marcello Panese (Lecce), who participated in the research on Italian telephone conversations reported in chapter 5, and Margret Selting, who commented extensively on a previous version of the manuscript. In addition, we are indebted to John Gumperz, Fred Erickson and Susanne Uhmann, all of whom contributed to the project in various ways.

Although this research grew out of intensive joint collaboration over a period of several years, the following authors are primarily responsible for the chapters indicated: Peter Auer for chapters 1, 5 and 8, Elizabeth Couper-Kuhlen for chapters 2, 3 and 4, Frank Müller for chapters 6 and 7.

Hamburg, Konstanz and Frankfurt   P. A.
November 1997   E. C.-K.
                                            F. E. M.

CONTENTS

Transcription Conventions ix

1 The Study of Rhythm: Retemporalizing the Detemporalized Object of Linguistic Research 3

2 Hearing and Notating Conversational Rhythm 35

3 Rhythm and Conversational Turn Taking in English 56

4 Rhythm and Preference Organization in English 92

5 Rhythm in Telephone Closings: An Analysis of Italian and German Data 116

6 Rhythm in Turn Construction: Scansions in Italian Conversation 152

7 Rhythm and Performance: An Analysis of an Italian Radio Phone-in Program 172

8 A Summary and Some Conclusions 201

Notes 209

References 221

Index 233

TRANSCRIPTION CONVENTIONS

((   ))   Transcriber comment
(   )   Transcriber doubt

Stress

'   Strong phonetic prominence
,   Weak phonetic prominence
"   Extra strong phonetic prominence

Pitch

.   Final falling pitch to low
;   Final falling pitch to non-low
?   Final rising pitch to high
,   Final rising pitch to non-high
–   Final level pitch
!   Final falling pitch from high, emphatic

Loudness

{f}   Forte up to next intonation phrase boundary
{ff}   Fortissimo up to next intonation phrase boundary
{p}   Piano up to next intonation phrase boundary
{pp}   Pianissimo up to next intonation phrase boundary

Length

:, ::, :::   Sound or syllable lengthening

Rhythm and tempo

```
non-proportional font
```
Rhythmically analyzed passages

```
(a) /'Jack and   /
    /'Jill; went /
    /'up the     /
    /'hill; to   /
    /'fetch a    /
    /'pail of    /
    /'water      /
```
Regular isochronous rhythm

```
(b) /'Jack and   /
    /'Jill; went/
    /'up the   /
    /'hill; to/
```
Faster tempo
```
    /'fetch a    /
    /'pail of    /
    /'water.
```
Slower tempo

```
(c) /'Jack and Jill; went   /
    /'up the hill; to       /
    /'fetch a //'pail of    /
    /'water.
```
Doubled tempo

```
(d)      /'Jack and   /
         /'Jill; went/
    /'up the/
         /'hill;
```
Syncopated beat

```
(e) /'Jack and   /
    /'Jill;      /
    /^     went /
    /'up the    /
    /'hill; to
```
Silent beat

```
(f)      /'Jack and   /
         /'Jill; went /
         /'up the     /
         /'hill; to   /
    /'fetch a    /
    /'pail of    /
    /'water.
```
Early beat, new (faster) rhythm

TRANSCRIPTION CONVENTIONS

(g) /'Jack and   /
    /'Jill; went/
    /'up the   /
    /'hill; to   /
        /'fetch a   /   Late beat, new (slower) rhythm
        /'pail of   /
        /'water.

(h)   /'Jack and   /
       /'Jill; went/
       /'up the   /
       /'hill to
  'fetch a pail of water.   Early beat, no further rhythm

(i) /'Jack and   /
    /'Jill; went/
    /'up the   /
    /'hill; to
        'fetch a pail of water.   Late beat, no further rhythm

Pause

(.)	Micropause
(-)	Short silent pause
(0.2)	Measured silent pause
.h, .hh	Inbreath
h, hh	Outbreath
?	Glottal stop

Turn Taking

[[	Simultaneous start or overlapping speech
=	Latching between two turns or two words within a turn

Language in Time

1

The Study of Rhythm

*Retemporalizing the Detemporalized
Object of Linguistic Research*

Rhythm is one of the most pervasive aspects of the human condition; it is in the world around us and in the world within us, in our bodies and our minds, our living and our thinking. This book argues that human language, quite predictably, is deeply rhythmic as well. In addition, we try to show that the rhythm of verbal interaction is synchronized between co-participants and, at the same time, *achieved* by co-participants. That is, the degree and kind of rhythmicity in everyday language may vary: Interactional rhythms may be shared or idiosyncratic, they may emerge or disintegrate, become more or less distinct. Finally, and most important, we argue that interactants' use of rhythmic structures is an important means for making interaction work.

Despite the obvious relevance of rhythm and tempo to verbal interaction, the linguistic textbooks we have been trained on for generations—from Hockett's *Course* (1958) through Lyons' *Linguistics* (1968) to Fromkin & Rodman's *Introduction* (1988)—have had nothing to say about them. In this introductory chapter, the *detemporalization* implied by this neglect of rhythm in the study of language will be related to how linguists theorize about their subject. Some of the ways in which linguists have occasionally worked with abstract (virtual) rhythms instead are mentioned, as are a number of attempts to reintroduce the notions of time and rhythm into research on verbal interaction outside linguistics 'proper', particularly in psycholinguistics and linguistic anthropology/microethnography. The final part sets out our basic aims and introduces concepts relevant for the subsequent chapters of the book.

1. The detemporalization of language: A brief excursion into the history of linguistics

Rhythms—patterned recurrences of events in time—form a large part of our lives. The alternation of night and day, of the seasons, of the phases of the moon, determine fundamentally the world we live in, and indeed the lives of most organisms in this world: the rhythms of the body (our heartbeat, breathing, hormonal cycles) as well as its basic needs (hunger, thirst, sleep) shape our experience of ourselves. The most automatic, basic human movement patterns, walking or running—and even the acquired and more complex movements of swimming, rowing or skiing—imply rhythmicity. Rhythmic movements provide comfort to the newborn baby and self-induced stimulation to the autistic child. Our minds and our perception rely on rhythmic patterns to such a degree that physically identical series of stimuli are quasi automatically heard or seen as rhythmically grouped, and that information is better understood and recalled when it comes in rhythmic chunks. The "process of civilization" (N. Elias) is in essential ways a process of imposing sociocultural rhythms on our lives, from the strict timing of life under the Benedictine rule up to modern working hours. And some of the most genuine and widespread cultural achievements of mankind (music, dance, poetry) are inextricably linked to rhythm. It seems in a way that the old *variatio delectat* is even more true when it is understood as *alternatio delectat*.

Yet, although a description of human walking would hardly be imaginable without a rhythmic component, the description of human language apparently is, as the nontreatment of this subject in many modern textbooks and introductions implies. This is so for reasons linked in subtle ways to our folk and scientific thinking about language, reasons that seem so natural that mentioning them might appear trivial; yet they have far-reaching consequences. Note first that—as surprising as it may seem—the evanescence of language in time, its one-dimensional nature, is part of our folk theorizing ('what's said is said') as well as our scientific thinking about language. (And this is still true today, some 1,000 years after the invention of a "technology" (Goody), which has neutralized the time-bound one-dimensionality of oral language, writing.) Thus, Hockett (1963) lists "rapid fading" among his "design features" of human language (i.e., among its definitional criteria); this, however, did not result in any serious consideration of time-specific or rhythm-specific features of language in his "Course" or other similar books. What sounds like a contradiction at first is easily explained by the equally commonplace conceptual distinction between language as a 'tool' to think and communicate thoughts with and the in-time discursive use of this 'tool' on the other. This distinction is so deeply rooted in the folk ideology of language that it is part of the everyday metalinguistic vocabulary of all Western languages; see distinctions such as *speech* versus *language, langue* versus *parole, Sprache* versus *Sprechen (Rede)*.

Those parts of language that can be described in grammars are abstracted out of the flow of linguistic communicative behavior in time.

The distinction between language as a tool and its usage is inseparable from a third metalinguistic presupposition of Western thinking about language, which is its "referential-and-predicational" (Silverstein 1992) bias: the focus on grammar as a tool for communication goes hand in hand with a focus on the (allegedly) stable referential functions of language as grammar, excluding "basic personality and . . . emotional orientation" (Hockett 1958:144). This implies the equation of grammar with repeatable and, therefore, time-neutral (detemporalizable and detemporalized) *signum-denotatum* relationships (or, to use a substitute neutral to this argument, *signifiant-signifié* relationships). It is this semantically neutral repeatability which is used to justify separating language from speech. Rhythm and tempo therefore not only elude the referential-and-predicational approach to grammatical description because it is difficult or impossible to define their denotations—in fact, they seem to index more than they denote—but even more important, they elude this description by the mere fact of being ephemeral in nature.

A fourth component of the Western folk ideology of language which has directly entered into linguistic thinking is its decontextualization, including in its broadest sense not only the exclusion of all those aspects of language that can only be appreciated when a particular instance of linguistic praxis is seen or heard in its linguistic cotext and with reference to its context of situation but also the embeddedness of this praxis in a particular 'culture'. Because contexts can only be construed as emergent in time (as we argue later), the decontextualized view of language must rid itself of time as a constituent feature. The detemporalization of language *qua* grammar is thus only one aspect of the more general decontextualization of language, which, in turn, has been made possible by the in-time stability of language as rendered in *writing*, a two-dimensional, preservable object resistant to time.[1]

Although the metaphorical distinction between language as a tool (or, in more academic linguistic parlances, a 'system of semiotic relationships', a 'cognitive ability', a 'collection of habits') and speech as its usage seems plausible enough at first sight, progress in linguistic research has taught us that, to pursue the metaphor, it is impossible to account for the 'meaning' of the components of this tool unless it is observed while being used to make real-world things. In fact, the distinction between linguistic praxis and language as the system that informs it collapses at precisely those points where the meaning of a sentence cannot be calculated, according to the so-called Fregean principle, from the meaning of its lexical components. Even the referential-and-predicational view acknowledges this collapse in the case of deixis, a referential process that hinges on contextual parameters. Deixis destroys the view of language as a context-independent reservoir of stable *signum-denotatum* relationships. At first sight, however, it does not seem to destroy its independence from time: When the context of a sentence is construed as a constellation of 'index points' (including a 'time point'), referential meaning does not depend on emergent time, and hence, language appears to be separable from it. Only on second thought does it become clear that including context into linguistic analysis—even the referential-and-predicational type—also unavoidably brings back into linguistics the unilinearity of language in time: Standard example sentences from formal pragmatics such as *Don't shoot now, but now, now and now* (Levinson 1983:95) cannot be analyzed unless the changing nature of context even within sentence boundaries is taken into account. More hermeneutically inclined, interpretive approaches to language would of course enlarge the field of indexical relationships between linguistic signs and elements of their context beyond these simple cases of deixis. In the end, the metaphor of language as a tool used to convey (denotational) meaning turns out to be basically flawed, although it continues to thrive in folk theories of language and, in various disguises, in linguistic theory: The tool has no existence without the praxis in which it is used, and this praxis unfolds in time. Given the fact that the neglect of rhythm is linked to some of the most basic presuppositions of Western linguistic ideology, it appears less than surprising that Meschonnic (1982), one of the most important French critics of atemporal linguistics, should exclaim: *qu'on ait pu être si longtemps indifférent à la voix, à ne voir que des structures, des schémas, des arbres, toute une spatialisation muette du langage* ('that one could have been indifferent to the voice for so long, seeing only structures, schemas, trees, a whole mute spatialization of language') (6). But by insisting on the temporal unfolding of language, by retemporalizing it, rhythm can indeed *mettre certains concepts de la linguistique en crise* ('create a crisis for certain linguistic concepts') (7).

The division of language into grammar and speech was crucial for the establishment of modern linguistics as structural linguistics in the first decades of this century. The work of 19th-century philologists (including Indo-European scholars) had been based exclusively on historical texts, on written and *eo ipso* delinearized/ detemporalized language, but nonetheless 'real' documents, each bringing along a particular co- and context.[2] It was with the emergence of what de Saussure later called synchronic description that the question of how the subject matter of linguistic research should be defined with regard to context and time was raised at all. At the beginning of the century it was by no means clear that this question should be answered in the negative (i.e., that linguists should be exclusively concerned with an abstract system of signs, but not with speech in context). On the contrary, the Humboldtian tradition, according to which language was inseparable from thinking (*Die Sprache ist das bildende Organ des Gedankens*; von Humboldt 1836), had gained impetus from progress in the new empirical discipline of psychology. Important work outside the Neogrammarian school, in particular Georg von der Gabelentz and Wilhelm Wundt in Germany, supported by developments in phonetics (E. Sievers), led to an integrative view of language that combined the structure of grammar with the act of speaking, tradition with performance, stability with variation (both of the diachronic and the dialectal kind).[3]

Von der Gabelentz (1901), for instance, who separated very clearly *Rede* ('speech'), *Sprachvermögen* ('language capacity') and *Einzelsprache* ('individual language') from one another (reminiscent of but prior to de Saussure's distinction between *parole, langage* and *langue*, as Coseriu 1969 reminds us), nevertheless included a long chapter entitled "Inhalt und Form der Rede" ('content and form of speech') in his *summum opus, Die Sprachwissenschaft*, where word-order problems (seen as problems in the linearization of language in time) and prosody are treated at some length as the two *ursprüngliche Mittel sprachlicher Formung* ('genuine methods of linguistic form giving', 376). To him, both word order and rhythm are techniques to structure information:

> It is true that speech moves forward linearly, ideas follow one another. . . . But it is not a straight line, and not an uninterrupted one either. Sometimes modulations of sound and tone indicate a climax, rough or mellow forms of various kinds; sometimes rhythm, whether fast or slow, fluent or cut off, whether with longer or shorter pauses, indicates the degree to which the parts of speech are to be connected to or divided from each other. (380; our translation)[4]

Here, rhythm and word order are seen as part of *Rede* ('speech'); yet they are also structured means to achieve linguistic functions which, however, are not on the level of denotational meaning. Instead, they convey emotional information on the one hand and 'connect and divide' linguistic materials on the other. Neither pragmatic nor emotional aspects of language are excluded.

The most detailed treatment at the time of what today might be called discourse prosody is found in Wilhelm Wundt's *Völkerpsychologie*.[5] Similar to von der Gabelentz in this respect, Wundt deals with word order and linguistic rhythm/ intonation in two successive chapters. He goes further than von der Gabelentz, however, when he introduces linguistic rhythm by outlining its psychological foundations. Building on gestalt-psychological principles, he develops basic insights into the perception and construction of rhythm which remain valid up to the present (see Fraisse 1974).

Apart from these comprehensive and monumental works on language, other authors published on aspects of speech and communication with a more restricted purpose in mind. In Germany, books on discourse (such as Wunderlich's seminal *Unsere Umgangsprache in der Eigenart ihrer Satzfügung*, 1894) and on the psychology of language use (e.g., Wegener's *Untersuchungen*, 1885) only mention prosody in passing. A systematic treatment of rhythm is given in Saran's *Deutsche Verslehre* (1907), however—a book with an inappropriate title, as half of it deals with rhythm (or, in Saran's words, "accent") in ordinary speech. Saran tries to account for the relative "weight" of each syllable in a spoken text depending on its position in a rich hierarchy of prosodic domains, in a fashion similar to recent work on Metrical Phonology (see discussion later).[6]

Rhythm remained a fashionable topic until the 1930s, particularly in speculative philosophy and the theory of arts; in the German *Rhythmusbewegung* ('rhythm movement'), most prominently articulated by Ludwig Klages (1934), an influential distinction was introduced between *meter* (*Takt* ['cadence'], the mechanical, machine-like recurrence of elements in time) and *rhythm*, the creative, even ecstatic, individual performance overlaying it.[7] However, this fascination with rhythm, which was from the very beginning associated with a neoromantic, anti-intellectual glorification of the body and/or nature and was in danger of being absorbed by all kinds of *Weltanschauungen*, does not seem to have affected more than the periphery of linguistics. For instance, Bally's lecture at the important 1er Congrès du

Rythme had the promising title *Le rythme linguistique et sa signification sociale* (Bally 1926), but it must have been quite disappointing to the 'rhythmologists' at Geneva: Structural thinking, which focused on virtual instead of actual rhythms, had already taken over.

All in all, there can be no doubt that time-related, prosodic aspects of language were an issue around the turn of the century. The development of instrumental phonetics and recording technology were not advanced enough to enable proponents to proceed to the prosodic analysis of actual spoken texts or discourse.[8] In fact, it was often practical, not theoretical, problems that excluded work on actual data. Today we can observe the opposite tendency: whereas the machinery to deal with spoken language is easily available, interest in prosody[9] is often restricted for theoretical reasons to the analysis of abstract systems. Is there any way to account for this shift in the history of linguistics?

If there is any legitimate place at which to pinpoint the shift toward the structuralist detemporalization of language, it is tempting to choose the treatment of the *syntagme* in the *Cours de linguistique générale* by de Saussure (and his followers). It is here that one can observe the in-time linearity of language being transformed into grammatical, timeless contiguity. The transformation proceeded, however, slowly.

In contrast to the works by von der Gabelentz or Wundt, the *Cours* does not contain a chapter on rhythm or prosody in general. This is in line with de Saussure's strict separation of a *linguistique de la parole* from a *linguistique de la langue*. Language as *langue* is a purely abstract system of relationships (*rapports*).[10] Among these, de Saussure makes his famous distinction between *rapports syntagmatiques* and *rapports associatifs*, later called "syntagmatic" versus "paradigmatic."[11] But although the latter clearly belong to language in the sense of *langue*, de Saussure's (1972) description of the former points to a real-time relationship of sequentiality in a number of ways and is for this reason deeply ambiguous:

- The syntagmatic axis is located in discourse, not in grammar; thus, the syntagm is a result of the fact that *dans le discours, les mots contractent entre eux, en vertu de leur enchaînement, des rapports fondés sur le caractère linéaire de la langue* ('in discourse words enter into relations with one another based on the linear character of language') (170). In contrast, relations on the paradigmatic axis are *en dehors du discours* ('outside of discourse'), *dans la mémoire* ('in memory'), *leur siège est dans le cerveau* ('their location is in the brain') (1972:171).
- Paradigmatic relationships relate linguistic structures to each other *in absentia, dans une série mnémonique virtuelle* ('in a virtual mnemonic series') (171), whereas the syntagmatic relationship is realized *in praesentia, il repose sur deux ou plusieurs termes également présents dans une série effective* ('it is based on two or more terms equally present in a real series') (171).
- Because the grouping of linguistic elements in time is not completely determined, or even not determined at all, by grammar at the level of syntax or below (see de Saussure's discussion of *ad hoc* compounding) but is open to the speaker's decision, and because this is precisely one of the criteria

according to which *parole* is delimited from *langue*, the syntagmatic relationship should belong, at least partly, to the former and not to the latter.[12]

It should be added—if only in passing—that Jakobson (1971), in his famous reformulation of de Saussure's distinction, which relies on the dichotomies "combination/context" vs. "selection" and "contiguity" vs. "similarity," deliberately retains the ambiguity in the notion of syntagma between context within the code and context within the message and uses it for his own purposes. However, structuralist practice, including many textbooks (for instance, Lyons 1968), has tended to eliminate the latter aspect entirely. For all nonlexicalized combinations of linguistic elements, particularly on the level of syntax and text structure, this alters the notion of syntagm fundamentally. It is now turned from an *in praesentia* coexistence or linearization in the speech chain (which de Saussure first had in mind, and which remains present in Jakobson's notion of 'syntagmatic') into a purely abstract contiguity/adjacency of abstract grammatical slots (categories, labeled 'nodes'), not in time but in grammar or 'competence'. All time-related aspects of language due to the unilinearity of the *chaîne parlée* are eliminated in this process.

2. Reflexes of time in detemporalized linguistics: Abstract rhythms

Yet reflexes of time-related linguistic processes have remained in various guises within the domain of structuralist and poststructuralist generative research. This applies first and foremost to lexicalized prosodic features such as word stress and tone. As part of the lexicon, word stress is mentally stored information and is clearly part of *langue*. In languages such as English, German or Italian its placement is almost exclusively governed by grammatical or lexical rules and it is only marginally at the speaker's disposition. This is not to say that rhythmic considerations, which by definition hinge on repeated patterns (rhythm can never be established by a single accent, virtual or actual), do not play a role within the lexicon: In more complex, multisyllable lexical entries, rhythmic weight is assigned on various levels and constraints on rhythmic well-formedness—avoidance of 'stress clash' and the like—may play a role for the distribution of lower-level weight (below primary stress). However, what has been exclusively analyzed with great sophistication in Metrical Phonology[13] during the past ten years has been *abstract* rhythms which may or may not be realized as such in actual speech. (In fact, how abstract and actual rhythms relate to each other has remained largely outside this research interest.)

Metrical analysis has been extended to units larger than the word as well (up to the sentence), although these tend to leave the domain of the referential-and-predicational approach to language called 'grammar' (recall de Saussure). This extension has several predecessors, most notably the structuralist, especially tagmemic treatment of prosodic features as quasi-phonemic units ('pitch phonemes' and 'juncture phonemes'). These early attempts failed for two reasons: First, they treated suprasegmental linguistic information in a fashion parallel to segmental information, which led to formally inadequate representations; and second, they treated prosodic phenomena on the sentence level as if they had a distinctive function just as segmental phonemes have for lexical items. But whereas structuralist phonemic analysis is perfectly adequate for segmental phonemes, which keep linguistic entities distinct on the referential-and-predicational level, it is quite incapable of capturing the 'meaning' of prosodic features beyond the word: This meaning is in large part delimitative or appellative, not representational, to use Trubetzkoy's phonological adaptation of Bühler's terminology.[14]

Recent advances in prosodic description within the detemporalized framework of language as grammar (Metrical and Autosegmental Phonology) have gone considerably beyond older approaches in overcoming drawbacks of the first type; that is, they have resulted in more advanced and more adequate descriptions of the form of prosodic representations within and beyond the word. However, they have not been able, nor have they even wanted, to address the question of the meaning of prosodic form beyond its representational function. From what has been said in the preceding section about the consequences of detemporalizing language, the reasons for this are immediately obvious: Because detemporalized language is also decontextualized language, those aspects of meaning that are not on the referential-and-predicational level will necessarily eschew analysis. But this is precisely how prosody beyond the word is typically meaningful in the first place: not by taking part in the symbolization (in the Peircian sense) of reality, as phonemes do via their distinctiveness—although this may of course also happen, for instance, in the famous category switches such as Engl. *'rebel : re'bel*—but by indexing (and/or iconicizing) it. Thus, any approach to language that restricts itself to abstract prosodic patterns devoid of contextual embedding will necessarily be unable to capture and analyze its meaning. This is true even for the crudest aspects of prosody (e.g., the placement of sentence stress in English—and many other languages). In one way or another, theories of sentence stress all rely on the idea that phonetic prominence marks or lies within units of particular 'relevance' in the utterance or sentence, a part of the sentence that may be called its 'focus', while less relevant ('old', 'known' or 'thematic') information appears in the nonfocal, 'topic' or 'background' part. Or, seen the other way, that it is by placement of phonetic prominences within the sentence/utterance/intonation unit that the speaker indicates how the information marked by such means is to be interpreted in a given context. This aspect of prosody then has the function of guiding the listener's attention within the utterance. In doing so, it constructs, relies on and is compatible with certain contexts. In short, it indexes but never symbolizes these contexts.

As far as the more narrow field of rhythm is concerned, Metrical Phonology restricts itself to building an algorithm for deriving abstract weight patterns in and above the word. Although this is only possible for a given context, the actual 'interface' between context and utterance is not focused on, for the reasons outlined previously. Selkirk's now classic *Phonology and Syntax* (1984), for example, presents an elegant but purely formal, nonsemantic and nonpragmatic algorithm for English rhythm.[15] Being process-oriented but lacking any interest in the emergence of rhythmic structures in actual time, it builds metrical grids by assigning demibeats or beats on various prosodic (or grammatical) levels, starting with the syllable and ending with the utterance. On the basis of the lexical stress patterns involved,

The Study of Rhythm

the algorithm specifies the metrical structure of the sentence, depending on morphonological, morphological and syntactic information. However, Selkirk argues that the output of this algorithm needs to be controlled by a filter which makes it conform with a teleology of optimal rhythmization, where optimal rhythms are those alternating between strong and weak elements. This teleology is implemented by so-called rules of rhythmic euphony, which may shift (or delete) rhythmic beats when two of them collide within the phrase; they resolve "stress clashes" and they add rhythmic beats when there are too many weak elements between two strong ones. Euphonic rules are optional; if, however, a stress clash occurs and no shift/deletion occurs to resolve it, pauses (silent beats) or lengthening must compensate. Silent beats are also added at the boundaries of syntactic constituents. Thus the sentence *Mary finished her Russian novel* has the following metrical structure without silent beats according to Selkirk:

```
                            x
   x         x          x   x
   x         x          x   x
   x  x   x  x      x   x   x   x   x
   Mary   finished her   Russian novel
```

Yet the 'correct', euphonic metrical representation requires the addition of a varying number of silent beats at phrase and sentence boundaries:

```
                            x
   x              x         x           x
   x              x         x           x
   x  xxxxx x    xx  x x x   x x   x xxxxx
   Mary     finished  her Russian  novel
```

It should be remembered that these structures represent abstract (virtual), not actual rhythms. They are assumed to be part of grammar, just like the rules of syntax. Their well-formedness is exclusively controlled by the competence of the speaker/hearer (or writer/researcher). Yet intuitions are sometimes on shaky ground when it comes to judging the necessity to delete or shift a beat, to add a compensatory (abstract!) silence when beat clashes have to be resolved or to mark the boundaries of constituents by pausing. (Especially in the latter case, Selkirk's beat additions appear idiosyncratic.) This, of course, confirms de Saussure's uncertainty as to the proper alignment of the syntagm with *langue* or *parole*: Nowhere is the syntagmatic axis of language so far from the grammatical system than in prosodic details like those of rhythmic euphony. Accordingly, normative metalinguistic knowledge is weak or absent. And when the predictions that can be derived from Selkirk's work or that of others are tested on the basis of actual speech data (a 'test' that is, however, antagonistic to the very idea of detemporalized, abstract rhythmic research), they quickly reveal themselves to be unsupported by speakers' actual behavior: Thus, Couper-Kuhlen (1992a) shows that stress shift is not restricted to the phonological phrase and that there is no compensation for lack of stress shift through compensatory lengthening via pause, both findings which are in disagreement with Metrical Phonology.

Not in contradiction to but rather in accordance with the exclusive (post-)structuralist interest in abstract or virtual rhythms, metrical theory has produced new insights into literary metrics (see Kiparsky et al. 1989), thus pursuing a marginal yet continuous tradition that has survived the general detemporalization of language (see early structural work by Jakobson 1923 and de Groot 1932). Rhythm has become *un accessoire poétique* ('a poetic accompaniment'; Meschonnic 1982:9); it is relegated to the domain of unusual, nonmundane language, which assumes meaning through rhythm to the degree that this meaning is expelled from ordinary language. The importance of literary meter underlines the irrelevance of rhythm for linguistic praxis in general.

The principled antagonism to data-based research in generative phonology and in particular in metrical theory does not apply to the second tradition of linguistic research, in which time-related phenomena (or rather, their abstract reflexes) have survived the structuralist detemporalization of language. In the Firthian tradition, Halliday and other British linguists have pursued a continuous interest in prosody. The approach has been comprehensive: It has included nonreferential, indexical meanings (see Crystal 1969), at least partly utterance-(instead of sentence-)related, close to the practical needs of language teaching (see Halliday 1970), but noninteractive (i.e., not related to conversational data) and largely prescriptive.[16] The merits of the Firthian tradition for research on intonation are not at issue here;[17] with regard to rhythm, however, it is not unfair to say that the interactional relevance of this prosodic parameter has not been seen or appreciated in it. The usual remarks on the rhythm of English are of a purely formal nature and tend to be confined to the problem of isochrony; the function or 'meaning' of rhythm, of arhythmicity, of rhythmic shifts and breaks is not taken into account. (The same, incidentally, applies to Kenneth Pike's [1945] work on prosody.)

An explanation for the way rhythm is treated in the Firthian tradition may be the impact phonetician David Abercrombie has had on it. Abercrombie (1964) describes the rhythm of English as follows:

> English utterances may be considered as being divided by the isochronous beat of the stress pulse into feet of (approximately) even length. Each foot starts with a stress and contains everything that follows that stress up to, but not including, the next stress. 'This is the 'house that 'Jack 'built has therefore four feet. (217)

Rhythm in English is equated with isochrony; isochrony, in turn, is defined strictly as the regular succession in time of all stressed syllables that occur in a particular stretch of speech (i.e., by equal duration of the feet in an utterance). (The only exception Abercrombie allows is that of a silent stress within the pattern.) Put somewhat differently, every phonetic prominence or stress has to be a *beat* in the rhythmic pattern. Because no stressed syllable can occur 'off beat', the criterion for rhythmicity becomes extremely restrictive. Consequently, subsequent phonetic research has found only short stretches of isochronous speech; in particular, no isochronous patterns are observed beyond the turn of a single speaker, and in fact, not even beyond sentence or intonation-unit boundaries.[18] We believe that interturn uptake of prosodic structures (i.e., rhythmic synchronization between participants) cannot be captured in this approach to rhythm. Adherence to an Abercrombian definition of rhythm, together with its lack of empirical basis in actual speech data, has hindered progress in understanding interactional rhythm in the Firth/Halliday tradition.

In sum, structural and poststructural—including generative—research on rhythm has restricted its object of study to abstract or virtual rhythms instead of actually performed ones. The difference between this approach and the one advocated here is similar to the difference between reading a piece of music and playing it. Quite obviously, "performing the music actually is a fundamentally different sort of activity from reading it over at a glance" (Erickson & Shultz 1982:98). We have argued that the prevalent restriction of linguistic thinking to abstract/virtual rhythms is congruent with modern Western language ideology, which prefers "segmental, referential, relatively presupposing indexes" to "nonsegmental, non-referential, relatively creative formal features," which have no "metapragmatic reality" for the user (Silverstein 1976:49).[19]

3. Language-related rhythm research outside linguistics, part I: Psychology

Outside linguistics, psychology has contributed to an understanding of the real-time deployment of language in three areas. The first, which deals with language as one among other motor and perceptual rhythms, involves research on the general gestalt-psychological foundations of rhythmic structures and their perception, starting with the early gestalt-psychological classics (e.g., Ehrenfels 1890), summarized by Fraisse (1974); the second is the more interactionally inclined research on 'synchronization' in the tradition of W. S. Condon; the third is psycholinguistic research on the relevance of rhythm to information structure and retrieval.

The most important result of *gestalt-psychological research* on rhythm is the recognition of the active role human perception plays in the construction of rhythms.[20] Since Wundt, we have known that for a given set of stimuli to be perceived as rhythmic, the factual durations making up this set are less relevant than the time structure we impose on it. As a consequence, the analysis of rhythm cannot begin with the detection of 'actual' rhythm structures in the acoustical data; it must start from perception and then relate this to the actual durational structures. The relationship is by no means simple. What Fraisse (1974) calls "subjective rhythmization" (74) is responsible for the well-documented finding that even physically identical stimuli (such as the dripping of a water tap or the tick tock [not tick tick!] of a clock) are heard as rhythmically structured in groups of two or, more rarely, three elements. In such a perceived (subjective) rhythmic structure, the interval between two rhythmic groups appears longer than the intragroup interval, and the first (or more rarely, last) element, the 'accent', longer than the others. Of further immediate relevance to linguistic research on rhythm is the finding that manipulation of equally timed stimuli with respect to length, pitch movement or loudness leads to the perception of accents. The result is a rhythmic grouping that adjoins the nonaccented elements to the right (or, more rarely, to the left) of the perceived accent.

According to Fraisse, subjective rhythmization can only take place within certain limits of interval size. Thus, if the stimuli are presented in intervals of less than 150–200 msec, or more than 1,500–2,000 msec, no rhythmic grouping takes place in perception. The optimal interval size for nonlinguistic stimuli seems to be around 400 msec. Likewise, the overall size of a potential rhythmic group must not exceed 4,000–5,000 msec and must not contain more than six elements.[21] However, the limits of rhythm perception and the exact time structure of optimal rhythms may vary from one individual to another, and even from one culture to another.[22]

These gestalt-psychological findings can be related directly to phonetic research on isochrony. For linguistic stimuli, a threshold for the perception of rhythmicity not below 50 msec has been reported.[23] In agreement with Fraisse, Couper-Kuhlen (1993) shows that this threshold depends on the tempo at which stimuli are presented and is more adequately expressed not in absolute time but in percentages of interval duration. According to her experiments, time deviations of 20% or less of the preceding interval do not usually disturb the impression of isochrony. The exact magnitude of permitted deviation may lie above or below this threshold, however, depending on a number of additional factors. For instance, boundaries of intonation units or speaker switches increase the tolerance for deviations beyond the 20% limit (see also Nooteboom 1997:655). Listeners also seem to judge the rhythmicity of a single interval not only relative to the immediately preceding rhythmic structure (interval) but on the basis of larger text segments in which some kind of rhythmic optimization is achieved. In addition, syntax and text structure—for instance, parallelisms such as lists—may influence the perception of rhythm (see chapter 6, in this volume).

For the investigation of conversational rhythms, gestalt psychology and subsequent research on perceptual thresholds for time and rhythm perception (including the 'P-center' [perceptual center] discussion[24]) suggest a cautious interpretation of instrumental measurements as the basis for an interactionally oriented, interpretive approach to the meaning and function of rhythm. There is good evidence that we perceive more and different rhythms than can be found in the physical data. What is called for is a combined auditory-perceptual and instrumental approach.

The second tradition of psychological research on rhythm, which, at first sight, relates much more obviously to the analysis of conversational rhythms, can be summarized under the heading *interactional synchrony*. In contrast to the investigations discussed previously, research in this tradition has been primarily interested in the adaptive processes by which two or more individuals synchronize their verbal and nonverbal behavior in terms of timing and duration. These temporal parameters are measured and quantified in various ways. Thus, Chapple, who was in many ways the first to follow this line of reasoning (see Chapple 1939), used a simple paper roll, moving at a constant speed from one wheel to another, on which the beginning and end of two interacting individuals' turns ('actions') were marked

The Study of Rhythm

by the observer with the help of a typewriter. It was the aim of this 'chronography' to compare the relative durations of these actions. Chapple (1939) speculated that the deviations could be used to measure "the degree of adaptation of the individuals to one another" (64).

Since then, infinitely finer hypotheses have been tested with highly sophisticated instruments.[25] One of the well-established findings on speaker synchronization is that adaptation between co-participants does indeed take place with respect to the *duration* of vocalizations (utterances) and with respect to intra- as well as interturn pauses (see Jaffe & Feldstein 1970).[26] Condon (1980), Condon & Ogston (1967) and others have also claimed that speakers synchronize the *timing* of their verbal and nonverbal activities in a very microscopic way, down to the level of phones. Similar timing coincidences between participants have been found by Kendon (1990).

However, the status and meaning of this 'synchronization' of timing remains unclear. Take, for instance, a statement such as the following in Kendon (1990), quite typical of the type of empirical result this line of research obtains. The author refers to an instance of 'internal' synchronization between verbal and nonverbal behavior within the same person: "From <frame> 810 to 815 B lowers his fingers over the bowl of his pipe. This movement coincides exactly with the middle syllable of 'possibly' in T's speech."[27] The statement presupposes that movements such as lowering one's finger and utterance parts such as the (unstressed, extremely short) midsyllable in *possibly* have boundaries that can be established with some reliability. But in the latter case, phoneticians would surely be at a loss to say where exactly the boundary between the first and second syllable, and again between the second and third syllable should be placed: /po&ssi&bly/, /poss&i&bly/ or /poss&ib&ly/? And leaving aside these problems, how can we be sure that "synchronization" at this microscopic level of temporal coordination is not simply a matter of chance?[28] The important questions from an interactional perspective might be: Is there any interactional relevance to the coincidence between a syllable and a movement such as lowering one's finger (provided it can be stated in reliable terms)? And if the two were out of synchrony by some hundredths of a second, would it make any difference for the interpretation of that utterance or movement? These questions, however, are not addressed in the chronographic approach to timing in interaction.

Synchronization of onsets in verbal and nonverbal behavior between co-participants, as well as adaptation of their mean speaking and pausing durations, may be regarded as an instance of accommodation between speakers. Although time is involved (in the sense of duration), issues of linguistic rhythm are not touched on; in fact, isochrony is sometimes explicitly denied.[29] Contrary to what might appear at first sight, the relevance of this research to the topic of the present volume is therefore rather limited.[30]

Psycholinguistic research on the relevance of rhythm to information processing, the third tradition of psychological research mentioned at the beginning of this section, focuses on *rhythmic attending* (Jones 1986). The basic idea is that rhythm is essential to information processing because it makes predictable the occurrence of certain events in time. Whereas attending to these events implies a state of heightened perceptory attentiveness, the time that elapses between expectable (rhythmic) events can be used for the processing of the perceived stimuli. Thus, on a larger, textual scale, filled and unfilled pauses have been investigated and found to cluster in certain loci while other text segments are relatively free of hesitation (see, e.g., Butterworth & Goldman-Eisler 1979 and Butterworth 1980). This has been taken as evidence for a model of speech production and perception in which phases of planning (evident as hesitancy) alternate with those of delivery (= fluency). At a lower level, that of the English foot, Allen & Hawkins (1980), building on prior research by Martin (1972) and Allen (1975), argue convincingly that verbal messages are easier to communicate when they are organized rhythmically, because the predictability of the next phonetic prominence (together with the fact that phonetically prominent, stressed syllables contain more salient information than unstressed ones) guides hearers' attention and enables them to switch cyclically between phases of perception and processing. Clearly, this line of reasoning requires isochrony as the 'best' rhythm: "Isochronous rhythms induce a stable and veridical 'locking-into' the reference beat of the unfolding pattern whereas non-isochronous rhythms tend to induce reliance on a less stable and shifted reference beat" (Jones 1986:28). A number of empirical results support this claim, showing that the perception of and reaction to certain targets are easier (faster) when they are in accented position.[31]

Furthermore, there is evidence that rhythmicized structures are remembered better than nonrhythmic ones (see Payne & Holtzmann 1986). One might speculate on a link between these psycholinguistic findings and the conversational analyses presented in chapter 6 (this volume), according to which focal events in extended sequences such as narratives are given extra prominence by (as we call it) rhythmic scansions. Made to stand out from their textual environment prosodically, these structures are perceived as particularly salient for the story, something 'to remember'. On the other hand, given the fact that rhythmicized structures are easier to remember, tellers who exploit this prosodic strategy can also be said to enhance the chance that their story (or its point) will be recalled (see Selting 1994).

4. Language-related rhythm research outside linguistics, part II: Linguistic anthropology

The rhythmic structure of speech has also fascinated and puzzled linguistic anthropologists for some decades; this holds for the 'ethnography of communication' and 'ethnopoetics' and their more recent offspring (e.g., 'performance studies') (Briggs 1988), as well as for the now thriving research on orality and oral cultures. Linguistic anthropologists working in these traditions have investigated oral genres from Homer to rappin' (see the subtitle of a recent survey by Edwards & Sienkewicz 1990). Such genres have been shown to make use of rhythmic patterns or 'metric' structures, often in crucial ways, to contextualize the genre (i.e., to mark it off from its conversational surroundings and to enhance the aesthetics of the performance). The rhythmic structuring found in the performance of certain genres is linked to the orality of a culture in more than one way (see Finnegan 1992:88ff). Above all, rhythm in performance is a direct or indirect consequence of the fact that rhythmic structuring facilitates memorization, to which we alluded briefly in the preceding section; rhythm therefore crucially contributes to the tradition of social knowledge through oral genres (see Parry 1930, 1932; Lord 1960). (One might want to add here that literate Western prescriptive rhetorics has developed elaborate rules for the rhythmization of oral genres as well; examples range from Classical Greek poetics, where the iambus was linked to the literary genre of mocking or abuse,[32] to 19th- and early 20th-century stylebooks on the composition of speeches. This is evidence for the polyfunctionality of rhythmization in oral performance and certainly cannot be explained by problems of memorization in nonliterate communities alone.)

A good example for the genre-specific usage of prosody is rhythm in Afro-American rhetoric. In an important article written on this topic in the tradition of ethnography of communication, Gumperz (1978) analyzes the rhetoric of a Afro-American Protestant sermon to show that the traditional concept of a dialect (which includes segmental-phonological and grammatical categories only) is not sufficient to capture the discourse structure of the speech event under discussion. The elegance and complexity of the event becomes visible only when prosodic features are taken into account, and particularly when their role in the various modes of participation uniting the preacher and the audience are seen:

> Instead of waiting for the audience's "Amen's", "Halleluyah's", and "Praise the Lord's" to die down, in order to begin, the minister actively joins the ongoing performance by repeatedly interpolating his own "Amen" and "Praise the Lord" in a rhythmically appropriate pause, each time with increasing emphasis. Having thus "taken his place" in the event, he repeats the theme of his sermon. His technique once more relies on rhythmic synchrony. (398)

> A typical sermon begins with an invocation or introductory phase which takes the form of dialogue-like interchanges representing the minister's, God's, and the audience's words. There follows a transitional phase marked by increasing rhythmic intensity, increasingly frequent audience responses and occasional stylistic cross-overs in which content appropriate to one of the characters is spoken with the stylistic characteristics of the other. The final culminating phase has trance-like performance characteristics: heavy breathing, staccato delivery, hyperventilation. (397)

But despite frequent references to rhythm, which underline the relevance of prosody for the 'performance' of oral genres, anthropologists have often contented themselves with intuitive descriptions of this layer of linguistic structuring via everyday vocabulary, or they have used the terminology of literary metrics, which may not always be able to capture the specifics of the non-Western data under analysis. This also holds for most work on ritual language and performance; for instance, Fox's introduction to a volume on parallelism in Eastern Indonesian rituals states that "the rhythm of a ritual language performance is one of its most essential and compelling features" (Fox 1988:28), yet none of the contributions actually deals with rhythm. There are, however, some exceptions, such as Woodbury's analysis of a subsection of a Central Alaskan Yupik Eskimo tale (Woodbury

1987:205–207) or Urban's analysis of South-American Indian (Shokleng) origin myths (Urban 1986), where the relationship between syntactic and content parallelism and rhythmical organization is discussed on the basis of transcriptions; here, the focus is on poetic genres, which are often distinct from everyday language and may border on musical performances.

A technical analysis of the interactional significance of rhythm for everyday language has been advanced by 'microethnographers' working on the small-scale detail of interactions in Western cultures on the basis of tape or film recordings. Pioneering work by Erickson (Erickson & Shultz 1982; Erickson 1981, 1992) and Scollon (1981, 1982) has demonstrated that the interactional significance of rhythm need not be confined to ritualized genres or speech activities but that it permeates everyday (American) verbal interaction. Its general importance for the maintenance of conversational involvement is that it gives conversationalists the temporal cues they need for deciding when the right moment for some next activity has come:

> Because of the need to decide *in time*, some continual sense of *what time it is* would seem to be crucial for moment-to-moment decision making in face-to-face interaction. It seems that temporal redundancy permits an interpretive sense of where one *is* in interaction, of what was a *moment before* and what will be a *moment to come*. (Erickson & Shultz 1982:97)

Because Erickson's work has been of special importance to the research presented in this volume, it is examined in somewhat greater detail here.[33] On close inspection, Erickson's conception of conversational rhythm in his work with Shultz on gatekeeping encounters is not entirely the same as in some of his other papers (Erickson 1981, 1992); this is already evident from the transcription, which, in the second case, is based on musical notation, while it is genuinely interactionalist in the first. Erickson & Shultz (1981) give a relatively detailed description of how rhythmic transcriptions such as the one reproduced in figure 1.1 are arrived at: A piece of interaction is rhythmically integrated when the stressed syllables (underlined) occur at equal intervals of roughly 1 second.[34] Body movements (their onset or apex) may take over the role of verbal emphases (see lines 3, 8).[35] Occasionally, an emphasis may occur elsewhere (e.g., before line 1), and sometimes a rhythmic beat may not be realized at all (the rhythmic representation then contains a 'silent beat'; see lines 6, 11, 13). This is roughly the notion of rhythm we use in the following chapters of this book (see §5).

By contrast, Erickson (1992:377–8) uses a musical transcription (see figure 1.2). It is linguistically more difficult to interpret and seems to imply a notion of rhythm at a 'deeper' level, abstracted out of the verbal and nonverbal co-occurring cues provided by various co-participants, just as the rhythm of a complex piece of romantic or modern orchestral music is abstracted out of the sometimes conflicting, sometimes congruent melodic, emphatic and phrasing patterns. The tempo is markedly slower than in the first case (1.7 seconds per interval, ± 0.3 sec.), which implies that more potential rhythmic emphases fail to fall 'on the beat'. As a consequence, it is not easy to find the alleged rhythm in the transcription: B-1's *wo::w!* and *it is?* occur clearly off beat, just as do B-3's *three days to*, where the stress is

The Study of Rhythm

Counselor's turn (c)

                                                A:11

                                    (*falling intonation*)

```
(1)   right      .         .            fine and
(2)   good       .         .         .
      (shifts postural position)
(3)   (clasps)   .         .         .
      (both hands together)
(4)   N o : w    .         .         .
      (steeply falling intonation)
(5)   A : : h    .         .         .
(6)        .     .         .   as far as
(7)   next semester        .         .
(8)   (reaches) .           .        .
      (for book)
(9)   Why don't       we    give    some
(10)  thought    .          to a:::h .
(11)       .     .         .        .   to
(12)  what you'd      like to take there
(13)       .     .         .        .   do you
(14)  plan       .         .        .   on con-
(15)  tinuing    a long    this     P::
(16)  E:: major?
```

Figure 1.1. Rhythmic transcription. From Erickson & Shultz (1982), *The Counselor as Gatekeeper: Social Interaction in Interviews* (New York: Academic Press).

most probably on *days*,[36] and possibly his *it is*, which is presumably stressed on *is*. In S's turn one would expect a rhythmic pattern like It 'cost even 'more than 'that to 'get his 'bike, which doesn't seem to fit into the rhythmic pattern very well either. In short, what forms the basis for Erickson's impression of rhythmic integration in this data does not seem to be captured by the information contained in the musical notation. In any case, phonetic and nonverbal emphases play a much less important role than in the counseling data. For the sake of clarity and intersubjectivity, as well as to maintain ties with prior linguistic and phonetic research

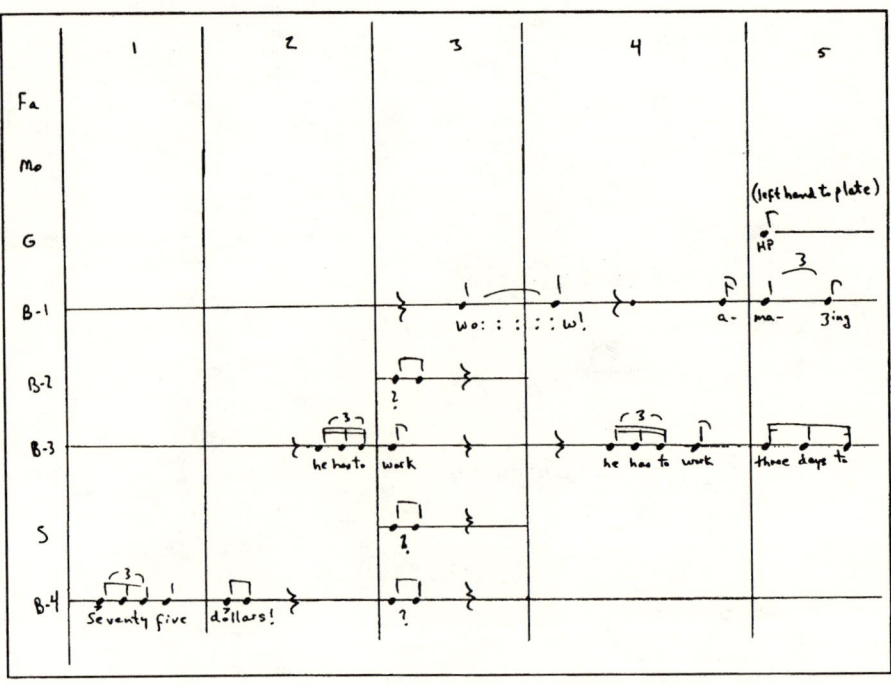
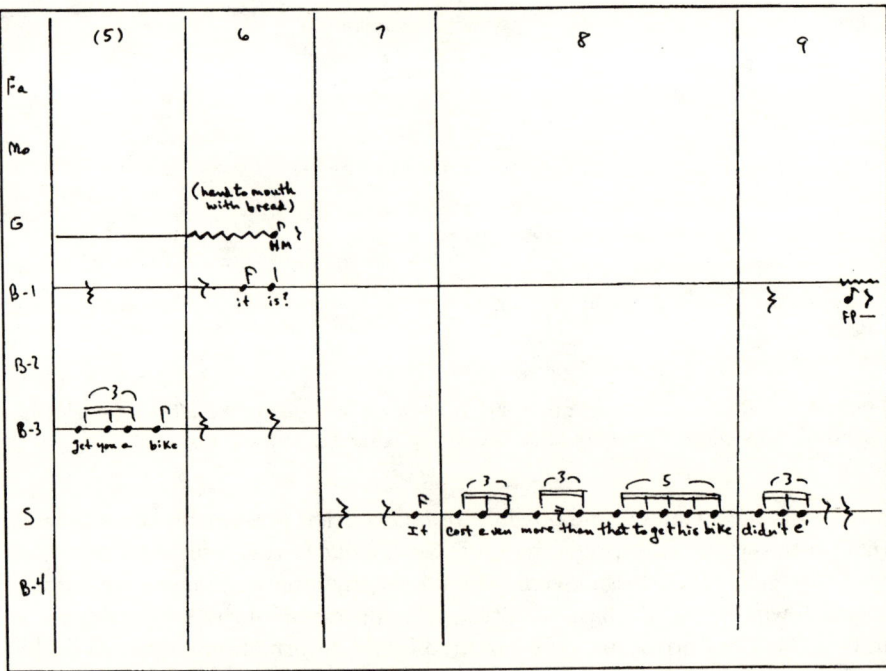

Figure 1.2. Musical transcription of conversational rhythm. From Peter Auer and Aldo di Luzio, eds. (1992), *The Contextualization of Language* (Amsterdam: John Benjamins).

on rhythm, we consider the first approach more useful for our own work than the second.

There is, however, a more fundamental reason why it has turned out to be difficult to apply either of Erickson's approaches to rhythm directly to our data and our analytical problems. This concerns the ubiquity of rhythmic integration, which is claimed for both sets of data (counseling and conversational) and which reflects the belief that rhythm is "constitutive for social meaning" (Erickson & Shultz 1981:96) and therefore a "normal condition" of interaction (1981:105). Interruptions of rhythmically integrated speech are, as a consequence, seen as dramatic events: They dissolve an elementary property of verbal and nonverbal interaction. In the conversational data (Erickson 1992), arrhythmicity does not seem to occur at all; here, on the basis of the rather 'deep' notion of rhythm, which is only loosely connected to the behaviorally realized emphases, everything is rhythmically integrated. In the counseling data, rhythmic 'disturbances' do occur and are shown to have dramatic correlates in (or consequences for) the sequential development of the interaction at hand (Erickson & Shultz 1981:103ff). The following types of arrhythmia are distinguished: (1) individual rhythmic instability (i.e., by one speaker only, whose rhythm begins to 'wobble' for a short period); (2) mutual rhythmic instability, where both co-participants 'wobble' together; (3) mutual rhythmic interference, where each partner insists on his or her own rhythm, which, however, is not compatible with that of the other; and (4) rhythmic 'tugging' (i.e., one participant comes in too early or too late to continue the rhythm of the other) (1981:114). Erickson & Shultz consider the two latter types of arhythmia to be indicative of "serious interactional trouble" (1981:103), and, indeed, they are able to show that rhythm tends to fall apart particularly at those loci in conversation where the counselor denies a student access to a course or negatively evaluates the student's achievements. In addition, they provide evidence that this is particularly true for intercultural encounters.

Our own research leads us to conclude that rhythmic integration in conversational English (and even more so in conversational German or Italian) is considerably less ubiquitous (see later). More exactly, although turn transitions in English seem to be rhythmically integrated in what could be called the unmarked case, the internal makeup of a speaker's turn (particularly, a complex one) usually does not show isochrony throughout but contains phases of 'wobbling' and/or rhythmic shifts. Although this finding is compatible with the previously mentioned psychological results based on pause distribution, which suggest an alternation between hesitant and fluent phases in speech, it contradicts the notion of ubiquitous rhythm constitutive of successful interaction as such (even though in the typology of arrhythmia given by Erickson & Shultz, it is of the less dramatic first type). And even when rhythmic disturbances can be observed at turn transitions (the 'marked' case), these often seem to have a less disruptive (although certainly highly relevant) impact on the interaction than that described in Erickson & Shultz's work.

The conflict can be resolved when the type of data investigated by Erickson & Shultz is taken into account. Their data come from institutionalized encounters based on a strict schema of question-answer sequences in which the counselor checks the student's results from the last term; after this highly routinized sequence the counselor proceeds to advise the student on his or her future career. From what we know about rhythm, it can be expected that in such prepatterned interaction, with predictable sequencing of usually short turns, rhythmic integration will be greater than in less patterned informal conversation. And, indeed, the examples for tight rhythmic structuring given by Erickson & Shultz are all of the type of interaction represented in figure 1.1. The higher degree of rhythmic integration found in their research may therefore be a consequence of the data investigated, whereas the looser rhythmization in our data (particularly in the internal part of extended turns) is more typical for conversational data. As demonstrated in the following section, subtle rhythmizations and derhythmizations require a more context-sensitive model for interpretation.

Apart from the work by Erickson and by Scollon, detailed rhythmic analyses related to specific interactional tasks or problems have been scarce. There is some evidence that rhythmicity (isochrony) in Canadian English is greater in spontaneous speech than in reading (Séguinot 1979) and, therefore, that rhythmic integration depends on linguistic 'channels'; that a transition to a greater or lesser degree of isochrony can be indicative of a transition to a different speech activity (see Selting 1992b for narratives); that rhythm can be coordinated even across two parallel constellations of speakers in a conversational schism (Komter 1983; also Erickson 1981:64ff); and that different modes ('keys') may coincide with different rhythmic patternings (see Kuiper & Haggo 1984 for 'drone' vs. 'shout' mode in Australian cattle auctioneers' speech and K. Müller 1992 for 'fun' vs. 'drama' in narratives).

All in all, it is surprising how little attention has been paid to the temporal unfolding of language production and reception even in those traditions of linguistic research that focus on interaction and partly follow a marked non- or even antistructuralist line. Particularly notable is the widespread neglect of rhythm in the now vast amount of research accumulated within the framework of conversation analysis. Several chapters in this book show that rhythm and tempo are constitutive parameters in the enactment of basic conversational patterns and are involved in issues that have been most central to conversation analysis (e.g., turn taking, preference systems, and the organization of closings). The argument has been made in detail for intonation elsewhere (Couper-Kuhlen & Selting 1996), which is sometimes incorporated but more usually denied substantive relevance (Schegloff 1996) for the organization of conversational interaction. It applies even more to rhythm and tempo. When temporal parameters have been considered at all (e.g., in Jefferson's discussion of a 1-second metric for conversational pausing; see Jefferson 1989), they are defined in terms of external (objective) time, not—as might be expected, given the ethnomethodological and phenomenological roots of conversation analysis—in terms of perceived time.

On the other hand, it is necessary for phoneticians and linguists to take into account (and profit from) the results of conversation-analytic research; indeed, we contend that no progress will be made toward a realistic analysis of rhythm unless its usage in everyday linguistic praxis is made the object of study. Conversation analysis has laid the groundwork for such an analysis of linguistic praxis in many ways. It seems possible now to combine various traditions of phonetic, linguistic, conversation-analytic and microethnographic research to come to a retemporalized—and thereby recontextualized approach to language.

5. Rhythm and tempo as contextualization cues: A new approach

5.1. Conversational rhythms as perceived gestalts

In this section, we present the picture of linguistic rhythm as it has emerged from our work. A discussion of further technical issues concerning the phonetic and phonological implications of this approach can be found in Couper-Kuhlen (1993); Chapter 2 discusses methodological and practical issues of rhythmic analysis.

Rhythm, as we said earlier, is not a property of physical signals such as acoustic waveforms; acoustic data may contain phonetic events such as f_o peaks and valleys, changes in amplitude or duration, and these may occur at objectively equal or similar time intervals. Yet the perception of rhythm is not directly or automatically related to (or derivative of) these physical events. It is the human mind which perceives certain physical cues as forming a rhythmic pattern or gestalt. More precisely, the human receptor of the acoustic signal must perform a number of interpretive tasks to hear its rhythm. Acoustic f_o variations must be interpreted as pitch chànges, amplitude variations as increases or decreases of loudness and variations of segment duration as changes of length. These features have to be combined into the perception of stress, the perceptory correlate of phonetic prominence. A series of stresses may be heard—on the basis of certain principles to be set forth later[37]— as a rhythmic pattern. To speak of rhythm therefore necessarily implies an interpretation of the physical data, a constructive process in the course of which these data become part of a holistic scheme, which is then able to incorporate further details from the incoming signal. Sonnenschein (1925) gave a definition that comes close to this view of rhythm:

> Rhythm is that property of a sequence of events in time which produces in the mind of the observer the impression of proportion between the durations of the several events or groups of events of which the sequence is composed. (16)

Rhythm always implies some kind of repetition in time; in the simplest sense this is the recurrence of events which, for the practical purposes of constructing rhythm, are considered to be of the same type and which are perceived to occur at a constant rate. Schematically, if $x_i \ldots x_n$ are such events, and / / symbolizes perceived equal distance, the simplest kind of rhythm may be represented as

/x_i /x_j /x_k ...

such as in English counting:

/one /two /three ...

Note that there has to be at least three events or two intervals of the type x to constitute a rhythmic pattern. As soon as such a rhythmic pattern has been formed in the mind of the hearer, an expectation for the next event x to occur within the pattern will guide perception and increase the likelihood of its rhythmic integration. The more established a rhythmic pattern is, the more it tends to integrate further events, even if they 'fit in' only poorly from the 'objective' view of the acoustic phonetician.

A more complex but also more prevalent rhythmic pattern emerges when further events intervene between the events that establish the rhythm. In this more usual type of rhythm, perception distinguishes on the basis of stress (but again, not entirely determined by it) between weak and strong elements. Rhythmic integration in this case requires the strong elements to occur at perceived intervals of equal duration; the weak elements are interspersed between the strong ones, in unpredictable numbers and varying proportions. Representing strong events as (s) and weak ones as (w), this pattern may be symbolized as

$$/s_i\ w_{i,1} \ldots w_{i,p}\ /s_j\ w_{j,1} \ldots w_{j,q}\ /s_k\ w_{k,1} \ldots w_{k,r}\ /\ldots$$

(In the more usual case, the strong element precedes the weak ones, although the inverse order may occur as well.) This, for instance, is the case in English when counting from 12 to 20; the number of weak syllables varies between zero and two:

/'twelve /'thirteen /'fourteen ... /'seventeen ...

A third type of rhythm imposes an even stronger regimen on the events involved: Strong elements are not only spaced equally, they are additionally followed (or preceded) by an equal number of *n* weak elements. Although the types of rhythm considered so far all involve *isochrony*, the perceived constancy of intervals between rhythmic events, the third type of rhythm additionally requires a constant *isometrical* pattern:

$$/s_i\ w_{i,1} \ldots w_{i,p}\ /s_j\ w_{j,1} \ldots w_{j,p}\ /s_k\ w_{k,1} \ldots w_{k,p}\ /\ldots$$

as in counting in English from 21 to 26 (with exactly two weak elements between the strong ones):

twenty /'one   twenty /'two   twenty /'three   twenty /'four ...

Finally, isometric patterns may occur without isochrony, constituting a fourth type of rhythm, which, however, will not play a central role in this book:

$$s_i\ w_{i,1} \ldots w_{i,n}\ s_j\ w_{j,1} \ldots w_{j,n}\ s_k\ w_{k,1} \ldots w_{k,n} \ldots$$

An example might be if the count from 21 to 26 were done without isochronous rhythmic spacing:

twenty 'one twenty 'two twenty 'three twenty 'four ...

The Study of Rhythm

Rhythm can thus be decomposed into a number of constituent parameters, two of which are central—one is the organization of strong and weak syllables in recurrent patterns (iambus, trochee, etc.) and the other is isochrony, the regular succession of beats in time.

Essential to the approach chosen here is the difference between rhythmic events and stresses. The first we call *beats*; the duration between two beats is a *rhythmic interval*. Not every stressed syllable need be heard as a rhythmic beat (i.e., as a 'strong' event in the sense of the second and third patterns above). (The categorization of stressed syllables, as we have seen, is in itself a construct from various parameters marking phonetic prominence.) At least three perceived stressed syllables are necessary for the formation of an isochronous pattern, but other stresses may occur off beat.

These two levels, the recognition of stress and the identification of rhythmic gestalts, must be distinguished carefully, although they influence each other. Note that there is no logical or temporal priority between them. It does not seem to be the case that hearers first identify stresses and then combine them into rhythmic gestalts. In a typical phenomenologically reflexive way, existing gestalts may also influence what is heard as a stress. An established isochronous rhythm prestructures future events; its essential property is to make the timing of a next rhythmically integrated event predictable. Therefore, at any point in time within an established rhythm, a next beat is anticipated. This expectation facilitates the perception of whatever event occurs 'on the beat' as a phonetic prominence and, indeed, as a stress. Schematically, the perception of rhythmic structures relates to stress as in figure 1.4, not as in figure 1.3.

Note that we do not distinguish between *meter* and rhythm, as is commonly done in musicology, literary metrics and dance. In music, 'time' or meter is the underlying structure, or the counting unit according to which a stretch of music is divided into bars, while rhythm may disregard and even violate this underlying scheme, as in the case of syncopations or hemiolae. In literary metrics, meter is an

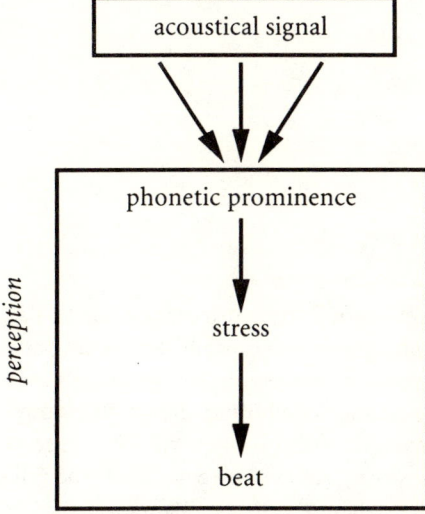

Figure 1.3. Incorrect relation between stress and the perception of rhythm

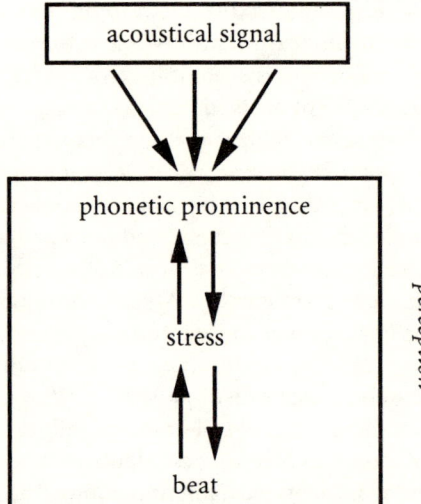

Figure 1.4. Correct relation between stress and the perception of rhythm

'objectively' given scheme of ordering, whereas rhythm covers all of its individual usages or even nonuses by the poet or the performer (see Paul & Glier 1970:17). Postulating underlying metrical schemes seems justified for the historically established and even codified transformations language has undergone in poetry and other forms of art; everyday language users, however, do not typically rely on such schemes. Instead, whatever rhythmic regularity they want to make use of for the production and interpretation of language is established in the speech situation itself. In this sense, there is no metrics of everyday language.

The following example serves as a preliminary illustration of the approach to rhythm used in subsequent chapters:

(1) [From a Radio Manchester phone-in program]

```
1   DJ:     ˌdid 'you get 'married with ehm
            /'all sorts of       /
            /'flowers in your    /
            /'hair
5   S:                       ˌno I /
            /'didn't
    DJ:                          you /
            /'didn't
```

Stretches between / / are rhythmically isochronous; the width of the slash-to-slash interval represents the duration of the rhythmic interval iconically. Phonetic prominences are marked by ' (strong stress) and, where necessary, by ˌ (weaker stress). Rhythmic patterns often extend over phrasal and turn boundaries. As the sample extract shows, two or more speakers may even contribute to one rhythmic interval (as in lines 4–5, where the DJ provides the strong element or beat, while the caller S contributes weak syllables, or in lines 6–7, where the reverse happens).

Although this passage is highly rhythmicized, nonisochronous stretches of talk are contained in it as well (in the first line). Syllables preceded by a lefthand slash are rhythmic beats; these beats coincide with stresses. Yet, not every stressed syllable is a beat; for instance in S's phrase *no I didn't*, the *no* carries stress although it is off beat.

It may be clear by now that our definition of an isochronous rhythm lies somewhere between the phonetician's (e.g., Abercrombie, who ties the notion very strictly to phonetic prominences) and the microethnographer's (e.g., Erickson or Scollon, who give rhythm a 'musical' treatment further abstracted from the phonetic surface than we do). We have found rhythm at an intermediate level, where it is neither ubiquitous nor unlikely over speakers' alternating turns, and where it is highly susceptible to being used as a resource for the construction of interactional meaning.

The approach outlined in the earlier part of this section implies that rhythmicity as an imposed temporal order is not an all-or-nothing affair; certain constellations of events lend themselves more easily to the perception of a clear rhythmic gestalt than do others. To capture the nature of these constellations, it is possible to formulate preferences for rhythmic gestalts, or *euphonic principles*. According to the euphonic principles we believe to be valid, a rhythmic gestalt is 'better' (i.e., more distinct and salient) when it has one or more of the following properties:

1. It contains few or no off-beat stresses.
2. The duration of the rhythmic interval does not exceed the upper limit of approximately 1 second or the lower limit of approximately 2/10th of a second.
3. Beats co-occur with stresses, and these stresses are realized by pitch obtrusion.
4. The number of weak off-beat syllables is fairly regular.
5. Prosodic rhythm is supported by lexicosyntactic properties such as repetition or parallelism.

The absence of these features do not render an utterance anisochronous or nonrhythmic. However, it may make its rhythmic gestalt more ambiguous: There may be more than one possibility of integrating stressed syllables into a rhythm.

5.2. The interactional work done through rhythm

The overall semiotic framework with which we have chosen to work for the interpretation of rhythmic structures is that of Gumperz's *contextualization* (see Cook-Gumperz & Gumperz 1976; Gumperz 1982, 1992, as well as the contributions in Auer & di Luzio 1992). Contextualization refers to the process by which conversationalists enable each other to bridge the gap between what is meant and what is said. They do so, among other things, by the use of indexical 'contextualization cues', which provide the contextual embedding indispensable for construing conversational meaning. Thus, contextualization cues evoke Goffman-like "frames" or contexts, which in turn are used for the understanding of a given utterance beyond its propositional content.

The extraordinary attractiveness of this approach lies in the fact that it enables us to come to grips with the interactional work done by prosodic cues such as intonation, tempo, loudness and rhythm (with their various component features) by showing how they acquire interpretive significance. Gumperz makes it clear that prosody is not an accidental or derivative addendum to the linguistic data proper (which can be safely neglected) but an essential part of interaction.[38] The meaning of these prosodic cues is of a basically indexical nature and cannot be captured by the traditional techniques of semantic description developed for representational or symbolic meaning. Prosodic cues only 'mean' in context. Analyzing the work done through prosody in interaction therefore necessitates a new theory of 'phonological pragmatics'.

In the contextualization approach applied to rhythm, it would be of limited value to ask what the interactional meaning of this prosodic cue is 'as such'. Instead, the ways in which rhythm contributes to the construction of meaning in interaction depend in essential ways on the local context. This is not to say that generalized descriptions of the meaning of rhythm—for example, that 'compactness of information' is signaled by 'compactness of speech rhythm', that rhythmic integration signals heightened 'interactional involvement', that the anapest signals a 'dramatic' mood and the iambus a 'funny' one—are necessarily wrong; at a sufficient level of abstractness, they may capture some kind of "meaning potential" (Auer 1992), which is at the core of many contextualization cues. However, it is a long way from the generalized meaning potentials of rhythm to the actual impact rhythmic structures have within and on the context of a particular utterance in conversation. Contextualization analysis is interested in the latter more than in the former. As a consequence, rhythmic structures and their changes must be seen in the light of what 'goes on' in conversation, in their relation to specific patterns of conversational structure.

5.3. Rhythm and tempo

Closely related to the notion of rhythm is that of *tempo*. The concept is not an easy one, as lay notions of 'fast' and 'slow' speaking do not seem to be used in a consistent way: They may refer, in their various occurrences, to quite different types of phenomena. For instance, the perception of tempo is influenced by the 'phrasing' of speech (i.e., its segmentation into intonation units) and by the duration of pauses within and between these units. It is also influenced by segmental phenomena such as the nature and degree of assimilation on the level of sentence/post-lexical phonology. But aside from these factors, the lay notion of tempo includes at least the following two parameters: the number of syllables produced within a given unit of time (e.g., 1 second), and the number of stresses per unit of time. The same parameters are the basis of the distinction between *speech rate* (i.e., the number of syllables per unit of time) and *density* (i.e., the ratio of stressed to unstressed syllables).[39]

Scollon (1982) and subsequent work in our research group (Uhmann 1992) show that constellations of these two parameters are used by conversationalists in interactionally meaningful ways. One of the most prevalent uses is to contextualize

The Study of Rhythm

an utterance or part of it by indicating its 'saliency' or 'relevance' to the point to be made. Low relevance in this sense is marked by a high number of syllables and a low number of stressed syllables per unit of time (i.e., by high speech rate and low density); high relevance is marked by a high number of stressed syllables (high density) and a low number of syllables per unit of time (low speech rate).[40] Tempo here contributes to information management on a small-scale 'utterance' level, just as do left and right dislocation, diathesis, word order and choice of referential techniques (full forms vs. pronouns vs. zero pronouns or clitics).

Consider the following extract from a German conversation. (Lines correspond to intonation units; speech rate was measured in syllables per second, excluding silence.[41] Where two values are given, they refer to speech rate, measured in phonemic syllables per second, and to density, the ratio of stressed to unstressed syllables, both within the intonation unit.[42])

(2) [From a face-to-face conversation]

1	C:	*ich hab jetz emol ne 'andre frage*	10.8/0.1
		now, I have another question	
		ich hab mir=s nämlich mal über'legt	11.5/0.13
		because I have been thinking about this	
		da liest=ma in letschter zeit immer wieder ar'tikel drüber	8.2/0.06
		there have been a lot of articles about it recently	
		(0.3)	
5		ähm	
		uhm	
		(0.37)	
		aso bei 'mir isch des zum beispiel 'so:,	6.8/0.2
		o.k. in my case for instance it's like this	
		+daß ich 'ganz ++mini'mal++ 'kurzsichtig bin;=+	5.4/0.3
		I am very slightly short-sighted	
	→	+also 'null'fünf.+	4.8/0.5
		I mean point five	
10		des heißt ich brauchs 'wirklich ,nur,	6.5/0.25
		which means I really only need them [sc. glasses]	
		wenn=ich (0.37) 'lange ,zeit auf 'einen ,punkt gucke muß.=	
		when I (0.37) have to focus on one point for a long time	6.4/0.3
	→	zum=beischpiel=m 'film oder im the'ater oder so:. ne*	8.1/0.07
		for instance in the movies or in the theatre or so, you see	
	B:	mhm	
		mhm	
		((*passage omitted*))	

C:	und etz ˌgibt=s ebbe so ar'tikel,=	7.8/0.2
	and now there are these articles ((*saying*))	
25 →	+daß=es ++'augeˌtraining++ gibt,+	4.9/0.57
	that there is eye training	
	+aso daß ich [es='auge trai'nieren kann.	5.7/0.18
	I mean that I can train my eyes	
L:	[?e?n ((*negation*))	

In this rather elaborate turn, the speaker introduces a new topic, the utility of 'eye training' for short-sighted people. Both speech rate and density vary greatly: Speech rate is relatively high in the first two lines (compared to the speaker's overall average in this conversational episode, viz., 6.72 syllables per second), then drops in line 3 and again in line 7 and reaches its minimum in the intonation unit in line 9; it goes up again in lines 10–11 and almost reaches the level of the beginning in line 12. After a subordinated clarification sequence (omitted here), C resumes talk at about the same speech rate as before but slows down considerably in line 25; line 26 is again slightly faster. Even more striking are the corresponding changes in density: Density is dramatically increased in lines 9 and 25 and just as dramatically decreased in line 12.

It is important to ask whether these changes in measured speech rate and density correspond to perceived speed. A survey carried out by Barden (1991) shows that they clearly do. (In the transcript, passages marked by informants as '(very) fast' are enclosed between (*)* ... *(*), those marked as '(very) slow' between (+)+ ... +(+).) The first three phrases and the last one in the first part were perceived as 'fast', the middle phrases 8 and 9 (particularly the word *minimal* in line 8[43]) and again lines 25 and 26 in the second part were perceived as 'slow'.

A look at the internal structure of C's elaborate turn demonstrates a strong correlation with how the speaker organizes her contribution on the content level. The first three lines announce a new topic without introducing it: They are 'pre-pres' to what is going to come (Schegloff 1980). The topic itself ('eye-training') is not mentioned explicitly until line 25—after a resumption of the 'pre-pre' in line 24; it is then reformulated in line 26. Intervening talk in lines 7 to 12 provides the background against which this topic must be seen as relevant to the speaker (i.e., that her own short-sightedness is only minimal and therefore potentially curable by eye-training). This 'pre' has a complex organization in itself and contains a series of phrases of different informational status. Lines 8 and 9 contain its central piece of information (that the speaker is only slightly short-sighted; line 9 is an elaboration of line 8), whereas line 7 relates this information to the speaker herself, and lines 10 to 12 give empirical evidence for the truth of the statement (line 12 being semantically dependent on lines 10 and 11) (i.e., both are more peripheral within this 'pre'). Thus, the turn can be divided into the mentioning of a new topic, a preparatory activity which demonstrates the topic's relevance to the speaker, and a prepreparatory activity which announces a topic change. This structure may be represented graphically as in figure 1.5.

The Study of Rhythm

In this diagram, passages perceived as 'slow' are surrounded by circles, those perceived as 'fast' by squares. As we have seen, speech rate and density vary in a parallel fashion in the intonation units marked as slow—particularly lines 8–9 and 25–26—and fast—particularly lines 1–3 and 12. There is then a strong correlation between tempo and informational 'saliency' or 'relevance': 'Fast' passages are second-order preparatory or elaborative activities (the pre-pres in the beginning and the example in phrase 12); 'slow' passages are the central components of the preutterance (line 8 and its first elaboration) and the new topic itself (phrase 25), together with its first elaboration.

A problem remains. Density and speech rate are doubtlessly used as contextualization cues, in this case for structuring information. However, it is difficult to integrate these notions with the approach to rhythm outlined in the last section. The reason is that density has been defined on the level of stress, not on that of the rhythmic beats (see figure 1.4). We now introduce slightly different definitions which are just as capable of capturing the interactional uses of speech rate and density but are natural parts of rhythmic analysis.

Rhythmic tempo is the duration of a rhythmic interval (the distance between two rhythmic beats). Because there may be stressed syllables outside the rhythm pattern as well as silent beats within it, rhythmic tempo is not identical with (but is usually not very different from) speech rate. *Rhythmic density* is then defined in terms of number of syllables per rhythmic interval, or, equivalently, in terms of the ratio between beats and off-beat syllables. Given the importance of rhythm for conversational interaction, we claim that tempo should be defined primarily on this level, where the interactional 'pulse' of a rhythmic ensemble becomes accessible to analysis: "It is the tempo that keeps the participants in touch with each other. It is through the tempo that the performers integrate their ensemble" (Scollon 1982:340).

In summary, the following terms and definitions apply:

speech rate = number of syllables per second

density = ratio of stressed to unstressed syllables

rhythmic tempo = duration of a rhythmic interval

rhythmic density = ratio of beats to off-beat syllables.

Note that rhythm and tempo in the new definition depend on each other. On the one hand, rhythmic tempo cannot be perceived, measured or interpreted without prior establishment of the rhythm of a conversational passage. On the other hand, tempo influences the perceptual clarity of a rhythmic gestalt according to the second principle of euphony (see earlier discussion): Rhythmic intervals (tempo) must be within a medium range to render a rhythmic pattern distinct and clear.

The following chapters show how rhythmic tempo contributes to rhythmic analysis. The notion of tempo makes it possible to capture subtleties of temporal organization that cannot be analyzed with the nonrhythmic notion of speech rate (see in particular chapter 5; also Couper-Kuhlen 1992b for tempo in conversational repair work).

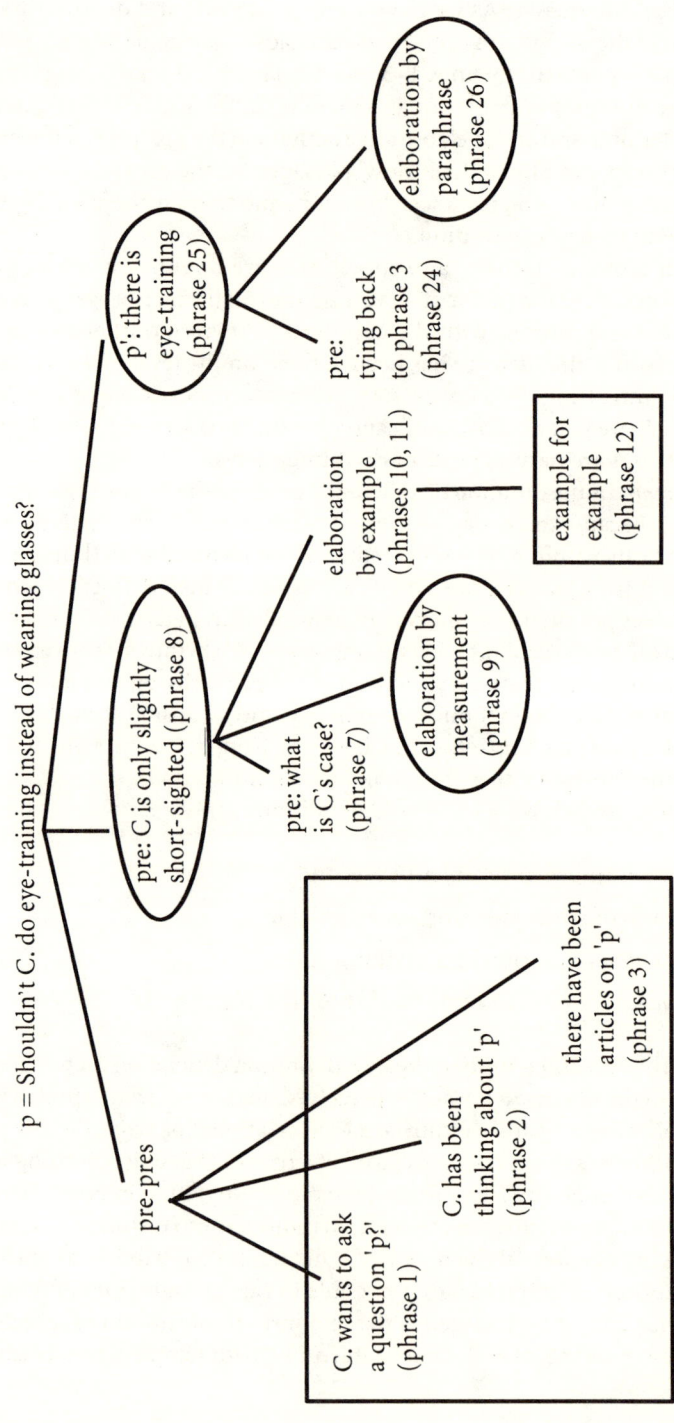

Figure 1.5. Structure of C's turn in example (3). The letter p = point to be made (here, the new topic).

6. Overview of the following chapters

In this book, we explore the contextualizing functions of rhythm and tempo in conversational data from three European languages: English, Italian and German. We believe that the contextualizing potential of time-related phonetic parameters can be located in two central aspects of spoken interaction—conversational organization and verbal performance—both of which are covered in the following chapters.

The first and—at least for English and German—possibly the most important aspect is that of conversational structure. As we show in chapters 3, 4 and 5, rhythm and tempo play a decisive role in turn taking, preference organization and conversational closings (i.e., those areas that research in conversation analysis has produced its most celebrated results in). We argue in these chapters that rhythmic patterns and their alternations are important cues for participants in deciding 'what to do next' *and when*. The incorporation of a notion of rhythmic timing means a substantial revision of, and precision in, the analysis of turn taking; moreover, it solves some of the thorny questions surrounding the problematic issues of overlap and pausing or 'gaps' in speaker transition, enabling the analyst to draw a clear line between interactionally irrelevant and interactionally relevant (or even problematic) cases of the two phenomena. As contextualization cues, rhythm and tempo are also shown to steer members' interpretation of preferred and dispreferred turns. The issue of 'preference structure' has warranted considerable debate in the last few years (see Bilmes 1988; Schegloff 1988). The disputed problem is whether a dispreferred conversational activity is noticeable as such by the very fact of being of a certain type (e.g., a 'disagreement', a 'refusal' or a 'rejection'), or whether an activity can only be seen as dispreferred when it is performed in a certain way (e.g., marked by delays, downgraders, and prefaces). We take the first point of view and argue that rhythm is an additional and independent means of contextualizing the interactional event (chapter 4). Finally, rhythm and in particular tempo are shown to play an important role in the enactment and resolution of closing sequences in telephone conversations; in fact, we argue that rhythmic integration is a prerequisite for the successful and conversationally unproblematic termination of a phone call (chapter 5).

The second large area in which rhythm and tempo work effectively as contextualization cues is that of verbal performance, particularly within more monological (although always highly recipient-designed) speech activities. This holds for all the three languages we have examined, but we sketch some of the most important usages of rhythm and tempo in verbal performance on the basis of our Italian materials, keeping in mind that Italian is generally less thoroughly isochronous than English or German. The results, however, generalize a *fortiori* to the latter languages as well. Extending the notion of performance from that of ritual texts to all (even partially) form-oriented verbal actions for which one participant takes over 'stylistic' responsibility toward an audience, we contend (with Bauman & Briggs 1990; Briggs 1988; and others) that performance refers at once to textual and contextual phenomena through which a speaker's words are turned into what is, according to lay norms, 'well-formed' speech. We show how this notion of performance can be applied to larger chunks of talk within everyday conversation. In chapter 6, we introduce the notion of scansions, densely organized, highly isochronous, loudly spoken passages with similar pitch movement on all stressed syllables, often co-occurring with syntactic or lexical parallelism and/or hyperbole as well as with list structures on the verbal level. We then elaborate on their contextualizing function as 'extreme-case formulations' (Pomerantz 1986) in the course of complex storytellings, commands, prohibitions and complaints. Finally, chapter 7 focuses on the more poetic functions of rhythm in an Italian moderator's performance on a radio phone-in program.

2

Hearing and Notating Conversational Rhythm

In the preceding chapter we stressed that our approach to rhythm relies on the notion of gestalt. Such an approach has of course its own methodological problems. How can rhythmic structures be discovered in reliable ways? Instrumental measurement of the acoustic data will not provide us with an unproblematic access to rhythm, given the highly interpretive steps we language users must go through to perceive language as rhythmic or nonrhythmic. From this it follows that an auditory analysis of rhythm must have priority over instrumental analysis as a research tool. However, to transcribe rhythms takes training: Although we believe that every competent language user is able to hear a given passage as more or less rhythmic or nonrhythmic, rhythm is probably one of the linguistic features to which language users have least access on a metalinguistic level. (It shares this property with intonation, a state of affairs undoubtedly brought about by the fact that writing and institutionalized language education do not provide an analytic apparatus for identifying or talking about prosodic phenomena.) In addition, changes in rhythm often co-occur with other changes in the prosodic makeup of an utterance, which makes it difficult for the lay analyst to tease them apart. For this reason, rhythm may not be immediately obvious to nontrained hearers (or even language professionals). Rhythmic transcriptions require the special skill of analytic hearing—a property they share with narrow phonetic transcriptions.

The examples used in subsequent chapters are based on auditory transcriptions usually made by several members of our project team. A common analytic apparatus—described later in this chapter—was developed during a period of joint work on a preliminary set of data: This apparatus has ensured the necessary degree of intertranscriber reliability. Yet rhythmic gestalts are not purely a matter of perception; perception relates to the physical stimuli only in indirect and complex ways. To make our transcriptions plausible even for skeptics (linguists or not), some of the ways in which perception transforms the acoustic signal in order to create a rhythmic gestalt have also been investigated. The results of these investigations are presented in detail elsewhere (Couper-Kuhlen 1993). They show that our auditory transcriptions of English rhythm are related in systematic ways to acoustic information; we can assume that the same holds true for the transcriptions of Italian and German rhythm in this book.

Our assumption, as noted earlier is that speech is not necessarily exhaustively rhythmic but that certain parts are more rhythmic than others. One of the aims of our analysis is to identify the strongly rhythmic passages in speech and to describe the patterns that contribute to this rhythmicity. In this chapter we set forth some of the steps analysts can take to "discover" conversational rhythms. The focus is on rhythmic patterns in the turns of single speakers. In the following three chapters (chapters 3–5) we discuss cross-speaker production of rhythm in conversation, and in the two after that (chapters 6–7) we return to turn-internal rhythms. The examples in the present chapter are taken from English.[1] The discovery procedures are the same in all cases.

What makes for an analytic mentality in the study of conversational rhythm? It is attention to the auditory shape of utterances as objects produced in and of time. In fact, little about the timing of English speech is prescribed by the words and abstract morphosyntactic structures of which it is composed. Syllable lengths and to a certain extent even lexical stress may be adjusted in production to suit rhythmic needs. Just as the sequential development of conversation—despite its *post hoc* appearance of 'seeming inescapability' (Schegloff 1982:89)—has been shown to be an achievement in real time, so the length and placement of syllables in time are eminently contingent. Sensitivity to the choices speakers make in 'putting to time' their syllables and utterances is a *sine qua non* of the rhythmic analysis of speech.

1. Discovery procedures for rhythmic analysis

In English speech, rhythmic patterns appear to be articulated primarily by the timing of stressed syllables. 'Stressed syllables', in our use of the term here, are those given prominence in the utterance via an increase in length or loudness and/or via a change in pitch. (Syllables with prominence due to pitch are also said to have a 'pitch accent' or to be accented.) Pitch prominence may be accomplished in two different ways: There may be a pitch movement up or down from the syllable in question, or there may be a pitch step up to or down to this syllable (Cruttenden

1986). We use the expression 'prosodic prominence' as a cover term for all kinds of syllables perceived to be stressed or accented.

It is important to remember that the prominences via which rhythmic patterns are articulated in speech are not abstract or virtual but concrete and real. Although the lexical stress of polysyllabic words in English dictionaries is abstract, indicating merely potential for prominence, the stressed and accented syllables of speech are due to concrete manifestations of length, loudness and pitch. In fact, the lexically stressed syllable of a polysyllabic word may not have much prominence at all, relatively speaking, in actual performance. And monosyllables, which lack lexical stress in the dictionary, may well be singled out for increased pitch, loudness or length in real utterances. To see this, consider the phrase *I'm very relieved to hear you say that*. According to the dictionary, the bisyllabic words *very* and *relieve* have primary lexical stress on their first and second syllables, respectively, whereas the monosyllabic word *say* has no marking for lexical stress at all. Yet in one actual realization of this phrase (see [12]) the first syllable of the word *very* is made strongly prominent, whereas the second syllable of the word *relieve*, adjacent to it, is 'destressed'.[2] Perceptually it fades into the background. The monosyllabic *say*, on the other hand, is made equally as prominent as the first syllable of *very* by virtue of being markedly louder, longer and higher than surrounding syllables. Thus, although the phrase has two lexical stresses and two utterance-level stresses, these sets are not identical.

The first step in analyzing conversational rhythm is to identify prosodic prominences. Prominence is a relative notion and accordingly the identification can be done with varying degrees of delicacy. To illustrate, consider the following attested example (figure 2.1), taken from a California radio phone-in program. The anchorman, Dr. Edell, is discussing emphysema and has just compared the human lung to soap bubbles.

In this utterance the syllables *hap-*, *-sem-* and *walls* have a step-up in pitch with respect to immediately prior syllables. In addition, *walls* and *down* have extra length and loudness, as can be seen in the waveform of figure 2.2 and the chart of syllable lengths in table 2.1.

Moreover, the syllable *down* has a downward movement on or following it, as does the syllable *-sem-*. Therefore *hap-*, *-sem-*, *walls* and *down* are all pitch accents and constitute prosodic prominences. The syllable *bub-* is also prosodically prominent because it is louder and longer than its neighbor *break*, relatively speaking.[3] Of course the syllables *em-* and *-tween* are also candidates for added prominence

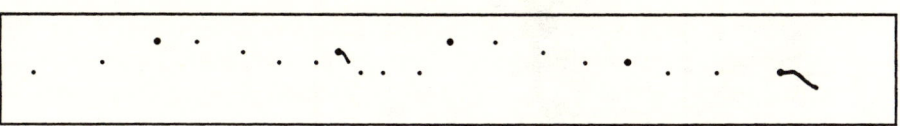

now what happens in emphysema is the walls between the bubbles break down

Figure 2.1. Impressionistic representation of pitch in example (1)

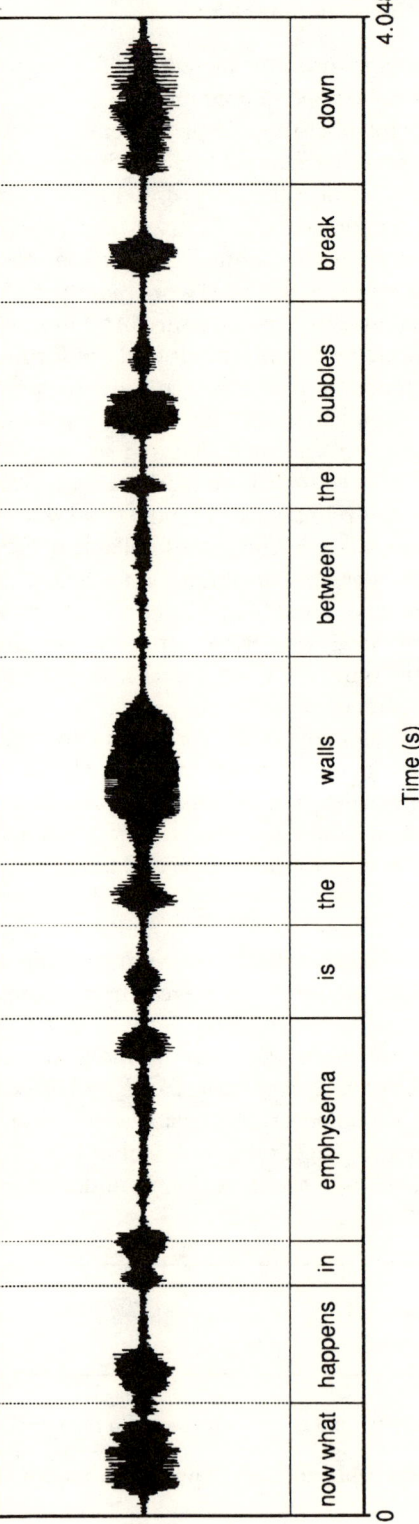

Figure 2.2. Wave form of example (1)

Hearing and Notating Conversational Rhythm 39

Table 2.1. Chart of Syllable Lengths in Example (1).

Time	Syllable	Duration
12.46	now	0.12
12.58	what	0.14
12.72	hap-	0.16
12.88	pms	0.15
13.03	in	0.08
13.11	em-	0.10
13.21	phy-	0.12
13.33	se-	0.27
13.60	ma	0.15
13.75	?is	0.24
13.99	the	0.17
14.16	walls	0.51
14.66	be-	0.14
14.80	tween	0.38
15.18	the	0.06
15.24	bub-	0.28
15.52	bles	0.13
15.65	break	0.27
15.92	down	0.52

by virtue of the fact that they have secondary and primary lexical stress, respectively, and upon close examination they will indeed be heard to be slightly louder and/or longer than the surrounding *-phy-* or *be-*.[4] Nevertheless to treat them as prosodically prominent would be assessing prominence at a finer level than is necessary for most rhythmic analysis. The syllables *em-* and *-tween* in this utterance can therefore be treated as nonprominent for all practical purposes.

Placing accent marks before the prosodically prominent syllables (raised for a strong accent, lowered for a weaker accent), we can now represent the utterance as follows:

now what 'happens in emphy'sema is the 'walls between the ˌbubbles break 'down

The next step in rhythmic analysis is to examine the placement of prosodic prominences in time.[5] One way to do this is to coordinate some kinetic activity, like tapping or nodding, with prominent syllables as the utterance is produced. Multiple listenings with a tape recorder or a computerized speech analysis program are helpful. When the tapping or nodding produces a sensation of temporal evenness or regularity, the prosodic prominences can be said to be perceptually *isochronous* (i.e., they are heard as coming at roughly equal intervals in time).[6] For the perception of temporal regularity to arise, at least three prosodic prominences are necessary: the first two to establish a temporal interval and the third to mark off an equivalent measure of time. A sequence of two prominences appropriately spaced may produce a gestalt-like group but it is by definition not an isochronous structure.

Applying these discovery techniques now to the demonstration phrase used previously, we note the following: *hap-* and *-sem-* form a gestalt-like group and the next prominence on *walls* comes at a point in time which is as far from *-sem-* as *-sem-* is from *hap-*. A temporally regular pattern is thus established: The three prominences form rhythmic beats. The next prominences on *bub-* and *down* are also perceived as being equally as far apart from preceding prominences respectively as were *-sem-* and *walls*. Therefore, they continue the regular temporal pattern as rhythmic beats. Placing slashes before the syllables that constitute these beats and aligning them underneath one another on the page to indicate perceived temporal regularity, this pattern can be represented provisionally as follows:

(1) [Curtis 3]

```
1      now what  / 'happens in emphy-
                 / 'sema is the
                 / 'walls between the
                 / ,bubbles break
5                / 'down
```

Having dissected a rather typical instance of rhythm in speech, we now survey some of the more common rhythmic patterns encountered in English speech.

2. Rhythmic patterns

All the examples used next are taken from genuine spontaneous verbal interactions and have been analyzed using the techniques described earlier. We begin with some of the more salient types of conversational rhythm:

(2) [Curtis 1]

```
1      / 'lots of
       / 'little
       / 'bubbles
```

(3) [Curtis 2]

```
1      / 'tons and
       / 'tons and
       / 'tons of
       / 'little
5      / 'teeny
       / 'bubbles
```

What characterizes these rhythmic patterns is that they are not only isochronous but also *isometric*: The rhythmic intervals, in addition to being perceived as temporally regular, contain an equal number of syllables (two in the case at hand).

Hearing and Notating Conversational Rhythm

(2a) Curtis 1   No. of syllables

```
1      / 'lots of          2
       / 'little           2
       / 'bubbles
```

(3a) [Curtis 2]   No. of syllables

```
1      / 'tons and         2
       / 'tons and         2
       / 'tons of          2
       / 'little           2
5      / 'teeny            2
       / 'bubbles
```

A comparison of these disyllabic intervals, however, reveals that the syllables involved need not have identical individual durations (see also Abercrombie 1964). For instance, in (2) the duration of the first rhythmic interval, which is 0.32 sec., is divided up between the two syllables *lots* and *of* in a ratio of 2:1 (*of* is actually proclitic to *little*), whereas the duration of the second rhythmic interval (0.31 sec.) is partitioned equally (1:1) between the two syllables of *little*.[7] At a more general level, although the rhythmic intervals in isochronous isometric rhythms are of approximately equal duration externally, time in a language such as English need not be distributed internally among the syllables in an equal fashion.

Trisyllabic rhythmic intervals are also common—and indeed even quadri- and quintosyllabic ones are not rare in English conversational rhythm. Following are examples of isochronous isometric patterns of each type:

(4) [Curtis 7]   No. of syllables

```
1      / 'mucus and        3
       / 'junk and in-     3
       / 'fections
```

(Note incidentally that this rhythm occurs on a three-part conversational list; this rhetorical device is highly conducive to rhythmic patterning, as is shown in more detail in chapter 6.)

(5) [Curtis 5]   No. of syllables

```
1      a= / 'vailable for       4
         / 'interchange of      4
         / 'gases
```

(6) [Hatch 28]   No. of syllables

```
1      you know you said
              / 'don't do that Missus       5
              / 'Soandso; and they          5
              / 'go on doing it
```

A final type of isochronous isometric pattern which deserves mention is the monosyllabic one:

(7) [Louise 6]   No. of syllables
1   it / 'just   1
        / 'sells   1
        / 'books

(8) [Louise 8]   No. of syllables
1   / 'dog (0.1)   1
     / 'bites (0.2)   1
     / 'man

This type of pattern is of interest because it belies the traditional belief that rhythm in language depends on an alternation of strong and weak syllables (Selkirk 1984). If rhythm is defined as a perceptually isochronous configuration of prosodic prominences, as here, then cases like the previous one clearly qualify as rhythmic, although they consist exclusively of strong syllables.

Despite the frequency of such isometric patterns in isochrony, it is worth noting that isometry does not guarantee isochrony. This can be seen from the following stretch of speech:

(9) [Louise 21–22]

     if I as'sume what we 'cannot as'sume

Although the first two accented syllables in (9) are each followed by exactly two unstressed syllables, in the actual realization of this stretch of speech there is final lengthening on the first *assume*, suggesting the presence of an intonation boundary between *assume* and *what*. Moreover, the prominences on *can-* and the second *-sume* are much closer together in time than those on the first *-sume* and *can*. Thus, because English syllables differ in inherent duration and may be given additional length in the service of, for instance, delimiting intonation phrases, isochrony does not automatically result when isometry is present. Rather, it must be achieved.

Furthermore, although isometric patterns like those in (2)–(8) may be frequent, English rhythm does not insist on isometry. In fact, isochronous patterns may contain intervals with diverse numbers of component syllables, as the following illustrate:

(10) [Louise 16]   No. of syllables
1   and it / 'makes   1
           / 'perfect   2
           / 'sense

(11) [Louise 21]   No. of syllables
1   it's a /'very   2
            /'nasty   2
            /'awful di-   3
            /'sease

(12) [Hatch 27]   No. of syllables
1   I'm /'very relieved to hear you   7
         /'say that because one   5
         /'does have to have some
       s kind of 'sympathy with them

Rhythmic patterns with varying numbers of component syllables in their intervals are actually more common than isometric ones in everyday English speech.

How do speakers achieve such amazing temporal regularity when the words and phrases they use do not necessarily provide them with the appropriate syllable lengths or stresses? From a close study of rhythmic patterns in English conversation, a number of phonetic strategies can be identified which speakers deploy to achieve rhythmic isochrony. For one, syllables may be stretched or compressed according to rhythmic needs:

(13) [Louise 21a]   No. of syllables
1   /'maybe you didn't get your   7
     /'ma:sk on: in   3
     /'time

Here the syllables -*be you didn't get your* are squeezed together, whereas *mask* and *on* are lengthened to fill an equivalent time interval.

Alternatively, micropauses of varying length may be inserted to ensure that prominent syllables will coincide with the rhythmic pulse, as in (8):

(8a) [Louise 8]   No. of syllables
1   /'dog (0.1)   1
     /'bites (0.2)   1
     /'man

Notice that two micropauses have been inserted between the rhythmic beats of this monosyllabic isometric pattern but that the second pause is longer than the first. One explanation for this may be that although *bites* /baits/ has more component sounds than *dog* /dog/, it has a final voiceless cluster /ts/, which shortens the vowel considerably. A slightly longer pause following *bites* than following *dogs* may be necessary to preserve temporal regularity.

In addition, prominence on a secondary rather than a primary lexical stress may be used to establish an isochronous rhythm, if it fits the potential pattern more readily. For example:

(14) [Louise 23]

```
1     'I don't know of any /'risk of the
                           /'anthrax
                           /ˌvacci'nation
```

The pattern initiated by the timing of *risk* and *anthrax* calls for a third rhythmic beat approximately 0.49 sec. later. And at the appropriate time, the stressed syllable *vac-* does occur, although it is not the main stress of the word in question. Preference is therefore given to the secondary stress in the establishment of the rhythmic pattern. Were one to hold out for the primary stress *-na-* instead, no rhythmic gestalt would take shape because this syllable comes too late to be perceptually isochronous with *risk* and *an-*.

Finally, the position of main lexical stress may be adjusted in speech to fit a local rhythmic pattern. Consider, for instance, the word *vaccine*. According to its standard lexical stress pattern, it has main stress on the second syllable: *vac='cine*. And this is the way it figures in the following pattern:

(15) [Louise 15]   *No. of syllables*

```
1     the person- /'nel should re-          3
                 /'ceive the vac-           3
                 /'cine
```

But on another occasion in this conversation the same speaker can be heard to say:

(16) [Louise 5]   *No. of syllables*

```
1     /'anti-              2
      /'vaccine            2
      /'stuff
```

This time the main stress on *-cine* has been shifted to *vac-*, yielding an isometric pattern that lends itself more readily to isochrony.[8] Stress shifts of this sort are not uncommon and have been widely investigated in Metrical Phonology (see, e.g., Selkirk 1984; Visch 1989; Gussenhoven 1991; Hayes 1995). Yet it has seldom been pointed out that the shifting occurs not only to further rhythmic alternation but also to facilitate isochronous timing.

The majority of the rhythmic patterns considered so far have been particularly salient ones in two respects. First, every prosodic prominence has constituted a rhythmic beat. Yet this is not necessary for the perception of isochrony, as the following example demonstrates:

Hearing and Notating Conversational Rhythm

(17) [Hatch 13]

```
1    of /'little old 'ladies
        /'sitting 'round sort of
        /'nodding their 'heads
```

In this pattern a rhythmic beat is created by the regular timing of *little, sitting* and *nodding*. Yet there are three other prominences on *ladies, round* and *heads*, which are *incorporated* into the rhythmic intervals rather than initiating ones themselves. Not every prosodic prominence thus need constitute a rhythmic beat in perceptual isochrony, although 'stray' prominences sometimes distract from the saliency of a gestalt-like pattern. Occasionally, the stray prominences are themselves part of a smaller rhythmic pattern incorporated into the larger one. This is the case in (17): the prominences on *ladies, round* and *heads* help form the following smaller (faster) rhythm:

(17a) [Hatch 13]

```
    /'little old
    /'ladies
    /'sitting
    /'round sort of
    /'nodding their
    /'heads
```

The prominences on *ladies* and *round* thus subdivide the intervals between *little-sitting* and *sitting-nodding* into two equal parts, or, in other words, the tempo has doubled. One way in which this can be represented notationally is as follows:

(17b) [Hatch 13]

```
1    of /'little old //'ladies      (double time)
        /'sitting     //'round sort of
        /'nodding their 'heads
```

When faster rhythms are incorporated into slower ones, as here, a multitiered rhythmic pattern is produced and the saliency of the gestalt as a whole is increased.

Second, the isochronous patterns considered previously are also relatively salient because they are located for the most part within a single intonation phrase. Example (1), however, shows that this is not a prerequisite for perceptual isochrony. Let us reconsider it:

(1) [Curtis 3]

```
1    now what /'happens in emphy-
                /'sema is the
                /'walls between the
                /,bubbles break
                /'down
```

As can be seen from the interlinear notation, the pitch configuration of this utterance suggests the possibility of an intonation phrase boundary between -*sema* and *walls* due to the step-up in pitch on *walls*. A consideration of relative syllable length substantiates this suspicion: *Is* has the final lengthening which tends to precede intonation phrase boundaries. Thus, using a semicolon to represent prior falling pitch to nonlow, the phrasing of this utterance can be transcribed as:

now what happens with emphysema is; the walls between the bubbles break down.

Yet the fact that there are two intonation phrases here does not prevent the prosodic prominences from being temporally regular. Although intonation phrase boundaries may on occasion disturb the perception of isochrony,[9] there are enough cases in English speech of highly salient rhythmic patterns encompassing two or more intonation phrases to preclude any principled restriction of isochrony to the intonation phrase. What appears to favor the perception of isochronous patterns spanning intonational boundaries is a series of pitch accents of comparable prominence in a succession of relatively short intonation phrases (see also Couper-Kuhlen 1993:98).

3. *Relative tempo*

A final notion with respect to isochronous rhythmic beats that deserves mention is relative tempo. Just as the tempo at which a piece of music is performed may vary, so in speech the rhythmic beat established by regularly occurring prosodic prominences may have different tempos. Often patterns whose rhythmic intervals have few syllables have a relatively fast beat. This is the case, for instance, in (2) and (7), where average interval duration is 0.32 sec. and 0.34 sec., respectively (we use righthand slashes as a roughly iconic indication of tempo):

(2) [Curtis 1]   *No. of syllables*   *Average interval duration*
1   / 'lots of /   2
     / 'little /   2
     / 'bubbles   Ø 0.32 sec.

(7) [Louise 6]   *No. of syllables*   *Average interval duration*
1   it / 'just   /   1
     / 'sells /   1
     / 'books   Ø 0.34 sec.

Similarly, rhythmic patterns whose intervals have many syllables are often slower: see, for example, (12) with an average interval duration of 0.98 sec.

(12) [Hatch 27]   No. of syllables   Average interval
                                                             duration

1   /'very relieved to hear you /   7
    /'say that because one   /   5
    /'does have to have some   /   Ø 0.98 sec.
    s kind of 'sympathy with them

However, on occasion, rhythmic patterns with few syllables per interval have longer average durations, a phenomenon likely to be perceived as 'emphatic' speech (Uhmann 1992; Selting 1994). This is the case in (16), where average interval duration is 0.60 sec.:

(16) [Louise 5]   No. of syllables   Average interval duration
1   /'anti-   /   2
     /'vaccine   /   2
     /'stuff   Ø 0.60 sec.

The tempo of the rhythm here is nearly twice as slow as that in (2), although both patterns have disyllabic intervals.

Conversely, rhythms with many syllables per interval may be encountered which have shorter intervals and the material they span may be perceived as 'parenthetic' (Uhmann 1992):

(18) [Limbaugh 1]   No. of syllables   Average interval
                                                             duration

    'he was
    /'here I 'didn't even
              know he was   / 7^{10}
    /'here but he 'ca:lled   /   4
    /'right before the uh   Ø 0.62 sec.
    .hh the 'program

This pattern has a tempo similar to that in (16), although in interval composition it is more like (12).

Reckoning average interval duration in a rhythmic pattern is useful to obtain an estimate of overall tempo. Yet it does not do justice to the phenomenon of tempo shift, which occurs often enough in English speech to deserve mention here. Consider, for instance, (3) once again:

(3) [Curtis 2]   No. of syllables   Interval duration
1   /'tons and   /   2   0.44 sec.
     /'tons and   /   2   0.40
     /'tons of   /   2   0.34

```
         /'little           /         2             0.30
         /'teeny            /         2             0.27
         /'bubbles                                  Ø 0.35 sec.
```

This pattern has an overall average tempo of 0.35 sec. Yet if the individual interval durations are considered, it will be seen that they gradually decrease: The tempo steadily accelerates throughout the pattern. Each successive interval is heard as approximately equivalent to the one before it, but continual undershooting of a prior durational goal results in an overall shift of tempo, with the pattern being faster at its conclusion than at its outset. Reverse shifts from faster to slower tempo are also encountered. Gradual tempo shifts of this sort do not generally disrupt the perception of rhythmic patterns.[11]

4. Silent beats

As pointed out in chapter 1, rhythmic patterns set up the expectation that they will continue; in fact, they make it possible to predict the moment in time when the next rhythmic pulse is due (see chapter 1, §5.1). It is this property of rhythmic gestalts that is responsible for the phenomenon of silent beats. A *silent beat* is defined as a rhythmic pulse which, at the moment it is expected, coincides with silence rather than with a prominent syllable. Consider, by way of illustration, the following example (we use the symbol ^ to represent a silent beat):

(19) [Louise 17]

```
1     with= /'out that vac-       /
             /'cine; (1.0)         /
             /^ if there's         /
             /'anthrax             /
5            /'used
```

The prosodic prominences on *without* and *vaccine* are timed so that they form a gestalt-like group (they are 0.72 sec. apart). This makes it possible to predict that the next prosodic prominence should come approximately 0.72 sec. after -*cíne*. But precisely this moment in time falls during a speaker pause of approximately 1.0 sec., so the pulse remains 'empty'. The next prosodic prominences on *anthrax* and *used*, however, hit the pulses after the empty one and the rhythmic pattern is confirmed, although it has a 'hole' in its middle. Another way of describing this phenomenon is to say that the speaker has paused 'rhythmically': He has used pausing to sustain a rhythmic pattern. However, in contrast to pauses incorporated between rhythmic beats such as those in (8), this pausing creates a rhythmic beat.

Two conditions must obtain for silence to count as a rhythmic beat: (a) there must be at least two clear rhythmic beats which establish a potential rhythmic interval prior to the silence, and (b) there must be at least one clear rhythmic beat following the silence to stabilize the pattern.[12] As condition (a) suggests, a situa-

Hearing and Notating Conversational Rhythm 49

tion like that in (20) would not permit positing a silent beat within the 0.4 sec. pause:

(20) [Curtis 12]

```
1     I am 'powerless (0.4)
      I am /'helpless in the      /
           /'face of this         /
           /'drug
```

Although the silence between *powerless* and *helpless* would theoretically allow an intervening pulse, thereby creating intervals of approximately the same duration as those that follow, silence cannot initiate a rhythmic gestalt. It can only aid in its prolongation. Therefore, the rhythmic pattern in (20) does not begin until after the 0.4 sec. pause.

Nor, according to condition (b), would the 0.2 sec. pause following *used* in (21) count as a silent beat:

(21) [Louise 17]

```
1     if there's /'anthrax/
                 /'used
      (0.2) uh your c your 'cousin's gonna be 'dead
```

Here the next pulse should come approximately 0.65 sec. after *used* and there is indeed silence at this point. But no prosodic prominence coincides with the next rhythmic pulse thereafter to confirm the pattern. (The next pulse is due when *c-* is broken off.) The word *cousin* comes too late to create a stable framework; therefore, the rhythmic pattern must be said to break down after *used*.

In English speech, strong rhythmic patterns can be found that tolerate more than one silent beat in their middle. In fact, as we shall see in chapter 3, two and even three silent beats are not unusual at certain kinds of marked turn transitions in conversation. However, four and more silent beats appear to overtax the average human capacity to 'keep time' silently and rhythmic patterns tend to disintegrate perceptually under these conditions.

5. *Syncopated beats*

Some strongly prominent syllables come too early to coincide with the expected pulse of a rhythmic pattern. They fall into two categories: (a) those that only temporarily cause an overriding rhythm to 'wobble', and (b) those that destroy a rhythmic pattern. The first case is illustrated as follows:

(22) [Louise 24]

```
1     that /'anthrax could be           /
           /'something that we come a-   /
```

```
                /'cro
        /'we've ex-
5               /'perimented with it in this      /
                /'country
```

In this pattern, the word *acro-(ss)* is cut short and the next word *we've* has sudden high pitch and loudness, creating a strong prominence. Because of its marked nature, it is difficult to hear this prominence as an incorporated one like those in (17), and it therefore destabilizes the pattern temporarily. Yet the following stresses on *experimented* and *country* coincide with the regular pulse and a stable framework is reestablished. Within this rhythmic frame the 'jog' on *we've* can be tolerated. When this happens we say that the prominence forms a *syncopated beat*.

The second sort of early prominence can be seen in:

(23) [Hatch 18]

```
1    to 'go on /'treating/
                /'people     /
                /'as
        'obviously they 'should
```

Here the strong prosodic prominence on *ob-* is far too early to be the next rhythmic beat in the pattern established by the timing of *treating, people* and *as*. But it is also too strong to be ignored. The next prominence on *should* comes too late to establish an overriding regular pattern and the initial rhythm now breaks down.

Syncopated beats are thus somewhat like silent beats in that they are local irregularities which can be tolerated within more globally regular patterns. In the case of silence, we speak of a *pause* (rather than of a silent beat) when global regularity is lacking. When the pulse is not postconfirmed, the next stressed syllable is said to be a *late* stress: see *cousin's* in (21). Because late stresses and silent beats involve the delay or omission of a projected beat, we shall say that they instantiate *delayed* timing. In the opposite case, we speak of *early* stresses (rather than of syncopated beats) when postconfirmation is lacking: See *obviously* in (23). Because early stresses and syncopated beats involve the anticipation of a projected beat, we shall say that they instantiate *anticipated* timing.

Syncopated beats and silent beats are also alike in that they require prior identification of a complete or partially complete rhythmic structure to be 'discovered' themselves. They thus entail a third, phenomenologically reflexive step in rhythmic analysis (see chapter 1, §5.1, in this volume): Pauses and 'stray' prominences in the vicinity of rhythmic patterns must be examined as potential silent or syncopated beats in overriding rhythms. Only once this step has been carried out can the analyst be sure of discovering all the rhythmic patterns in conversational speech.

Hearing and Notating Conversational Rhythm

6. Instrumental measurement and rhythmic gestalts

The point was made previously that an auditory analysis of rhythm, as we have described it here, must have priority over an instrumental analysis. Yet this does not mean that rhythmic intervals cannot be measured instrumentally once isochronous gestalts have been identified. In fact, when this is done, a number of interesting observations can be made about the acoustic durations of intervals between prosodic prominences and how they relate to the presence of a perceptually rhythmic pattern.

6.1. Interval variability

First, it can be observed that the rhythmic intervals of perceptually isochronous gestalts are hardly ever absolutely identical in acoustic duration when measured from a constant point such as the onset of the syllable or the vowel. Even highly salient patterns such as the ones discussed earlier display durational variability, although it may on occasion be rather minimal:

(2) [Curtis 1] Interval duration[13] Percent difference vis-à-vis *prior interval*

1   /'lots of /   0.32
    /'little /   0.31   −3%
    /'bubbles

(12) [Hatch 27]   Interval duration   Percent difference vis-à-vis *prior interval*

1   /'very relieved to hear you / 0.98
    /'say that because one   / 0.97   −1%
    /'does have to have some
    s kind of 'sympathy with them

In both these patterns the second interval is 0.01 sec. shorter than the first. This represents a 3% decrease in (2) and a 1% decrease in (12) compared to the duration of the prior interval.[14] Such figures are, however, well below the *just noticeable difference* (j.n.d.) in the comparison of empty intervals (e.g., separated by clicks), which is reported to be on the order of 10% for interval durations of 0.2–1.5 seconds (Woodrow 1951:1224–5). The majority of perceptually isochronous patterns examined here display variability in absolute interval duration greater than this j.n.d. Consider, for instance:

(5) [Curtis 5]   Interval duration   Percent difference vis-à-vis *prior interval*

1   a-/'vailable for   /   0.70
    /'interchange of   /   0.79   +13%
    /'gases

(20) [Curtis 12]   Interval duration   Percent difference
                                                   vis-à-vis *prior interval*

1   / 'helpless in the /   0.76
    / 'face of this   /   0.85   −15%
    / 'drug

As these measurements show, a second rhythmic interval may represent either an increase or a decrease in duration as compared to the first interval in a perceptually isochronous pattern. And, as the following measurements suggest, sometimes the difference exceeds 20%:

(11) [Louise 21]   *Interval duration*   *Percent difference*
                                                     vis-à-vis *prior interval*

1   / 'very   /   0.36
    / 'nasty   /   0.41   +14%
    / 'awful di-   /   0.52   +27%
    / 'sease

(16) [Louise 5]   *Interval duration*   *Percent difference*
                                                     vis-à-vis *prior interval*

1   / 'anti-   /   0.54
    / 'vaccine /   0.67   +24%
    / 'stuff

Notice that it is not necessarily variability in the number of syllables in an interval which is responsible for greater deviation in absolute interval duration: The pattern in (16) is isometric but has greater variability than that in (20), which is nonisometric. Moreover, the patterns in both (5) and (16) are isometric but (16) has greater variability; the pattern in (20) is nonisometric but has less variability than the nonisometric second part of (11). Thus isometry does not seem to increase the likelihood of equivalence in absolute duration in English. In fact, it is sometimes isometric patterns (especially ones with a relatively fast tempo) that display the greatest durational variability:

(7) [Louise 6]   *Interval duration*   *Percent difference*
                                                     vis-à-vis *prior interval*

1   it / 'just /   0.29
    / 'sells   /   0.38   +31%
    / 'books

But intervals in nonisometric patterns may also vary by as much as 30%:

Hearing and Notating Conversational Rhythm

(1) [Curtis 3]

		Interval duration	Percent difference vis-à-vis *prior interval*
1	now what / 'happens in emphy- /	0.74	
	/ 'sema is the /	0.82	+10%
	/ 'walls between the /	1.05	+28%
5	/ bubbles break /	0.70	−30%
	/ 'down		

How can this much acoustic variability be accounted for? One factor which suggests itself immediately is the way the acoustic measurements are taken. If we reckon interval duration from the syllable onset of one rhythmic beat to the syllable onset of the next (i.e., including any and all initial consonants), a certain amount of variation in interval duration may be attributable to the presence or absence of initial consonants and, in case they are present, to different inherent durations of consonants.[15] In fact, initial consonants appear to influence the location of so-called P-centers (perceptual centers), which determine when syllables are heard as occurring (see the discussion in Couper-Kuhlen 1993). Measuring perceptually isochronous intervals from vowel onset to vowel onset produces better empirical results, in part because P-centers tend to be located more in this vicinity than at the beginning of syllables. However, until the factors that determine P-center location are better understood, there will always be some variability in absolute interval duration when a constant point for measurement is chosen.

Why are hearers (and analysts) able to tolerate interval variability which is much greater than the j.n.d. in the perception of isochronous patterns? Part of the explanation may lie in the fact that in conversation we are dealing not with empty intervals bounded by clicks but with intervals containing linguistic 'bites', whose meanings must be deciphered and/or inferred. Presumably cognitive attention is in such heavy demand for the reconstruction of meaning that much acoustic variability above the j.n.d. goes unnoticed.

6.2. Constraints on interval variability

Yet the interval durations of perceptually isochronous patterns do not vary infinitely. No perceptually isochronous pattern has intervals whose acoustic duration departs by more than roughly 35% from that of prior intervals. Thus there is clearly a limit beyond which intervals will be perceived as anisochronous. That the cutoff point lies somewhere above 31% is substantiated by a comparison of regular rhythms with maximal variability (e.g., [7]), and rhythms with early stresses or syncopated beats as in the following:

(23) [Hatch 18]

		Interval duration	Percent difference vis-à-vis *prior interval*
1	to 'go on / 'treating /	0.42	
	/ 'people /	0.32	−24%
	/ 'as	0.16	−47%
	'obviously they 'should		

(22) [Louise 24]   *Interval*   *Percent difference*
                                                    duration   vis-à-vis *prior*
                                                                    interval

1   /'anthrax could be   /   1.08
        /'something that we come a-   /   1.02   −6%
        /'cro   0.31   −70%
    /'we've ex-
        /'perimented with it in this   /   1.01   −1%[16]
        /'country

Here the early/syncopated syllables create intervals whose durations decrease by 47% and 70%, respectively, compared to prior interval duration. As these are clearly anisochronous intervals, the border b8etween perceptual isochrony and perceptual anisochrony must lie somewhere between 31% and 47%.

It is worth observing, however, that prosodic prominences whose measured distances in time should make them fall fully within the bounds of perceptual isochrony do not always contribute to the construction of rhythmic gestalts. This can be observed in the following:

(14) [Louise 23]   *Interval duration*   *Percent difference*
                                                           vis-à-vis *prior interval*

1   'I don't know of any
        /'risk of the /   0.49
        /'anthrax   /   0.58   +18%
        /₁vacci'nation

Although the accented syllable *I* comes 0.53 sec. before *risk* and should fit nicely into the subsequent pattern established by *risk*, *Anthrax* and *vaccination* (the duration of the interval between *risk* and *Anthrax* would be a mere 8% less than that between *I* and *risk*), it is not perceived as part of the rhythmic figure. One reason may be that the three syllables *risk*, *An-* and *vac-* are alike in having no pitch obtrusion, whereas *I* is different, being accented with extra high pitch. In this case, three like events form a gestalt which excludes the odd fourth.

6.3. *Tempo variability*

Finally, the interval durations of attested isochronous rhythms suggest that there are limits as to how small or how large temporal intervals may be and still create rhythmic gestalts. No rhythmic patterns have been found in our English data with interval durations of less than roughly 0.23 sec. or more than roughly 1.2 sec. These figures suggest that rhythmic beats must be a minimal distance apart, presumably to be perceived as separate events, but at the same time that they must be close enough together to permit perception as a group. How much the tempo of rhythmic patterns may vary is therefore subject to psycholinguistic constraints. It is interesting to compare these figures for speech rhythm to tempo variation in music, where metronome values range from approximately 40 beats per minute (as, e.g., with *grave*) to approximately 200 beats a minute and more (e.g., *prestissimo*). Speech rhythms cover approximately the same range: Interval durations of 1.2 sec. correspond to 50 beats per minute and those of 0.23 sec. to 258 beats per minute. Moreover, a moderate tempo in speech rhythm (interval durations of approximately 0.50 sec.) corresponds to *moderato* in music (120 beats per minute).

As these comparisons suggest, rhythm in speech is not unlike meter and tempo in music. In fact, Lerdahl & Jackendoff (1982, 1983) have shown that both are constrained by the same perceptual and cognitive factors. Yet in contrast to meter in music, rhythm—in our understanding of it—is less pervasive in speech, although potentially more meaningful as a contextualization cue by virtue of its nonpredictability.

3

Rhythm and Conversational Turn Taking in English

Isochronous beats, syncopated/early beats and silent/late beats as described in chapter 2 may be thought of as a set of rhythmic tools with which speakers configure their speech in time. We argue in this chapter that the temporal configuration of speech is something to which speakers attend not only within single turns but also across turns at talk. Although coordinating turns at talk is *prima facie* different from coordinating stressed syllables with one another, we shall see that the same set of rhythmic resources is used for the temporal configuration of speech across turns as for that within turns. The main difference between interturn and intraturn rhythm is that in the former it is two or more speakers who are configuring speech in time. Time, for these speakers, is 'shared', in a sense to be explicated later.

It is customary to think of the coordination of speakers' turns in conversation as governed by the turn-taking system—a self-regulating, locally managed, interactional mechanism for the allocation of turn order and size in two-party and multiparty interaction (Sacks, Schegloff & Jefferson 1974). Although it often goes unsaid, the assignment of speaking rights according to the turn-taking system is an eminently temporal affair: At an initial transition relevance place (i.e., following a first possible turn-constructional unit), a current speaker may select a next speaker, in which case the transfer of the floor occurs *at that place*.[1] If no next speaker is selected by the current speaker, other participants may *then* self-select, with the *first* one to do so gaining access to the floor. If no other party self-selects, *then* the floor reverts to the current speaker and the cycle repeats (adapted from Sacks, Schegloff & Jefferson 1974:704). The italicized temporal expressions (taken from the original) make clear that the turn-taking system depends crucially on time for its proper functioning in conversation. In this chapter we argue that the temporal notions inherent in turn taking may be interpreted rhythmically in English conversation. The coordination of turns at talk thus yields *interactional* rhythms, rhythms similar to those described in chapter 2 but produced by two or more speakers.

In addition to its turn-coordinating function in conversation, interactional rhythm makes an important contribution to the interpretation of utterances as conversational activities. It provides interlocutors with a means for designing and evaluating the way in which an activity such as, for instance, assessing or informing is carried out or responded to; in the extreme case, it may even partially constitute an activity such as repair. Rhythm performs both turn-coordinating and activity-signaling tasks, we argue, by helping to create interpretable contexts for linguistic utterances in the speech event: Isochronous beats, syncopated/early beats and silent/late beats function as *contextualization cues* indexing interpretive frames which guide conversational inferencing (Gumperz 1982; Auer & di Luzio 1992). Interactants rely on such frames in forming hypotheses about matters of interactional concern such as 'Where are we now in discourse?' (at a transition relevance place [TRP], at the beginning or end of a sequence, into closing, etc.), 'Whose turn is it?' (e.g., yours or mine), 'What are we doing with one another?' (e.g., greeting, questioning, assessing, complaining, etc., or arguing, narrating), and 'How are we doing this?' (e.g., unexpectedly, insistently, fearfully, confidentially, etc., or affiliatively, disaffiliatively) (Auer 1986).

Rhythm can thus be seen as having a twofold contribution to make to interaction: To speak with Goffman, it participates in the framework of *system requirements*, those features an interaction system must have, given the anatomical, physiological and cognitive constraints holding on those who participate in it, and in the framework of *ritual requirements*, those rules governing interaction, given that its participants are moral beings with reciprocally held norms of what constitutes appropriate behavior (Goffman 1981; Kendon 1988). In this chapter and the next we investigate both 'system' and 'ritual' aspects of interactional rhythm, examining the various forms found in English conversation and at the same time attempting to assess their contribution to the interpretation of situated utterances in focused encounters.

Beforehand, however, we must consider the notion of *shared* time, a prerequisite for temporal coordination in discourse. Shared time is related to the concept of 'focused gathering', a term Goffman introduced to refer to the maintenance of a sustained focus of attention in situations in which a collection of individuals is co-present (Goffman 1963, 1967; also Kendon 1988). As Schegloff & Sacks (1973) have pointed out, it is only within focused encounters that the constraints of the turn-taking system hold. When two speakers are not in focused interaction with one another, the absence of next-speaker selection by current speaker will not necessarily lead immediately to self-selection by other speakers for the floor: It may instead be followed by a lapse in talk. Nor in the absence of self-selection will the floor revert to current speaker at some specifiable moment in time; nor will self-selection, in the event of its occurrence, be based on a 'first come, first serve' basis. In fact, whether someone 'comes in' and who comes in 'first' are not relevant considerations for nonfocused interaction, because the floor and its temporal counterpart, time, do not function there as an economy. In focused encounters, on the other hand, time and the floor are limited resources: Participants 'compete' for the floor and they 'use up' floor time for their turns at talk. Just as the turn-taking mechanism requires a single focus of interaction to be operative, so interactional rhythm requires a common 'clock' to be functional in the conduct of conversation.[2] In taking turns at talk, participants are drawing from the same supply of time and this supply is continuously in demand.

In the following sections we show how adopting the notion of shared time as a background assumption makes it possible to distinguish different types of turn transitions with respect to timing. 'Well-timed' turn onsets within conversational sequences are those that establish or prolong a rhythmic pattern across the transition; they are said to be *integrated* with the rhythm of prior talk (§1.1). Rhythmic integration is shown to be not happenstance but an interactional achievement (§1.2). 'Ill-timed' turn onsets, by contrast, are those that cause a cross-transitional rhythm to wobble or to break down altogether: The rhythmic *nonintegration* can be due to anticipated or delayed prominences. It is especially nonintegrated onsets that trigger inferential processes. Yet a comparison of anticipated onsets (§2.1) and delayed onsets (§2.2) in a variety of conversational activity sequences shows that the type of inference likely to be drawn is highly context sensitive.

1. Rhythm at turn transitions

When and where are interactional rhythms found in conversation? Let us begin by considering situations in which the coordination of turns at talk is by nature at a maximum, namely, in joint productions (Lerner 1987, 1991). Suppose that two or more interactants wish to collaborate in the construction of a conversational list. If so, they may be concerned to coordinate their turns temporally such that the joint product will be perceived as a single list produced by one speaker rather than as two separate lists. On this assumption, linking the members of the list via isochrony is arguably a useful strategy. (Recall that conversational lists favor isochronous beats.[3]) This strategy, we propose, is the one used in the following exchange[4]:

(1) [Hodge 40[5]]

```
1   G:    my corner shop is very good. (0.9)
          they'll give you a couple of slices of
          / 'bacon if you                    /
          / 'want it.
5   H:                      (0.1) and a/
        →/ 'couple of ounces of       /
```

```
        /'cheese. and
        [that sort of thing
   G:   [that's right (0.2) and that sort of thing
```

In this excerpt Mrs. Giles is extolling the merits of her local grocery, in particular the fact that they are willing to sell in small quantities to people who live alone. As one instantiation of this, she mentions *they'll give you a couple of slices of bacon if you want it*. The prominences on *bacon* and *want* are configured as the beginning of a potential rhythmic pattern. Mr. Hodge, despite the fact that he is not personally acquainted with Mrs. Giles or her neighborhood and is consequently unlikely to be familiar with the habits of her corner shop, nevertheless treats Mrs. Giles's instantiation as a partial list and volunteers another instantiation to match it: *and a couple of ounces of cheese*.

The fact that Mr. Hodge's phrase is designed to create a list whose first member is the prior instantiation by Mrs. Giles is manifest in three ways: (a) it is organized lexically as a coordinative construction using *and*; (b) it is structured syntactically on the model of the first instantiation:

   a couple of slices of bacon
   and a couple of ounces of cheese

(c) it is treated prosodically like the first instantiation. The intonation of *and a couple of ounces of cheese* is identical to that of *a couple of slices of bacon* and the timing of its prominences matches the timing of those at the end of the first instantiation: Mr. Hodge's *couple* and *cheese* establish an isochronous pattern with Mrs. Giles's *bacon* and *want*. Thus these interlocutors produce, together, a partial list of things available at the corner shop in small quantities,[6] and they employ prosody, especially rhythm, to do so.

As this example suggests, participants are sensitive to their interlocutor's rhythm and indeed are able to 'tune in' to it with enough precision for an isochronous pattern to arise across turns. The pattern is created through a pooling of appropriately timed prominences by two or more speakers. Why would speakers wish to do this? In (1) above, the fact that Mr. Hodge is contributing to the partial construction of a list begun by Mrs. Giles provides a possible motivation for the rhythmic coordination of his onset with prior turn. Having a common rhythm counts as a display of mutual endeavor; it turns the sequence of turns into a conversational 'duet' (Falk 1980) with speech rhythm serving as a unifying frame.

1.1. Intrasequential vs. intersequential rhythms

On other occasions interlocutors who produce interactional rhythms, rather than carrying out a joint activity, are engaged in complementary conversational activities which together form an interactional sequence. The common rhythm provides a prosodic display of sequential cohesion. Consider, for instance, the following exchange, which occurs as the conversation in (1) is coming to a close:

(2) [Hodge 50–51–52]

```
1   DH:    lovely to talk to you (0.1)
           thank you very much for coming
                  /'on, you've really/
                  /'set me up for the/
5                 /'day
    MG:                         (0.1) well/
         →    /'I'm
           I'm 'really pleased to 'tell you (0.5)
           and I 'think that
10                /'Wythington is/
                  /'absolutely   /
                  /'marvelous
    DH:  →                  (0.2) /
                  /'super (0.2)
15         thanks
                  /'very much in-/    (faster)
                  /'deed Missis  /
                  /'Giles        /
    MG:  →    /'right
20  DH:                           bye-/    (slower)
                  /'bye now
    MG:                           good-/
         →    /'bye
```

This sequence contains four different isochronous patterns, each of which spans a turn transition. In the first case, Mr. Hodge establishes a rhythmic pattern with the regularly timed prominences *on*, *set* and *day* (lines 3–5). Mrs. Giles orients to this rhythm in her response by placing her first accented syllable *I'm* on the next pulse (line 6). In doing so, she manages to achieve a smooth transition for her entry to the floor, although the rhythmic pulse subsequently disintegrates. She now begins a new pattern on *Wythington*, *absolutely*[7] and *marvelous* (lines 10–12), which Mr. Hodge orients to in timing his next entry: His first accent on *super* (line 14) coincides nicely with the next pulse of Mrs. Giles's prior rhythm. Having assured a smooth takeover of the floor himself, Mr. Hodge now initiates a new, faster rhythm on *very*, *indeed* and *Giles* (lines 16–18), which Mrs. Giles picks up adeptly for the timing of her next response *right* (line 19). Finally, notice the rhythmically smooth farewell sequence,[8] which Mr. Hodge initiates with a more slowly paced *bye-bye now* (lines 20–21) and Mrs. Giles closes with a well-timed *good-bye* (lines 22–23).

As the exchange in (2) demonstrates, speakers do not necessarily maintain a single rhythmic pulse throughout their turns at talk. In (2), Mrs. Giles shifts to a new rhythm within her turn in line 8; Mr. Hodge shifts to a new rhythm in line 13 and to a new tempo in line 18. Changes in rhythm and tempo such as these are sometimes used to contextualize the beginning of a new activity sequence in conversation. But *within* activity sequences, speakers routinely attend to rhythm and tempo at the projected end of their interlocutors' turn and they coordinate their entry to the floor accordingly. If new rhythms are initiated within turns prior to turn endings, the roles of rhythmic leader and rhythmic follower alternate at successive turn transitions.

Yet when interlocutors' turns are short and no rhythm or tempo shifts occur within them, it is not uncommon for a succession of conversational activity sequences to be timed around a single rhythmic pulse. As an example, consider the following conversational opening from a California radio phone-in program[9]:

```
(3)  [Gulf 1]
        M:      hel-/'lo:. I'm                    /
                /'calling from El                 /
                /'Centro Cali-                    /
                /'fornia.
10      L:                                    El/
                /'Centro:.                        /
        M:      /'yeah:.                          /
                /'yeah. down [there
        L:                  [any                  /
15  →           /'protests in El                  /
                /'Centro—                         /
        M:      /'no:- ,everything is             /
                /'pretty cool here.
```

In this exchange, the caller, Max, sets up a moderately paced rhythm in announcing the location of his call with regularly timed prominences on *hello, calling, Centro* and *California* (lines 6–9). The moderator, Leo, picks up this rhythm when he echoes Max's location (lines 10–11) and Max prolongs the rhythm when he confirms the location in the next turn (lines 12–13). Leo now times the onset of his next activity, questioning Max about protests in El Centro, to coincide with the same common pulse (lines 15–16) and Max responds negatively within the same rhythmic frame (line 17). Even Max's turn expansion *everything is pretty cool here* does not change the established rhythm or tempo (lines 17–18).

Speakers then have more than one option for configuring successive turn-constructional units at sequence boundaries: They may preserve the pulse of a prior sequence or they may shift to a new rhythm and tempo. But what most conversational activity sequences have in common is that speakers collaboratively work at achieving isochronous transitions within them. At these moments there appears to be a premium on rhythmic coordination between new turns and prior turns; it is departures from the expectation of smooth interactional rhythm within sequences that trigger extra inferencing by interlocutors.

1.2. Achieving interactional rhythm

Just as with individual rhythms, interactional rhythm does not happen by chance: It must be jointly achieved. A closer look at some of the interactional rhythms discussed previously reveals that interactants need considerable technical skill to produce isochrony collaboratively.

To appreciate what is involved, let us consider what must be done to make interactional rhythm succeed. First, current speakers must set up prominences susceptible to rhythm at potential transition relevance places in discourse. These prominences must either (a) establish an isochronous rhythmic pattern themselves, or (b) provide rhythmic beats for a potential isochronous pattern. As an example of the first option, where a current speaker establishes a complete rhythmic pattern alone, consider:

```
(2a)  [Hodge 50-51-52]
      DH:    thank you very much for coming
             →/'on, you've really       /
             →/'set me up for the       /
  5          →/'day
      MG:                      (0.1) well/
             /'I'm
             (. . .)
 10   MG:    →/'Wythington is           /
             →/'absolutely              /
             →/'marvelous
      DH:                      (0.2) /
             /'super
             (. . .)
 16   DH:    →/'very much in-           /
             →/'deed Missis             /
             →/'Giles                   /
      MG:    /'right
```

In each of these instances the first speaker sets up an isochronous rhythm with three or more regularly timed prominences, thus assuming the role of rhythmic leader. The second speaker prolongs the established pattern by timing the first prominence of the next turn accordingly, thereby assuming the role of rhythmic follower.

An example of the second option, where a current speaker contributes only one or two beats to a potential rhythmic pattern, can be observed in (1):

```
(1a)  [Hodge 40]
      G:     they'll give you a couple of slices of
             →/'bacon if you            /
             →/'want it.
  5   H:                       (0.1) and a/
             /'couple of ounces of       /
             /'cheese.
```

Rhythm and Conversational Turn Taking in English

Here a first speaker contributes two prominences to the potential pattern and a second speaker adds more. Mrs. Giles is consequently the rhythmic leader, whereas Mr. Hodge, in completing the pattern with a third and fourth prominence, assumes the role of rhythmic follower.

Alternatively, the rhythmic pattern may be built up by single prominences from each speaker, as happens in the last sequence of (2):

(2b) [Hodge 50–51–52]

```
19   MG:  → /'right
     DH:                    bye-/
          → /'bye now
     MG:                    good-/
               /'bye
```

In this case it is difficult to distinguish a rhythmic leader from a rhythmic follower: Both Mrs. Giles and Mr. Hodge contribute equally to setting up a pattern for subsequent completion.

Second, for interactional rhythm to succeed, a next speaker must time the first prominence of his or her new turn so that it coincides with the pulse established by the rhythm at the end of a prior speaker's turn. This often requires a fine sense of timing, especially in speech at extreme tempos. A relatively slow pulse, for instance, may mean that a next speaker must wait to come in; a relatively fast pulse may mean that a next speaker must rush to be on time. But how long to wait or how much to rush depends on the tempo at hand—and on whether there are unstressed syllables following the last prominence of the prior turn and/ or preceding the first prominence in the new turn. The fewer unstressed syllables there are between the two prominences that must be coordinated, the more 'room' there is for maneuvering. Thus, a speaker whose next turn has no 'upbeat' or anacrustic syllables may be able to 'pause' if the tempo of the ongoing rhythm is slow, whereas a speaker who wants to squeeze in a large number of unstressed syllables at a fast tempo may need to encroach upon the prior speaker's territory.

To illustrate, consider the following pattern:

(4) [Gulf 6]

```
1    L:     we're con-/'tinuing to take 'calls    /
                      /'Debby on the line from    /
                      /'San Jose you're on the    /
                      /'Giant sixty-eight /        (faster)
5                     /'KNBR I'm         /
                      /'Leo Laporte
     D:  →                         (0.3) /
                      /'hi Leo
     L:  →                         (0.1) /
```

10   /'hi Debby
     D: →   (0.3) /
                     /'uhm:

The tempo as of line 4 is moderate (Ø 0.67 sec.), yet Debby nevertheless allows 0.3 sec. to go by before coming in with *hi Leo* (line 8), whereas Leo waits only 0.1 sec. before responding *hi Debby* (line 10). Another 0.3 sec. elapses before Debby continues with a rhythmically placed *uhm* (line 12). Because both greetings (*hi Leo*, *hi Debby*) are alike in having three syllables, the amount of micropausing between the latter three turns cannot be directly related to the number of syllables in the rhythmic interval: rate of articulation must also play a role. In fact, Debby is articulating more slowly than Leo, which accounts for why he does not need to wait as long as she does before coming in.

Another variant of "precision timing" (Jefferson 1973) can be observed in (1a):

(1a) [Hodge 40]

     G: they'll give you a couple of slices of
           /'bacon if you   /
           /'want it.
5   H: →   (0.1) and a/
           /'couple of ounces of   /
           /'cheese.

In (1), Mr. Hodge must not only gauge the onset of *couple* such that it coincides with the pulse established by the timing of *bacon* and *want*; he must also be sure to get in the unstressed syllables *and a* after the post-tonic *it* of the prior turn but before the first prominence of the new turn is due. This is precisely what the pause of 0.1 sec. allows him to do. Micropausing between rhythmically coordinated turns then is sensitive to the presence of post-tonic and anacrustic syllables.

Finally consider an excerpt from (3) once again:

(3a) [Gulf 1]

10   L: El/
           /'Centro:.   /
     M: /'yeah:.   /
           /'yeah. down [there
     L: →   [any   /
15   /'protests in El   /
           /'Centro—

In this excerpt Leo synchronizes *protests* with the pulse, but to do so, he must get the unstressed *any* in beforehand. Max has appended two unstressed syllables *down there* following his rhythmic beat *yeah* (line 13), so that the interval between this *yeah* and *protests* is for all practical purposes 'full'. Given the tempo and rhythm constraints holding at this moment, it is hardly surprising that Leo's *any* overlaps

Rhythm and Conversational Turn Taking in English 65

there in the tail of Max's turn. Such minimal incursion into prior speaker's 'territory' at a legitimate TRP we shall call *transitional overlap* (see also Jefferson 1984, 1986). Transitional overlap is rhythmically motivated and should not be confused with nontransitional overlap or 'interruption'.

1.3. Rhythmic transitions and sequential well-formedness

We claimed earlier that there is a premium on rhythmic coordination between turns within conversational activity sequences. How binding is rhythm at these transitions? If it is not achieved, is the sequence ill-formed? To answer this question, let us first consider greeting sequences.

Exchanging greetings is one of the most widespread of conversational routines. As the literature has pointed out, the exchange serves not only the function of mutual salutation but also of 'cranking up' the turn-taking mechanism, ensuring that it is in place and working for the upcoming interaction (Schegloff 1972; Levinson 1983). The temporal coordination of greeting sequences is thus more than aesthetic embellishment: It is the crucial testing ground for the coordination of subsequent interaction. Consider, for instance, the beginning of the following phone calls:

(5) [Hodge 1a]

```
1   H:       /'welcome Missis     /
             /'Giles,
    G:  →                  (0.2) /
             /'hello Mister       /
5            /'Hodge,
    H:                    how d'you/
        → /'do madam.
```

(6) [Brain teaser 50]

```
1   D:       /'hello Ron,    /
    R:  → /'hello Dave,      /
    D:  → /'how are ya;      /
    R:  → /'not so bad thanks.
```

In the first case Mrs. Giles times her entry (lines 3–4) so that, together with the beats provided by Mr. Hodge's greeting (lines 1–2), a collaborative rhythmic structure is created. In the second case, the moderator, Dave, and the caller, Ron, provide single beats with each of their turns in order to establish a common rhythm.

When moderators do not issue a formal greeting themselves, callers' greetings tend to be synchronized with the prior announcement of the call. For example:

(3a) [Gulf 1]

```
1   L:       /'Max on the line; from      /
             /'Sacramento. you're on the  /
             /'Giant sixty-eight          /
             /'KNBR.
```

```
5   M:                     hel-/
      →/'lo:. I'm          /      (faster)
        /'calling from El/
        /'Centro Cali-     /
        /'fornia.
```

In announcing the next caller, Leo provides several regularly timed prominences which establish a clear rhythmic pattern (lines 1–4) and Max's entry to the floor (lines 5–6) is timed so that it integrates rhythmically with this pattern. Once Max has assumed the floor, he shifts to a faster tempo.

Synchronization of greetings with the moderator's announcement and/or greeting can also be observed in the following telephone calls to radio phone-in programs:

(4) [Gulf 6]

```
1   L:  we're con-/'tinuing to take 'calls    /
                  /'Debby on the line from    /
                  /'San Jose you're on the    /
                  /'Giant sixty-eight /        (faster)
5                 /'KNBR I'm         /
                  /'Leo Laporte
    D:                              (0.3) /
       →          /'hi Leo
    L:                              (0.1) /
10                /'hi Debby
    D:                              (0.3) /
                  /'uhm:
```

(7) [Hodge 49]

```
1   H:  Mister /'Butler.           /
                /'hello Mister     /
                /'Butler,
    B:                       (0.2) /
5       →       /'hello Dick,
    H:                       (0.2) /
                /'how're ya;
```

Yet consider what happens when synchronization is not achieved, as in the following exchange:

(8) [Brain teaser 60]

```
1   D:  so I think we'll kick off; with er—
                /'sexy Nora; who             /
                /'lives in Heaton Chapel.    /
                /'hi!
```

```
 5  N: →    (0.7) 'hi        (late)
    D:     / 'hi!       /    (faster)
           / 'how are you /
           / 'Nora?      /
    N:     / 'oh    hel-/
10         / 'lo
    D:              he-/
12         / 'hello,
```

Although this moderator also furnishes his caller with regular prominences for the timing of her entry, she misses his cue. Nora's *hi* (line 5) is noticeably late with respect to the next pulse which Dave's rhythm makes expectable. Dave now recycles his greeting (line 6), using an animated voice, and expands it with a routine question concerning his caller's health (lines 7–8). In doing so, he starts up a faster rhythm. This time Nora picks up his cue and places an *oh* plus a new greeting token on the next pulses (lines 9–10). Dave now responds with a replicate of the new greeting token.[10] Ill-timed greetings such as Nora's in line 5 thus seem to call for repair, the repair entailing the replacement of 'faulty', uncoordinated parts by well-timed, coordinated ones.

But Dave and Nora do not appear to consider the matter closed yet, as the continuation of this exchange shows:

(8a) [Brain teaser 60 (*continued*)]

```
    N:              hel-/
           / 'lo!        /
15  D:     / 'hello!
           you're on the /
           / 'radio!     /
    N:     / 'well
           that was a surprise
20  D:     surprise surprise
```

Nora and Dave now go through another cycle of even more animated greetings. And they produce explicit accounts for what they are doing: Dave's *you're on the radio* appears to be motivating the necessity of lively voice behavior, Nora's *that was a surprise* accounting for her rhythmic 'error'. This example suggests that a well-timed exchange of greetings in conversation is not only expectable: If it misfires, correction and accounting may ensue.[11]

A similar expectation appears to hold with respect to closing sequences. In the closing section of conversation, the turn-taking machinery must be jointly brought to a halt in a process that requires delicate negotiation between participants (Schegloff & Sacks 1973). Like openings, closings are a locus for strong temporal coordination between turns, often accompanied by an acceleration of tempo (see also Auer 1990 and chapter 5, in this volume):

(9) [Brain teaser 12]

```
1  DJ:   /'thank you Sue         /
   C:    /'thank you very much   /
   DJ:   /              bye-  /
         /'bye
5  C:    /bye-//'bye    (double time)
```

(10) [Brain teaser 24]

```
1  DJ:   /'thanks for [coming/
   C:                 [oh::::
   DJ:   /['on
   C:        [h:::      you're a/
5        /'darling.      bye-/
         /'bye
   DJ:                   bye-/
         /'bye
```

(11) [Brain teaser 28]

```
1  DJ:   /'okey dokey              /
         /'thanks for coming on    /
   C:    /'okay then
   DJ:                    see ya/
5        /'soon
   C:          //see ya  (double time)
   DJ:                    bye-/
         /['bye
   C:      [bye-bye
```

(12) [Brain teaser 33]

```
1  C:    /'okay                /
   DJ:   /'thank you Julie    /
   C:                   bye-/
         /'bye
5  DJ:                  bye-/
         /'bye
```

(13) [Brain teaser 36]

```
1  DJ:       'okay
         /'thank you Doreen      /
         /'nice to have you on   /
   C:    /'thank you
```

```
5   DJ:                    bye-/       (faster)
                /'bye               /
    C:          /'bye
```

(14) [Brain teaser 42]

```
1   DJ:     /'how's that for you Nora    /
    C:      /'right. 'thank you.
    DJ:                               bye-/
                /'bye                     /
5   C:          /'bye
```

(15) [Brain teaser 49]

```
1   DJ:     /'thank you Ron for     /
            /['coming on            /
    C:       ['thank you
    DJ:                         bye-/
5           /'bye
    C:                          bye-/
            /'bye
```

In these radio phone-ins either the caller or the moderator initiates preclosing, often with a new rhythm. His or her partner follows up with a rhythmically timed return token in next turn. The closing *good-byes* are then exchanged in tight synchronization.

Contrast these routine patterns now to a closing section in which timing goes awry:

(16) [Brain teaser 69]

```
1   DJ:     it's been lovely to have you on the radio Nora
    C:      thank you [very much indeed
    DJ:             /['thank you for
                       coming on and            /
5                   /'being a good caller    /
    C:              /'okay
    DJ:                                 bye-/
                /'bye Nora
    C:      →/'thank you. bye-/
10          /'bye [dear
    DJ:           [bye-
                /'bye
    C:              bye-/      (faster)
                /'bye
15  DJ:         bye-/
                /'bye
            .hh go on like that all night!
```

Following a rhythmic exchange of preclosing tokens (lines 3–6), Dave moves into closing (lines 7–8). Yet Nora decides to append another *thank you* (line 9) and in doing so anticipates the established pulse, thereby throwing the rhythm off. Dave and Nora must now establish a new rhythm, which entails an extra round of *bye-byes* (lines 13–16). That this constitutes a deviation from the expected pattern is evident in Dave's metacomment (*we could*) *go on like that all night!* (line 17). Like nonrhythmic openings, participants also appear to orient to nonrhythmic closings as ill-formed products which require recycling and repair.

Yet openings and closings are rather special kinds of sequence: They constitute recognizable sections of conversation concerned with getting the turn-taking apparatus going and bringing it to a halt (Levinson 1983). In this sense they frame the body of conversation, where other activities (news reporting, assessing, questioning, thanking, complaining, etc.) 'develop' less constrainedly. The nonachievement of rhythmic synchronization at transitions within these other sorts of activity does not appear to be susceptible to repair in the same way it is susceptible in openings and closings. Nevertheless, there is a background expectation that rhythmic coordination will also be achieved at other sequence-internal turn transitions. Where it is lacking, we find interactants engaging in supplementary inferencing.

1.4. Rhythmic integration as unmarked transition timing

On what grounds do we regard rhythmic coordination—or rhythmic *integration*, as we call it here (see chapter 2)—as a background assumption for turns within activity sequences? Our argument is based on quantitative, but also—and especially—on qualitative evidence. Rhythmic integration in English is not only more prevalent than nonintegration but also, when it is lacking, the interaction has a special, marked quality. If turns within activity sequences are rhythmically coordinated with one another, interlocutors do not find it necessary to make additional inferences to construct conversational meaning. Their behavior suggests that they assume interactional business is proceeding as usual. But if a second turn within an activity sequence is rhythmically 'off', interlocutors will be observed to engage in supplementary inferencing to account for the departure from expectation. Therefore, we shall say that rhythmic integration is the *unmarked* option for timing conversational turns within activity sequences.

To see this, let us take the case of assessments. It has been pointed out in the literature that an assessment by one speaker generally sets up a strong expectation in conversation that the interlocutor will provide a second assessment agreeing with the first in next turn (Pomerantz 1984).[12] Excerpt (2) contains an example of such a sequential development:

(2) [Hodge 50–51–52]

```
    MG:   I'm 'really pleased to 'tell you (0.5)
          and I 'think that
10        / 'Wythington is /
          / 'absolutely    /
          / 'marvelous
```

```
DH:                     (0.2) /
    → / 'super
```

When Mrs. Giles assesses the hospital she stayed in as *absolutely marvelous* (lines 11–12), Mr. Hodge produces a congruent assessment in next turn (line 14).[13] Notice now that the second assessment is rhythmically coordinated with the first.

Similar synchronization between second and first assessments can be observed in the following conversational extracts:

(17) [Afternoon tea 82]

```
1  P:      / 'oh it's 'nice around the    /
           / 'ha::rbour there, {p}but     /
   L:  → / 'oh it ˌis.                    /
           / 'yes.
```

(18) [Hodge 81]

```
1  H:      / 'what a silly                /
           / 'fellow. he's                /
           / 'talking through his         /
           / 'head; 'isn't he;            /
5  W:  → / 'isn't he ri-                  /
           / 'diculous.                   /
   H:  → / 'yeah!
```

If a second assessment is rhythmically delayed with respect to a speaker's first assessment, that speaker may use the delay as a cue to a supplementary inference, for instance, that the recipient is reluctant to agree:

(19) [Sister talk 88]

```
1  T:      so it's twenty for you;
           and twenty for Zara. so
           / 'keep that in the /
           / ['back of your    /
5  L:         ['forty dollars.
   T:      / 'purse.           /
   L:      / 'yes.             /
   E:      / 'I think it's a   /    (slower)
           / 'cheat!           /
10 T:  → / ^                (0.6) /
       → / ^                .hh .hh/
           / hnuh huh           /
           / 'well:::-          /
```

```
15         / 'yes; 'I           /     (faster)
           / 'think it's a bit /
           / 'steep my-        /
           / 'self,
```

Tina is advising her sister Lea to reserve money for the airport tax on her upcoming trip to Australia. When Lea's husband, Ernest, now throws in the assessment *I think it's a cheat* (lines 8–9), not only is Tina's response—despite its lexically agreeing nature (*yes; I think it's a bit steep myself*)—preceded by audible outbreaths and other hesitation markers, it is also rhythmically delayed. Rather than setting in on the next pulse following Ernest's *I* and *cheat*, Tina allows two silent beats to elapse before placing a hesitation marker (*hnuh*) on the third pulse and finally beginning her response on the fourth with *well*. It is this rhythmic delay (in addition to the various markers and the downgrading *a bit steep*) that cues Tina's reluctance to agree with Ernest's assessment. In fact, as the development of subsequent discourse makes clear, she is indeed constructing an opposing position (with her husband [Bernie's] help):

(19a) [Sister talk 88 (*continued*)]

```
15   T:    / 'yes; 'I           /     (faster)
           / 'think it's a bit /
           / 'steep my-        /
           / 'self, but
     E:    yeah
20   B: →  but then they do it to cover their ground costs and
     T:    mm
     B: →  and pay for the airport [presumably
     T: →                          [pay for the airport
           → yes (.) that's the only reason (.) they do it
```

Now consider the case of questions, in particular those which are out of the blue and initiate new topics or trigger topic shifts in conversation. For instance:

(20) [Sister talk 27]

```
1    L:    'does 'Lily play the
                 / 'organ;    /
                 / 'Tina,
     T:                (0.3)/
5        →       / 'yes she has a (0.6)
                 I really don't know— very much about organs,
                 but she's got a magn (...)
                 she's got a magnificent organ.
```

Tina has been telling her sister Lea about her recent trip to Australia, where she visited a common relative Lily. With Lea's out-of-the-blue question in lines 1–2

Rhythm and Conversational Turn Taking in English

(the prior topic was the meat the participants are eating), she reactivates the topic of Lily and initiates talk on a new aspect related to it, namely Lily's organ playing. Notice that Tina's answer (lines 5–8) is timed to complete the rhythmic pattern set up at the end of Lea's question.

Similar rhythmically integrated out-of-the-blue question sequences can be seen in the following:

(21) [Sister talk 28]

```
1   L:      have we got 'time for a
                    /'cigarette; before we have a- /
                    /'nother course,
    B:                                              we/
5   →       /'certainly have,
    L:                              (well)/
                    /'I don't want any more to eat,
```

(22) [Sister talk 30]

```
1   L:      /'will it incon-       /
            /'venience her(-)at    /
            /'all(-)
    T:                      (0.1) oh/
5   →/'no
```

(23) [Sister talk 20]

```
1   T:      you /'don't feel       /
                    /'cold          /
                    /'do you        /
    L: →            /'no ((laughs))
5   B:      no I can feel the wind coming in  [from there
    T:                                        [er yeah
            I feel the difference because we haven't got the heat on
    B:      that's where the door is
```

(24) [Sister talk 29]

```
1   L:      /'what's her 'house            /
            /'like,
    T:                              well I can/
          →/'show you a 'photo of it;      /
5           /.if you want to 'see it,
```

Notice that regardless of whether such topic-shifting questions are answered affirmatively, negatively or evasively, the answers are timed to complete or prolong the prior rhythmic pattern. Moreover, interaction proceeds smoothly in subsequent discourse.

Compare this unmarked sequential development now to the following:

(25) [Sister talk 41]

```
 1  B:      do you/'like our new /
                    /'coasters.    /
    L: →            /^        (1.1)/
       →            /^          [oh
 5  T:                          [she/
    L:              / ['yes
    T:                ['never even /
                    /'noticed them!
    L:                             I/
10                  /'have,
            they are rather nice, aren't they.
```

Bernie's question *do you like our new coasters* (lines 1–2)—addressed to his guest Lea—comes as much out of the blue as does Lea's question to Bernie *have we got time for a cigarette* in (21): Neither cigarettes nor coasters have been mentioned in prior discourse. Yet in (25) Lea mistimes her response. She allows two silent beats to go by before setting in with *oh yes* (lines 4 and 6). That this delay is noticeable and accountable is evident in Tina's lateral comment to Bernie: *she never even noticed them* (lines 5, 7 and 9), which 'accounts' for Lea's delayed response.

Summing up the argument so far, it is the quality of interaction at rhythmically integrated versus rhythmically nonintegrated transitions which justifies calling the former unmarked. Whether an interlocutor is thought to be about to disagree or whether some other 'account' is sought/rendered, the common factor in nonintegrated transition timing within activity sequences is a rhythmic sign that something is 'off'. For moves within sequences to proceed smoothly, we conclude, they must be 'on cue'.[14] *Prima facie* then, rhythmic timing within sequences appears to tie in with the discussion of different formats for second pair-parts, where immediate versus delayed formatting has been associated with the distinction between preferred and dispreferred turns (Levinson 1983; Pomerantz 1984; Davidson 1984). We return to this issue in chapter 4. But beforehand, we wish to take a closer look at rhythmically marked turn transitions in interaction.

2. Rhythmic nonintegration at turn transitions

To say that rhythmic integration is the unmarked way of timing turn onsets within most conversational activity sequences does not mean that all sequence-internal transitions display rhythmic integration. On the contrary, there is the rather trivial case of rhythmically unstable sequences where no potential rhythm at the close of a first turn can be detected. These sequences are trivially arrhythmic.[15] But there is also the fact that sequences in which a second turn is noticeably ill-timed with respect to prior rhythm and tempo, as in (19) and (25), are not uncommon. Nonintegration due to anticipation or delay can create mere temporary rhythmic instability or it can cause a prior rhythm to collapse altogether. In both cases interactants will be seen to draw inferences concerning the interaction and/or their interlocutors, inferences whose nature depends (a) on the kind of sequence in which the nonintegration is embedded and (b) on how disruptive an effect it has on interactional rhythm. If incoming speakers time the first prominence of their new turn as a syncopated beat or an early stress, their turn onsets will be heard as *anticipated*. If, by contrast, they time their first prominence late with respect to prior rhythm (i.e., if they use one or more silent beats or a late stress), then their turn onsets will be heard as *delayed*. In the following sections we examine first anticipated and then delayed turn onsets, considering how the type of activity in which speakers are momentarily engaged interacts with different kinds of timing to cue context-sensitive interpretations.

2.1. Anticipated onsets

Anticipated onsets can be subclassified as temporary wobblings within overriding rhythmic frames (*syncopated beats*) or as perturbations with more far-reaching consequences leading to the disintegration of a prior rhythm (*early stresses*) (see chapter 2, §5). When encountered within the same type of conversational activity sequence, the former tends to be milder in effect. To see this, consider first the case of interactive repair.

2.1.1. ANTICIPATED ONSETS IN INTERACTIVE REPAIR SEQUENCES Conversational repair is a relevant action in situations involving misspeaking, mishearing and misunderstanding, although whether and how it is carried out is subject to delicate negotiation among participants (Schegloff, Jefferson & Sacks 1977). Often the type of problem involved and whether it is speaker's or recipient's problem is cued prosodically (see Selting 1987, 1988). One of the preferred formats for addressing an instance of misspeaking or misunderstanding interactively is for a recipient to single out the trouble spot in next turn, thereby *initiating* repair, and for the prior speaker to repeat, rephrase or otherwise clarify the problem in the following turn, thereby self-*repairing*. Alternatively, speakers may themselves elicit help in producing an utterance: The repair can then be proffered by recipients in next turn. It is above all in the repairing turn—whether performed by self or other—that anticipated onsets are encountered. For instance:

(26) [Afternoon tea 122]

```
1   L:    actually— you see, they haven't got a garage,
          erm— (2.1)
          the thing was kept out in the open, (0.9)
          uh which (1.0) ((clears throat))
5         it was deteriorating; wasn't it;
          through— (0.5) being left out, (1.5)
    E:    don't say that,
          mine's out.
```

```
      P:      well so is mine.
10    L:      yes but yours
              / 'wasn't— a new         /
              / 'car to 'start with.   /
              / 'was it. I mean,       /
      P:      / 'who d'ya mean;        /
15            / 'Ernest's?
      L: → / 'I mean      (syncopated)
              / 'theirs— I mean  /     (faster)
              / 'theirs wasn't a /
              / 'new car to      /
20            / 'start with.
```

Lea is explaining here that her daughter and son-in-law have had to sell their car because it was deteriorating from being left out in the open (lines 1–6). When Lea's husband, Ernest, and her son Peter comment that their cars stay outside too, implying that this does not justify selling a car (lines 7–9), Lea's next move (lines 10–13) aims at invalidating their point via the implicit assumption that new cars fare better (i.e., deteriorate less) without a garage than those that are not new. The actual wording of her turn, however, is at best ambiguous and at worst erroneous. Because Peter's car is new and both he and she know this, it is somewhat silly for her to state to Peter, *yours wasn't a new car to start with*. This may be why Peter initiates repair with *who d'ya mean; Ernest's?* (lines 14–15). By assuming that her reference was unclear rather than that her assertion was patently wrong, Peter is opting for the lesser of two (socially stigmatized) evils (Pomerantz 1984).

Rhythmically, Lea's repair in lines 16–20 is oriented to the timing of prominences in the prior initiation: her stress on *theirs* coincides with the pulse established by Peter's *who* and *Ernest's* (lines 14–15). Yet before *theirs* (line 17) there is a strong stress on *I* (line 16), creating a syncopated beat which gives the repair turn a noticeably anticipated onset.

What is the effect of this anticipated onset? Notice first that it is part of the design of a turn that corrects Lea's statement, *yours wasn't a new car to start with* to *theirs wasn't a new car to start with*. Goffman (1969) pointed out that the correction process is invoked when an event that is incompatible with current judgments of interlocutors' social worth receives accredited status as an incident (14). One or more of the interactants is thereby placed in a state of ritual disequilibrium or 'disgrace'; the corrective process is required to restore the ritual equilibrium. Seen in this light, the syncopated beat in Lea's turn onset becomes a quasi-iconic cue to the temporary disequilibrium in talk and to the urgency of setting things right. Her verbal repetition of *I mean theirs*, with *theirs* heavily stressed both times, is indicative of the extra effort being invested to reestablish the ritual balance. The rhythm, the increased tempo and the doubling of the corrected form draw attention to the repair, lending it urgency, extra weight and length, thereby attesting to its status as a conversational 'incident'.

Yet a syncopated beat is by nature less disruptive of interactional rhythm than is an early stress, which destroys a prior rhythm altogether. Consider what happens when an early prominence is used in repair (in this case the early prominence forms the first beat of a new faster rhythm):

(27) [After dinner 113]

```
1   E:              / 'what is this a-      /
                    / 'partment;            /
                    / 'like;                /
    M:              / 'oh the
5                   / 'place I'll be moving /    (early)
                    / 'into?
    E: → / 'no; I mean the        /    (early, faster)
                    / 'place 'he's {p}in.
    M:                       oh/
10                  / 'his?                 /
    E:              / 'yeah;                /
    M:              /^ (1.0) it's           /
                    / 'big,
```

Ellen has not yet seen her son Nate's new apartment and asks Nate's girlfriend Martha what *this apartment* is like (lines 1–3). However, because Martha herself is planning to move soon, Ellen's question is referentially ambiguous: Martha thus initiates repair with *oh the place I'll be moving into?* (lines 4–6), which is followed up immediately by Ellen's repair *no I mean the place he's in* (lines 7–8). Notice that Ellen does not synchronize the onset of her repairing turn to the rhythm of prior talk but uses an early stress which initiates a new, faster rhythm. This early stress arguably cues more of an interactional incident than the syncopated beat in (26) above: Participants here must engage in more interactional work to set things right, as is evidenced by the fact that they expand the remedial exchange, with Martha requesting confirmation of the corrected reference with *oh his?* (lines 9–10) and Ellen providing this confirmation with *yeah* (line 11), before resuming the business at hand.

A similar incident is observable in the following instance of repair, this time with an other-repair format (here too the early prominence initiates a new, faster rhythm):

(28) [After dinner 114]

Participants are discussing a do-it-yourself yoga course with 300 weekly lessons.

```
1   E:     well if / 'I'm not mis-      /
                   / 'taken;            /
                   / 'three hundred     /
                   /^                   /
5                  / 'years-            /
                   / 'three hundred-    /
                   / 'how many is       /
                   / 'tha-
```

```
        N:  →    /'weeks. /        (early, faster)
10      E:  →    /'weeks. /
        N:  →    /'six    /
            →    /'years, /
        E:       /'three hundred    /      (slower)
                 /'weeks; are       /
15               /'six years!
        M:  well it's supposed to be a lifetime,
            [you know study it's something you continue;
        N:  [yeah that's the point,
            yoga is something you do:
20          over a continuous—
```

When Ellen misspeaks by saying *three hundred- years* (lines 3–5), Nate 'other corrects' with *weeks* (line 9), which Ellen confirms in next turn (line 10). Nate now additionally provides the equivalent number of years (lines 11–12), thus introducing the sum which Ellen was arguably seeking in prior discourse. Ellen now repairs her initial turn *three hundred weeks; are six years!* (lines 12–15), thereby confirming Nate's corrections. Here too the (first) repairing turn (line 9) has an early onset which initiates an accelerated tempo, and the remedial exchange (lines 10–12) involves more interactive work.

Thus the type of anticipated onset, whether syncopated or early, appears to link up with how noticeable corrective repair is made to be in interaction, and this in turn has consequences for how much remedial effort must subsequently be invested before participants can return to ongoing business. Yet all cases of anticipated onsets in repair have in common that they call attention to the fault-implicative nature of the activity (see also Couper-Kuhlen 1992b, 1993). Indeed, their indexical value is in an important way codetermined by this very activity.[16]

2.1.2. ANTICIPATED ONSETS IN ARGUMENTATIVE ASSERTION SEQUENCES

The context-sensitivity of anticipated onsets becomes more evident if a second sequential environment in which they occur is examined: Let us take now the case of argumentative assertions. These conversational moves embody an assertion made to warrant a speaker's position in argumentation. They make confirming or disconfirming responses in next turn expectable. By *argumentation* we refer not to the lay notion of 'having an argument' but to a special frame or modality for conversational interaction which, once evoked, has consequences for the preferential organization of activities within it (Jacobs & Jackson 1981). Recall that assessments in everyday interaction, for instance, set up a strong expectation that they will be *agreed* with in next turns (see §1.4). Within an argumentative framework, by contrast, the expectation is that assessments will be *disagreed* with (Goodwin 1982, 1983; Vuchinich 1984, 1990; Kotthoff 1993). This is because in argumentation speakers' primary goal is to weaken alter's position and thereby strengthen their own (opposing) position. The overriding aim is not affiliation and cooperation but disaffiliation and conflict. Disagreements, denials and rejections are therefore at a premium. The preference reversal is reflected in the way such activities are carried out. Whereas

Rhythm and Conversational Turn Taking in English

disagreeing second pair-parts in nonargumentative discourse are likely to be carried out reluctantly, if at all (Pomerantz 1984), disagreeing turns in argumentation tend to be immediate and unmitigated (Goodwin 1982, 1983). For this reason *disconfirmation* must be viewed as the preferred next for argumentative assertions: It works toward a rejection of interlocutor's point and thereby a weakening of the opposing position.[17] Following is an example:

(29) [Amstrad 102]

```
1   C:    we just accept that we don't
          we don't get luxuries like holidays.
          and things like that. (.)
    Z:    oh we could've done;
5         if we hadn't /'spent what we      /
                      /'spent on the        /
                      /'house;
    C: →             /'no; no       (syncopated)
                    /'come on;
10                /'no; I don't think you/   (early, new rhythm)
                    /'could.
```

Charles and Zara, a married couple, are talking with their in-laws about how they make ends meet. Charles' position is that he and his wife have not had money to spare because the price-wage relation has been unfavorable (lines 1–3), whereas Zara's position is that it is because of expenses for the house (lines 4–7). Charles denies Zara's assertion (lines 8–11), thereby rejecting it as a valid point, and he does so in a turn that sets in with a syncopated beat (line 8).

Similarly, somewhat later in the same conversation, we find:

(30) [Amstrad 103]

The topic is getting a loan for the purchase of a house.

```
1   Z:    now; it's better.
          it's easier.
          because, like Ray and Ruth;
          they didn't have a deposit for a house,
5   C:    well they were lucky.
          they were /'dead lucky— {p}and I/
                   /'mean—
    Z: →          /['no;       (syncopated)
    P:             [yeah that
10  Z:           /'no. because
                 /'some building so—    /   (early, new rhythm)
                 /'cieties now will—
          (.)'give a hundred percent 'mortgages.
```

This time it is Charles who advances a claim (*Ray and Ruth*) *were dead lucky* (lines 5–6) to warrant his position that buying a house is difficult because it requires getting a loan; Zara's disconfirming response *no; no. because some building societies now will give a hundred percent mortgages* (lines 8, 10–13) begins with a syncopated beat (line 8).

In contrast to (26), where a syncopated beat was used in repair, the syncopated beats here have little to do with a corrective process made necessary by a problem of speaking or understanding. Instead, they accompany turns that address the task of defending one's own position against a position established by other. In this case the anticipated onsets appear to be cueing the readiness (and strength) of the speaker's countermove. By anticipating the pulse, next speaker displays not only that he or she is not at a loss to provide a counterargument but also that this counterargument is a particularly forceful one. The force of the responses in (29) and (30) is reflected both in the prosody (strong stress and syncopated rhythm) and in the verbal means deployed: repetition of *no*, additional negative expressions (e.g., *I don't think you could*) and reasons for the denial (e.g., *because some building societies now will give a hundred percent mortgages*).

Yet in argumentative assertion sequences, just as in repair, syncopated beats do not cue as extreme a disruption as do early prominences. Compare, for instance, the following extract:

(31) [Sack 3]

```
1   H:      yes I I'm not erm veterin ((babble))
            or whatever it is qualified
            but is it not true that we (1.1)
            animals of various types can tolerate certain
5           kinds of
            what we would regard as dangerous (0.1) er
                    /'substances for     /
                    /'u:s:
    S:   → /'yes I       /      (early, faster)
10          /'know but I /
            /'don't see
            why they should tolerate sawdust and er (0.9)
            nails or whatever it was
```

This excerpt is part of an extended argumentative episode on a radio phone-in call, initiated when Mrs. Sack expresses dismay at the use of contaminated meat in the preparation of pet food. Prior to this exchange Mr. Hodge has implied that Mrs. Sack may be overly concerned about the welfare of animals. Here he suggests that animals can tolerate more contamination than human beings (lines 4–8). Mrs. Sack's response *yes I know but I don't see* . . . (lines 9–11) is not only much too early for the next pulse following the prominences on *substances* and *us*; she also adopts a faster tempo. The early stress on *yes* initiates a new rhythm, preventing the former potential one from taking shape at all.

Within the argumentative framework, Mrs. Sack's response can be seen as an attempt to deflect the thrust of Mr. Hodge's point, which is interpretable as an attack on her position. She does not deny his assertion outright but attempts to thwart it via a strategy of *reductio ad absurdum*. It may be this strategy which calls for more marked prosody than that of outright denial as in (29) and (30). In any case the early beat and the accelerated tempo of Mrs. Sack's response together create a stronger prosodic break in the flow of interaction and thus cue a more extreme form of rebuttal.

A final example demonstrates that early prominences also co-occur with explicit denials:

(32) [Gulf 11/2]

```
1    R:      I'd like to say (.) that eh:::
             I I think eh eh burning the flag;
             is a (.) is a slap;
             in the face; of every American. (.)
5            and I think (.) people should have respect for the flag. (.)
             and ((clears throat))
             if protesters; (.)
             are gonna to burn the flag;
             people are /'not going to                    /
10                      /'side                            /
                        /^                    (0.8) with/
                        /'them.                           /
                        /^                    (1.1)      /
     L: →               /['I don't think a lot of these
15   R:                  ['they don't have any re-       /
                        /'spect;                          /
     R:                 /^ for their country.
     L: →       /'I don't think a lot of these    / (early)
                /'protesters are much              /
20              /'worried if anybody's gonna       /
                /'side with them un-               /
                /'fortunately.
```

This caller's point is that burning the flag is un-American (lines 2–6) and that Gulf War protesters who make use of this tactic will not gain public support (lines 7–12). Leo's first attempt to counter this point (line 14), which comes one silent beat after a potential TRP in Ron's current turn, is thwarted when Ron unexpectedly extends his turn with *they don't have any respect; (.) for their country* (lines 15–17). At the next TRP, Leo now anticipates the pulse with a strong early stress on *I* (line 18). This strategy not only ensures him the floor; it also adds a gloss of forcefulness to his turn's business, which is to detract from Ron's stance by claiming that the protesters are not concerned about finding support in the first place (lines 18–22).

Thus, the use of early prominences in argumentative assertion sequences is independent of whether the turn is explicitly or implicitly defending speaker's own position and/or countering opponent's position. The argumentative assertion is, however, cued as being more forceful if it is timed *early* with respect to prior talk.

2.1.3. ANTICIPATED ONSETS IN CONVERSATIONAL OPENINGS   Anticipated onsets also occur in conversational openings,[18] where their signaling value is different once again. For example:

(33) [Brain teaser 51]

```
1   D:      /'hi Gary,
    G:            hel-/
                /'lo,
    D:      hel//'lo! /      (double time)
5           /'how are ya.
    G:          /'I'm not so bad       /    (late)
                /'Dave; how's your-    /
                /'self;
    D: → /'excellent;/        (early)
10          /'thank you,/
            /'excellent.
```

Following an initial exchange of greetings with Gary (lines 1–4), Dave expands the opening sequence of this telephone call with *hello! how are ya* (lines 4–5), accelerating the tempo. But Gary's response *I'm not so bad* (line 6) comes late with respect to the pulse established in prior talk. Moreover, he continues with a new, slower rhythm on *Dave; how's yourself* (lines 6–8). Notice now that Dave's next incoming on *excellent* is early with respect to the new pulse (line 9).

How are anticipated onsets such as Dave's interpreted in conversational openings? To answer this question, it is necessary to compare other greeting exchanges on this radio program. Recall example (8): Here Dave was also observed to increase tempo in a (recycled) greeting sequence. On occasion, he even deploys early onsets in the absence of dragging or delayed rhythm by a caller:

(34) [Brain teaser 53]

```
1   D:          /'Bert Dawson,          /
                /'first in Withenshawe. /
                /'hi Bert,
    B:                              hel-/
5               /'lo there;
    D: →    /'how are ya;    /   (early)
    B:          /'fine;
    D: →/'good!/     (early, faster)
            /'welcome to the program
```

Rhythm and Conversational Turn Taking in English

Anticipated onsets are generally heard as signaling something akin to vivacity or pep in conversational openings and, when deployed by moderators on radio phone-in programs, are arguably designed not only to prod immediate addressees into more animation but also to have a stimulating effect on the larger radio audience.

To summarize the discussion so far, each sequential activity type examined provides a different context with respect to which anticipated onsets are interpreted. Thus anticipated onsets can be thought of as design features which contextualize the various sequential turns they serve as formats for in a context-sensitive fashion. Yet the contextualizations are not wholly unrelated to the nature of *anticipated* rhythm, a point which becomes clear when we contrast them with *delayed* rhythm.

2.2. Delayed onsets

Similar to anticipated onsets, delayed onsets can be subclassified into two types: those created by one or more *silent* beats, which produce temporary disturbances in an overall rhythmic pattern, and those created by a *late* prominence, causing a prior rhythm to break down (and optionally initiating a new one). As with anticipated onsets, the difference in effect between these types is one of degree and the particular signaling value is highly context dependent. In the following, we examine instances of delayed onset as they occur in argumentative questioning, in out-of-the-blue questioning and in repair initiation.

2.2.1. DELAYED ONSETS IN ARGUMENTATIVE QUESTIONING SEQUENCES Consider first the use of a delayed onset following a question asked within an argumentative framework:

(35) [Amstrad 43]

Peter, who lives in Switzerland, has been describing the high price of housing on the Continent.

```
 1  C:      would it not be worth your while though;
            to buy maybe a little small property in
                    /'England; to              /
                    /'keep—
 5  P:                                    not/
                    /'really; I mean what     /
                    /'for;                    /
    C:  →           /^                 (1.0) /
                    /'well,                   /
10
    P:                          (0.5) and what/
                    /'on;                     /
    C:  →           /^                 (1.4) /
        →           /^            well you're/
```

15   / 'never
            gonna 'lose on it. 'are you.

As is evident from this exchange, Charles and Peter hold different opinions on whether it would be advisable for Peter to own property in England. Peter's questions *what for* (lines 6–7) and *what on* (lines 11–12) are intended to elicit answers that will serve as warrants for his position. Charles's delay in providing these answers (see lines 8, 10 and 13–14) cues not only the fact that he does not have them immediately available but also that he is in danger of having to concede the points in question.

Delayed answers of *I don't know* to argumentative questions are a related phenomenon:

(36) [Amstrad 42]

Peter and Ernest are talking about apartment owners who rent their property rather than convert it into cash.

```
1    E:    would he get a bigger income (0.5)
           from his cash deposit than (.)
           owning that property with all its problems (.)
           and / 'you just paying the /
5          / 'rent for it.              /
     P:    /^                           /
     →     / 'I don't know.
     E:           d'y'see what I'm/
           / 'getting at?
```

(37) [Amstrad 46]

```
1    E:    'what— is the— 'going
           / 'rate; for a de-     /
           / 'posit in            /
           / 'Switzerland.
5          / 'interest       /    (late)
           / 'rate.          /
     P:    /^         (1.8) /
           /^                /
     →     /^          I/
10         / 'don't know;
           I've never I've never had to have interest rates.
```

In each case here Ernest's questions are attempting to get Peter to provide answers that will enable Ernest to construct an argumentative stance. And in both instances Peter's verbal response *I don't know* (line 7 in [36] and lines 9–10 in ([37]) claims lack of knowledge. All things being equal, this is a perfectly legitimate conversational move. Yet within an argumentative frame and accompanied by noticeable onset delay, as here, these turns take on an additional gloss. Similar to (35), lack of an immediate response to an argumentative challenge signals that the speaker is in a predicament, being unable to rebut immediately. The claim to lack of knowledge is a convenient way to avoid explicitly conceding the point. Yet here too the rhythmic 'holes' are iconic of a 'lack' on the part of the interlocutor responsible for them.

Onset delays following argumentative questions which couch an implicit face threat are likely to create a more serious 'uncomfortable' moment in interaction (Erickson & Shultz 1982; Auer, Couper-Kuhlen & di Luzio 1990):

(38) [Hodge 44]

```
1   H:     what about wrapped meat and that sort of thing.
            how d'you go along for a
            for a bit of joint.
            do you / 'ever   /
5                   / 'get a /
                    / 'joint /
    G:              / [ 'oh no
    H:                [{p} 'Missis Giles
    G:     I never get a joint.
10         it's either chops [stew (0.5)
    H:                       [mm
    G:     or erm (1.0) braising steak (0.2)
    H:     but isn't that
           I mean I think you're the kind of lady who
15         deserves to have a joint occasionally.
           don't you think that's a bit bad that you
           / 'really    /
           / 'can't af- /
           / 'ford a    /
20         / 'joint     /
    G: → / ^       (0.5) /
        → / '? uh         /
        → / 'we::::ll
           I suppose it is in one way.
25         but on the other hand if you've got a joint
           you see I live al I'm a childless widow (0.1)
    H:     yes
    G:     er (0.4) I'd be chewing it all week wouldn't I
    H:     hn heh heh I suppose you would (0.3)
30         I suppose you would Mrs. Giles
```

Mr. Hodge is engaged in an attempt to argue that old-age pensions are insufficient. His elderly interlocutor, Mrs. Giles, on the other hand, does not hold this opinion:

She *manages to manage,* as she puts it earlier. Nonetheless Mr. Hodge pursues his side of the argument by asking *do you ever get a joint* (lines 4–6). The answer reveals that Mrs. Giles buys only small pieces of meat rather than whole legs or shoulders (lines 7, 9–10, 12). When Mr. Hodge now asks his interlocutor to agree that it's *a bit bad* that she *really can't afford a joint* (lines 17–20), her response is noticeably late (see lines 21–23). In contrast to Mrs. Giles's earlier response with unmarked rhythm (line 7), this timing suggests that something is 'off'. Given its position in the argumentative frame—namely in a reply to Mr. Hodge's attempt to establish a point which would strengthen his position—one interpretation of the onset delay is that Mrs. Giles is about to have to concede the point, the silent beat cuing her predicament and unwillingness.[19]

Because of the strong sequential implication in argumentation that a move by one opponent will be immediately countered by the other, delayed onsets in this framework seem to imply that the speakers find themselves in a predicament, either being unable or unwilling to furnish the requisite rebuttal immediately. They are not only 'embarrassed' for an answer but also—due to the constraints of the genre—in a position of thereby having to concede the point under construction. The seriousness of the concession depends in the cases at hand on the seriousness of the prior 'attack'.

2.2.2. DELAYED ONSETS IN NONARGUMENTATIVE QUESTIONING SEQUENCES In contrast to argumentative questions, delayed onsets following nonargumentative questions may make quite a different set of interpretations relevant. Consider, for instance, the following exchanges:

(39) [Edell 3.38]

```
 1   D:      she's /'starting to        /
                   /'cough              /
                   /'out of the         /
                   /'blue. now          /
 5                 /'how old a woman    /
                   /'is she?            /
     C: →         /^              (0.6) /
                   /'she uh'll turn
                      /'fifty this      /     (late, new rhythm)
10                    /'year
     D:      yeah
             what's her attitude towards it all
     C:      well
             if you (even) bring it up
15           she gets mad at you
```

(40) [After dinner 109]

```
 1   A:      I'm 'so 'happy that I 'stopped,
     N:            /'when did you /
                   /'quit;        /
```

```
         A:  → /^            (1.2) /
    5        → /^                 /
                / 'uh:::—              /    (slower)
                / 'when Robert and I   /
                / 'met each other,
                we quit together,
    10          we both smoked,
                and we decided we'd quit together,
```

In (39), Dr. Edell is inquiring about the age of his caller Curtis's mother (lines 5–6); in (40), Nate is asking Ann when she quit smoking (lines 2–3). In both cases, responses in next turn are delayed by one or more silent beats.

Silent beats suggest in general that recipients have a problem with responding in the expected way to a prior conversational move. Yet determining what the problem is requires context-sensitive inferencing on the part of interlocutors (and analysts). In nonargumentative questioning sequences, rhythmic delay in a response can often be accounted for by the nature of the prior question. As the questions in (39) and (40) are ones that may require recipients to do some mental reckoning, this is one plausible account for the delayed onset of responses to them. The need to reckon is, however, hardly an issue in the following exchange:

(41) [After dinner 106]

Martha is telling her interlocutors about a marathon race in which she and her girlfriend ran.

```
    1   M:      but 'she was feeling 'wonderful;
                and 'I was feeling—
                / 'just like—            /
                / 'garbage.              /
    5   K:      /['why didn't you just   /
        N:       [yeah but
        K:      / 'stop;                 /
        M:  →   /^                 (1.8) /
            →   /^
    10  S:                         {p}'pride;/
        M:  →   / 'I— hhh I              /
                / 'would have
                if I had been alone,
                pride in a way,
    15          a sense of cameraderie;
                with my girlfriend,
```

In this episode Martha, an amateur marathon runner, has been describing the 'bad experience' she had in a recent race. At about the halfway point she began to feel weak and nauseated; yet despite this, she dragged herself through to the finish. When Karen innocently asks *why didn't you just stop* (lines 5 and 7), Martha's response is delayed by two silent beats (lines 8–9). Yet clearly it is not numerical calculation that is at stake. Instead, as Sam's proffered *sotto voce* answer suggests (line10), the motive behind Martha's staying in the race despite her acknowledged discomfort may have been that she was too proud to drop out. If so, this account impinges upon her 'moral' self or its public 'face'. Questions susceptible to being interpreted or answered in a way that invokes the moral order may influence the way the timing of a recipient's response is interpreted. A recipient who delays in answering such a question draws attention to its face-related implications; lack of a filled beat is in a sense iconically related to signaling loss of face.

This is at its most evident when the rhythmic configuration of talk breaks down altogether following such a question:

(42) [Brain teaser 107]

```
 1  D:    couple of callers (.) .h
          er firstly to Bolton and Gary McDonald (.)
          hi Gary
    G:    hi
 5  D:    hi how are ya
    G:    not so bad thanks
    D:    good (.)
              / 'whereabouts in /
              / 'Bolton do you  /
10            / 'work.
    G:  → (0.5) ' eh-  I       (late)
              / 'don't; I'm unem-  /
              / 'ployed (-) well a /
              / 'student;          /
15            / 'part-time.
    D:  → (0.2) a 'student (-)  'uh     (late)
              / 'part-time unem- /
              / 'ployed.         /
    G:        / 'yeah.
```

When Dave asks his caller Gary *whereabouts in Bolton do you work* (lines 8–10), Gary's response is noticeably delayed (line 11). It is prefaced with *eh*, whose timing does not fit into an overall rhythmic frame or contribute to establishing a new rhythm. It is therefore maximally disruptive for the flow of interaction.

Now as Dave's question tacitly assumes that Gary does indeed work somewhere in Bolton, the only straightforward answer to this question is a place of employment (Boots, Securitor, etc.). Considerable more conversational work is required, however, if—as here—the presupposition of employment does not hold. Moreover, as in (41), a moral order is invoked by this question which potentially affects the caller's public face. Rhythmic delay here thus cues the fact that the next speaker's face is at stake. In contrast to (41), however, the perturbation of interactional rhythm persists: Gary later establishes a new rhythm in his response (lines 12–15), but Dave now misses Gary's new cue, causing the latter's rhythm to disintegrate (line 16). In effect, over a series of within-sequence turns, these participants are unable to 'get together' rhythmically. In this case then, prosodic nonintegration reflects a lack of common ground between participants and cues a rather serious interactional incident.

2.2.3. DELAYED ONSETS IN REPAIR INITIATION   In contrast to lack of rebuttal or loss of face, delayed onsets in repair initiation cue a different kind of lack:

(43) [Hodge 116]

```
1   H:     what d'you wanna argue about.
    L:     the Grand National Appeal.
    H:     oh yes, ((laugh))
           have you seen in the paper,
5   L:     aye
    H:     that it failed; (0.3)
    L:     u? (0.3) yes.
           I'll tell you why.
           em 'cause that's what I'm explaining
10  H:     go on then,
    L:     now in my opinion,
           it is not a /'paying propo-       /
                       /'sition.             /
    H: →     the /'Grand National as a/    (faster)
15                  /'whole.               /
    L:              /'yeah,                /
    H:              /'mhm,
    L:          'otherwise,
```

(44) [Women 123]

```
1   O:     well I don't know whether you're a gardener.
           Marvin,
           but but uh if [you are—
    M:                   [hhh
5   O:     or even if you [aren't;
    M:                    [(I'm not really.)
    O:     you might know that science;
           has been /'creeping into the   /
                    /'garden as           /
10                  /'well;               /
                    /'lately— for
    M: →             /['slugs did you /    (late, faster)
    O:                [(???)—
    M:                  /'say?           /
```

```
15   O:                    /'science.
     M:                                    oh/
                           /'science.
     O:                              'and—/
                           /'well I suppose  /     (slower)
20                         /'slugs 'too;
```

In both these extracts recipients initiate repair by proffering a possible correction—in (43) *the Grand National as a whole* for an unclear anaphoric reference and in (44) *slugs did you say* (jocularly) for a putative misspeaking. Moreover, in both cases the repair initiations set in with late beats and are accompanied by a noticeable acceleration of tempo. There are thus clear prosodic signs of the fact that a new activity is under way, and indeed one which—judging from the increase in tempo—is endowed with a certain urgency. Why the delayed onsets?

The answer appears to lie in the preference order for different types of repair. As Schegloff, Jefferson & Sacks (1977) have shown, it is *self*-repair which has structural preference in everyday conversation. There are a number of structural opportunities for self-repair of a trouble spot before repair initiation by other. Among these are (a) turn components following the trouble spot, (b) the transition space at the end of current speaker's turn, and (c) an extra space before the onset of next turn. Rhythmically delayed onset of repair initiation constitutes this third opportunity space: It provides current speakers with a pulse following the end of their regular turn on which they can self-correct.

Delayed onsets in repair initiation thus have a structural (or system-related) function in conversation, as well as cuing inferences of a more evaluative nature. Evaluation, however, becomes relevant when the onset delay is maximally disruptive of interactional rhythm as happens, for instance, in the following:

(45) [Hodge 115]
```
1    J:    /'what I'm—what I'm       /
           /'saying Dick,            /
           /^               is a-/
           /'bout these er:          /
5          /^            (0.9) kerb/
           /'crawlers.
     H: →      (0.7) 'these 'what;      (late)
     J:    these /'people that    /    (faster)
                 /'go around, these /
10              /'men in
           /'cars; you        /      (early)
           /'know,
     H:    oh
           /"kerb::   /      (early, faster)
15         /'crawlers. /
           /'yes I'm   /
```

```
            /'sorry; I
               didn't/
            /'catch
20             what you /
            /'said
```

When June announces the reason for her call as being *about these er: kerb crawlers* (lines 4–6), Mr. Hodge manifestly has a problem, for which he initiates repair with *these what* (line 7). Not only does this repair initiation have a delayed onset; it also has maximal prosodic prominence by virtue of the fact that both words are loud and strongly stressed. Moreover, they can be heard as breaking with prior rhythm. The result is that *these what*, already prominent by virtue of its stress clash, is made even more prominent by being disengaged from the rhythm of surrounding talk.[20]

That this prosodic treatment contributes to the creation of a conversational 'incident' can be seen from the course of subsequent interaction: Once June has paraphrased the trouble item *these people that go around, these men in cars* (lines 8–11), Mr. Hodge repeats the now repaired item in a display of understanding (lines 13–15), but he appends an 'apology', thereby making explicit the moral question of who was responsible for the error.[21]

In sum, just as with anticipated onsets, delayed onsets are prosodic signs that something is 'off'. They make additional inferences relevant, inferences about the interaction or the interlocutors which are often evaluative in nature. What kind of inference is appropriate, however, is contingent upon the embedding sequential context. In nonargumentative questioning sequences, rhythmic delay may cue that something has put the recipient in a predicament (e.g., the need to reckon or a face threat), whereas within argumentative frames, delayed onsets may cue the (impending) loss of a point. In repair initiation, on the other hand, a delayed onset may serve as a hint to prior speaker to look for a trouble spot and self-repair. Late onsets in such sequences have in common that they signal that something is interfering with business as usual. How severe this interference is depends to a large extent on the degree to which interactional rhythm is interrupted.

Comparing delayed with anticipated onsets, it will be seen that although both can be said to contextualize their turns in a context-sensitive fashion, they are not wholly arbitrary in function. One indication that these contextualization cues are 'motivated', however weakly, is the fact that they are not interchangeable in a given sequential environment. Take the case of argumentation: The production of a rebuttal earlier than expected (as, e.g., in [31]) conveys quite a different sort of implicit message compared to a rebuttal produced with delay (as, e.g., in [38]). Early rebuttal is indicative of forceful self-defense, whereas delayed rebuttal is more suggestive of weakness hinging on a threatened loss of point. Granted, in most cases the contextualization does not depend on rhythm alone: There are likely to be clusters of verbal and other prosodic cues—the latter including stress, loudness, intonation—which point in one direction or the other. However, many of the prosodic cues—including rhythm—are seen to have an iconic core of meaning, rhythmic integration cueing business as usual and rhythmic nonintegration, some untoward interference with same.

4

Rhythm and Preference Organization in English

The last chapter emphasized the context sensitivity with which marked rhythmic transitions must be interpreted in conversation. Syncopated beats and early stresses as well as silent beats and late stresses in turn onsets, it was argued, are indexical of diverse interpretive frames for talk depending on the type of activity and conversational genre in which participants are momentarily engaged. But there may be some more abstract level at which generalizations concerning marked conversational rhythm can be made. In conversation-analytic literature, temporal delay has been identified as one of the formal features of dispreferred second turns in conversational sequences. Can marked rhythm be regarded as a sign of dispreference? To answer this question, it is necessary to determine how the notion of preference should be understood, whether as a purely formal distinction or as one with some face-related substance. Preference organization can then be examined within selected activity sequences and compared to the attested rhythmic patterning. In the following sections we examine the empirical data for potential correspondence first between rhythm and preference understood formally (§1) and then between rhythm and preference understood substantively (§2). The discussion shows that interactional rhythm does not correlate neatly with either a formal or a substantive definition of preference but constitutes instead an independent 'gloss' which interacts in predictable ways with preference options (§3).

1. Formal preference

1.1. The notion of preference in conversation analysis

In contrast to adjacency pairs in the restricted sense (e.g., summons/answers), whose first pair-parts make particular second pair-parts conditionally relevant, some conversational first moves allow a set of alternative next actions. The term *preference* has been used in conversation-analytic work to describe the ranking of these alternative but nonequivalent next actions (Atkinson & Heritage 1984; Levinson 1983). Some next actions can be shown to be 'invited' while others are avoided, withheld or delayed; the former are said to be *preferred*, the latter *dispreferred*. Preferred responses, in the canonical view, are not characterized by their psychological desirability but, rather, by the presence of certain formal features that mark their status as unproblematic conversational moves: They are performed immediately, in a verbally direct fashion and with no delay—all features designed to maximize the actions they accompany. Dispreferred responses, on the other hand, have a format designed to minimize the actions they are designed to constitute: They are typically hedged in one way or another and are performed indirectly and with noticeable delay.

It is a corollary of preference organization that silence following a first conversational move which 'invites' a particular response will be interpretable as implicating the dispreferred option (Pomerantz 1984; Davidson 1984). Speakers are sensitive to such implications and may be observed to preempt the upcoming dispreferred activity by subsequently modifying their original move to make it more likely to achieve the preferred response. Preference organization has thus been said to be instrumental in furthering conversational cooperation and affiliation (Atkinson & Heritage 1984:55).

One sequential context in which preference organization has been well described is assessments and statements of opinion (Pomerantz 1978, 1984; Goodwin 1986; Goodwin & Goodwin 1987). In assessing some person, object, event or state of affairs in terms of 'good' versus 'bad' or in expressing some opinion about a person, object, event or state, a first speaker is carrying out an action that makes either agreement or disagreement by a second speaker in next turn sequentially relevant (Pomerantz 1984; Davidson 1984). Typically, one of these options will be structurally preferred—that is, it will be oriented to as the 'invited' next action. Following assessments that evaluate a third party or some event/state in which neither ego nor alter has any stake, it is *agreement* that is generally preferred. In other words, subsequent agreeing turns will be performed in a verbally direct way as, for example, in the following assessment sequences:

(1) [Brain teaser 58]

```
1   DJ:    are you working
    C:     yeah I am
           I work at Robert Fletchers
```

	DJ:	{p}but what about what [a
5	C:	[it's a paper mill
		in Stoneclough
	DJ:	ahh
		what sort of hours do you do down there
		Colin
10	C:	eh we work the continental shift system
		eh six two two ten ten six
	DJ:	→ mm can be quite confusing that
	C:	→ yeah it can be (hh)
		you believe me

(2) [Brain teaser 10]

	DJ:	did you ever see the Stones live Sue
1	C:	no I've not
		I'd love to
	DJ:	I saw the Stones (.)
5		many years ago back a at the Palace
		(. . .)
	C:	→ I still don't think there's anybody to
		beat them
	DJ:	→ very true
10		→ and I it's good to see that they're still
		around really

(3) [Brain teaser 102]

1	DJ:	I- I mean I look at them and I think (.)
		er: it'll never go that
		and [I'm
	C:	[yeah
5	DJ:	really surprised when they
		some of them I think
		yeah that'll go dead easy
	C:	mm
	DJ:	but you know the
10		the reference in the Latin dictionary
		→ I thought that would go on for [years
	C:	[I know
		→ it baffled me that one
	DJ:	→ I I thought I'd be here till the year two
15		thousand doing that

In (1), when DJ qualifies the continental shift schedule as *quite confusing* (line 12), Colin immediately agrees in next turn. In (2), Sue makes an assessment of the Stones *I still don't think there's anybody to beat them* (lines 7–8); in next turn DJ seconds this assessment immediately and elaborates on it with *it's good to see that they're still around really* (lines 10–11). In (3), talk centers around the riddles which are an essential part of the brain teaser program. When DJ assesses the one concerning *reference in a Latin dictionary* (line 10) as threatening to *go on for years* (line 10), Corinne agrees immediately in next turn that the riddle was baffling. DJ immediately appends another assessment in third position: *I thought I'd be here till the year two thousand doing that* (lines 14–15).

By contrast, it is *disagreement* that is structurally dispreferred in routine assessment sequences. This is evident from the fact that disagreeing seconds following such assessments tend to be carried out in an indirect or weak fashion and with temporal delay:

(4) [Gulf 13]

```
1   L:      I think you have to talk to Mayor Hancock
             I was very surpri
     A:      {p}you're kidding
     L:   → I was very surprised to hear that,
5   A:   → (1.2) you were surprised with her?
     L:      well maybe not
     A:      ha ha ha ha
```

(5) [Amstrad 89]

```
1   C:      what's that guy called now;
     Z:      what works in Comet's.
     C:      yeah!
     Z:      Jack Barnes;
5   C:      Jack Barnes.
          → he told me Amstrad was rubbish!
     Z:   → (1.3) well I don't know;
     C:      he sells them.
```

(6) [Brain teaser 86]

```
1   DJ:     if you'd like to stay on the line Bert
              because we haven't got your: eh
              full address
     C:      no
5   DJ:     we've only got Bert Dawson of Withenshawe h
          → and I don't think the postman'd find that
     C:   → (0.3) oh I think they would you know
              er: because I am one you know h
              and they're very good
```

When Leo expresses surprise in (4) at a decision by the mayor (line 4), his interlocutor pauses and then requests confirmation: *you were surprised with her?* (line 5). Following an assessment such as Leo's, the avoidance of immediate agreement in next turn and the use of a repair-initiating strategy is sequentially implicative of upcoming disagreement. This is what Leo now preempts by backing down in next turn with *well maybe not* (line 6). In (5), following Charles's report of Jack Barnes's assessment that Amstrad is *rubbish* (line 6), Zara also avoids agreement in next turn, first pausing, then prefacing her turn with *well* and claiming lack of knowledge. This lack of knowledge serves as a warrant for her to decline making any kind of second assessment. Yet her interlocutor, Charles, manifestly interprets the disclaimer as implying disagreement, as his next move is addressed to establishing the credibility of Jack Barnes as a judge: *he sells them* (line 8). In (6), when DJ underestimates the postman's ability to locate residents without a proper address, Bert disagrees in next turn. But his action is delayed (see the 0.3 sec. pause) and is hedged with *I think* and *you know*. The counterassessment, viz., that postmen are *very good* (line 9), is presented as being justified by personal knowledge: *because I am one* (line 8). Thus, whereas agreeing seconds are immediate and straightforward, disagreeing seconds are accomplished, if at all, with reluctance and more interactional 'work'.

In the canonical view, preference organization is not wholly insensitive to local context, in particular to the kind of assessing action being carried out. If a first assessment negatively evaluates the speaker or something related to the speaker, as, for instance, in self-criticism or self-deprecation, this kind of move is seen as inviting disagreement rather than agreement in next turn (Pomerantz 1978). The preference reversal is evident from the fact that instead of agreeing next actions, disagreeing next actions are carried out in a direct and immediate format:

(7) [Women 86]

```
1   O:   → now you can see what a funny old clutter;
         → we work:: in here.
           there's even a cooker;
           in the corner.
5   M:   → I think it's glamorous and magical;
```

In (7), Olga's guest in the studio, Marvin, explicitly disagrees with her critical evaluation of the studio as being in *a funny old clutter* (line 1) and having *a cooker in the corner* (lines 3–4) by unhesitatingly qualifying it as *glamorous and magical* in next turn (line 5).

All in all, the concept of preference advocated in standard conversation analysis (CA) literature is a predominantly form-based one. And one important formal marker of preference in this view is the timing of a next response. This now raises the question of whether the *rhythmic* distinction between unmarked and marked speaker transitions can be exploited in the description of preference organization. In the following section we propose to investigate empirically whether there is a rhythmically sensitive way to distinguish preferred from dispreferred turn shapes.

Rhythm and Preference Organization in English 97

1.2. Rhythm and formal preference status

If interactional rhythm is a formal marker of preference, we should expect unmarked, integrated rhythmic transitions (chapter 3, §1.4, in this volume) to be found when responses are 'immediate' (or preferred), but marked, nonintegrated rhythmic transitions to occur when the responses are 'delayed' (dispreferred). Let us first consider the rhythm of the preferred second assessments previously discussed:

(1a) [Brain teaser 58]

```
1   DJ:    mm can be /'quite con-     /
                     /'fusing         /
                     /'that           /
    C:  →            /'yeah it 'can be
```

(2a) [Brain teaser 10]

```
1   C:     I /'still don't think there's  /
             /'anybody to                 /
             /'beat them                  /
    DJ: →    /'very true. and I it's      /
5            /'good to see that they're   /
             /'still around               /
             /'really
```

(3a) [Brain teaser 102]

```
1   DJ:    /'I thought that would    /
           /'go on for               /
           /['years
    C:  →  ['I know it               /
5          /'baffled me              /
           /'that one                /
    DJ:    /'I thought I'd be        /
           /,here till the year two  /
           /'thousand doing
10         /'that
```

Following these routine first assessments, next turns which agree have rhythmically integrated onsets.

Subsequent to self-critical assessments (with preference reversal), on the other hand, it is disagreeing next turns that have rhythmic integration:

(7a) [Women 86]

```
1   O:     'now you can see what a
                     /'funny old       /
                     /'clutter; we     /
```

```
                    /'work:: in          /
    5               /'here.there's
                                even a/
                    /'cooker in the     /
                    /'corner.
        M: →                I think it's/
    10     →        /'glamorous and     /
                    /'magical;
```

By contrast, the dispreferred responses illustrated earlier all have nonintegrated rhythmic transitions with late stresses or silent beats:

(4a) [Gulf 13]

```
    1   L:   I think you have to talk to Mayor Hancock
             I was very surpri-
        A:   {p} you're kidding
        L:   I was /'very surprised to   /
    5            /'hear that,            /
        A: →    /^              (1.2)  /
                 /'you were sur-/    (faster)
                 /'prised with  /
                 /'her?         /
    10  L:       /'well maybe   /
                 /'not
        A:   ha ha ha ha
```

(5a) [Amstrad 89]

```
    1   C:   what's that guy called now;
        Z:   what works in Comet's.
        C:   yeah!
        Z:   Jack Barnes;
    5   C:   Jack Barnes.
             'he told me /'Amstrad was   /
                         /'rubbish!      /
        Z: →             /^      (1.3) well/
                         /'I don't know;
    10  C:                              he/
                         /'sells them.
```

(6a) [Brain teaser 86]

```
    1   DJ:  /'I don't think the /
             /'postman'd         /
             /'find that
        C: → (0.3) oh I
                 /'think they    /    (late)
```

Rhythm and Preference Organization in English

```
5              /'would you      /
               /'know           /
               /'er:
       because I am one you know
```

These disagreeing turns following routine first assessments are delayed: Transitions have either a silent beat (4a, 5a) or the next turn begins late with respect to prior rhythm (6a). Thus there is some *prima facie* evidence in favor of regarding rhythm as a formal marker of preference. Yet there are also some serious objections.

1.2.1 EARLY RHYTHM AND PREFERRED COURSES OF ACTION   The first of these objections is the rather trivial observation that marked, nonintegrated rhythm, as we have defined it, includes not only silent beats and late stresses but also syncopated beats and early stresses. The latter two (cases of anticipated rhythm) are not found with dispreferred turns. In fact, if there is any potential correspondence, it is between anticipated rhythm and *preferred* turn shapes: Witness Pomerantz's observation that invited agreements are often performed in slight overlap with first assessments (1984:69).

Of course, as we have shown in chapter 3, not all latched and/or minimally overlapping transitions constitute early rhythm. Some transitional overlap may be rhythmically induced and should not 'count' as being rhythmically marked at all. This is arguably the case in the following:

(8) [Brain teaser 192]

```
1   P:     did you /'see it tonight
    DJ:                                    I/
                   /'did; the last         /
                   /'one Phil
5   P:                             it was in-/
                   /'credible [wasn't it
    DJ:                       [oh           /
 →                 /'excellent program
```

Phil is referring to a well-known television program which has just had its last show. Both DJ and Phil agree in their positive evaluation of the program as *incredible* (lines 5–7) and *excellent* (line 8). Yet despite the fact that the onset of DJ's second assessment overlaps the end of Phil's first assessment, it is not heard as having anticipated timing because the overlap involves only post-tonic and anacrustic syllables (see also chapter 3, §1.2).

But on occasion, genuine syncopated beats are encountered in agreeing seconds following assessments:

(9) [Hodge 100]

```
1   G:     I think when you've got a nice name like Richard;
           why they call you Dick—
```

```
            I'll never know.
      H:    well d'you know—
 5          privately;
            I agree entirely with you;
            but when you've been Dick as long as I have;
            because your family started it;
            there's(.)
10                    /'no point in 'arguing     /
                      /'really,                  /
      G: → /'no—    (syncopated)
                      /'quite.
```

(10) [Hodge 101]

```
 1    N:    but she was getting really—
            awkward;
            and— (.)
            and everything.
 5    H:    it becomes a /'twenty-          /
                         /'four-'hour       /
                         /'job for          /
                         /'you; [didn't it.
      N:                        [it
10    →             /'was.      (syncopated)
                    /'it 'was.
```

In (9), when Mr. Hodge proffers the opinion that it is useless to try to go against a nickname one's family uses, Mrs. Giles hastens to agree (lines 12–13). Rather than waiting for the next beat, she places her agreeing token *no* well before the moment in time when it is due, producing a noticeable syncopation. In (10), Nora also anticipates the beat (line 10) in agreeing with a prior turn, in this case Mr. Hodge's estimate that caring for an elderly person is *a twenty-four hour job*. In both cases the first prominences of the second assessments are too salient to be regarded as incorporated prosodic prominences.

Thus, marked rhythm—when understood to subsume both syncopated beats/early stresses and silent beats/late stresses in transition timing—displays no consistent pattern with respect to preference status. However, even if the claim that marked rhythm is related to formal preference were to be restricted to well-timed versus delayed rhythm, it would still be difficult to establish a satisfactory rhythmic correlate for formal preference, as we shall argue below.

1.2.2. INTEGRATED RHYTHM AND DISPREFERRED COURSES OF ACTION   Surprisingly, given the canonical view of preference, dispreferred courses of action—ones that do not appear to maximize cooperation and affiliation but potential conflict instead—are sometimes carried out with integrated rhythm. For instance:

Rhythm and Preference Organization in English

(11) [Teatime 92]

```
 1  L:     we'd sit around the table; (0.3)
           and have our sausages— and whatever, (0.8)
           and— (1.4) he:::;
           would be the only one, (0.5)
 5         to have gristle.
    E:     no he's not the only—
           no he wasn't the only (to eat the) (0.4)
           if you don't like a thing;
           you eat it slowly;
10         and you
                    /'find all the            /
                    /'faults in it. the       /
                    /'rest of you,            /
                    /'liked them, and         /
15                  /'shot them     /   (faster)
                    /'down,         /
                    /'gristle as    /
                    /'well.
    L:     (0.4) 'n:o::::!      (late)
20  E:     'it /'is!=             /
    L: →       /[='no::          /
    P:         ['no::
    E:                    'it/
       →       /['is.
    P:         ['come on;
25  L:                      it/
       →      /'wasn't;
```

(12) [Brain teaser 73]

```
 1  C:     it's not Marilyn
           she won't get on the phone actually
           [she's a bit shy
    DJ:    [aw has her bottle¹—
 5         has her bottle gone
    C:         [yeah
    M:         [no it has-[n't
    DJ:                   [aye
    C:                    [it has
10  DJ:    your bottle's gone
           I can hear you in the background
    C:     hee hee hee
    M:     I didn't phone
    DJ:    you're a/'coward!
```

```
15    M:                            I'm/
      →              /'not
      DJ:                  you're an/
      →              /'out and out/
                     /'coward!
20    M:                            I'm/
      →              /'not
      DJ:                       you/
      →              /['are:
      C:              [he h h
```

In (11), Ernest disagrees with Lea's statement that only her son Peter used to get the sausage with gristle in it. He counters that if you like sausage, you don't notice the gristle because, as he later puts it, *there's gristle in all sausage*. Lea now expresses strong disagreement in her next turn, whose onset is late, whereupon Ernest rebuts with an equally strong token of disagreement. Thereafter, Ernest and Lea exchange disagreement tokens three times in perfect rhythmic synchronization. Thus, what begins as rhythmically marked disagreement (line 19) develops into an argument which is rhythmically unmarked (lines 20–26).

In (12), DJ accuses Marilyn, who reportedly *won't get on the phone* (line 2), of being a coward (line 14). At this point Marilyn does join in to rebut: *I'm not* (line 16). Over the next three turns, DJ and Marilyn engage in a 'duet' of reciprocal denials which display neat rhythmic synchronization. Yet the rhythmic integration attested in examples such as these is not associated with actions that are maximizing affiliation but with ones that are ostensibly maximizing conflict. This suggests that rhythmically integrated transition timing does not correlate consistently with what is canonically considered to be a preferred action.

2. Preference as a substantive notion

2.1. A face-related view of preference

Conceivably, some of the objections to treating interactional rhythm as a correlate of preference status can be overcome if preference is defined more substantively. Indeed, by stressing that preferred structures have in common the maintenance of "sociability, support and solidarity," whereas dispreferred ones are "impolite, hurtful, or wrong," Pomerantz herself acknowledges that there is a functional difference between the two types of action (1984:77). But it is Atkinson and Heritage (1984) who invoke a workable basis for the nonformal ranking of alternative courses of action:

> [I]t may be suggested that the design features associated with the production of preferred/dispreferred activities may inform and be informed by a logic of 'face' considerations (Brown and Levinson 1978, Goffman 1955) at the levels of both form and usage. (56)

The crucial step in a functional approach to preference is to think of *face* as determining what is regarded as a preferred or dispreferred course of action. Preferred actions contribute to the maintenance or preservation of one's interlocutor's face, whereas dispreferred actions, accordingly, threaten or impinge upon the face of an interlocutor (see also Owen 1983). According to this view, agreements to assessments and disagreements with self-criticisms fall neatly into the preferred category because both types of action pay face to alter, whereas disagreements with routine assessments and agreements to self-criticism fall into the dispreferred category because they are face threatening for the interlocutor. Does interactional rhythm correlate better with a face-based understanding of preference?

2.2. Rhythm and face-related preference status

The distinction between face-preserving (preferred) and face-threatening (dispreferred) second actions provides an alternative, equally satisfying account for the distribution of unmarked and marked transitional rhythm in the assessment sequences previously illustrated. The unmarked or integrated rhythm of the second assessments in examples (1a)–(3a), for instance, can be motivated by the fact that the (agreeing) actions being carried out are face preserving for the first (assessing) speaker; likewise the integrated rhythm in (7a) can be linked to the face-preservation work that the (disagreeing) second assessment is doing vis-à-vis alter's self-criticism. By contrast, the marked rhythm of the seconds in (4a)–(6a) can be linked to the fact that these turns are disagreeing with assessments by alter, a course of action which *ceteris paribus* threatens interlocutor's positive face.

More interestingly, however, a face-related understanding of preference offers a possible explanation for the use of rhythmic integration in cases such as those illustrated in (11) and (12). Here, it can be argued, there is a suspension of 'normal consensus expectations'; instead of consensus and solidarity, opposition and dominance are the relevant interactional goals (see also Goodwin 1982, 1983; Vuchinich 1984, 1990; Kotthoff 1993). Preservation of face—current speaker's as well as prior speaker's—thus demands immediate disagreement or contradiction of a prior claim, given the prevailing oppositional frame. Assuming that the frame for talk in (11) and (12) is argumentative, the rhythmic integration of the 'aggravated' disagreeing turns can be motivated by their preferred (i.e., face-saving) status.

Within an argumentative frame, lack of strong disagreement or immediate provision of a counterclaim is consequently a sign of weakness and may mean that alter's argument or point is being conceded. This constitutes a threat to current speaker's face. And it is in cases like this that we would expect marked transitional rhythm. The following exchange appears to bear out this prediction:

(13) [Sack 4]

```
1   S:   but there was also the other point
         that wha that (.)
         that the fact that the food factory even
         ha::d stuff (.)
5        of that quality on their premises
    H:   oh yes that's very frightening indeed and
         and somehow the
```

```
              these villains got hold of it
              and were able to put it into tins for pets
10            is there any /'evidence that they       /
                           /'actually                 /
                           /'did that                 /
    S:  →                  /^              (1.5)      /
                           /^                         /
15                         /^                         /
                           /hherh                     /
    H:                     /['I mean
    S:                      ['no
    H:     surely I I've opened tins of pet food for
20         our cat
    S:     and it looks all right [yeah
    H:                            [and it looks fine
```

The point Mrs. Sack has raised in her phone call is that standards for the manufacture of pet food are not high enough, as contaminated meat and other indigestible products are often used. Mr. Hodge has questioned whether animals cannot tolerate more than humans (see example [31] in chapter 3, in this volume). This exchange cues an oppositional frame which remains active throughout a substantial part of ensuing talk. With his question *is there any evidence that they actually did that* (lines 9–11), Mr. Hodge can now be heard to express latent doubt about the authenticity of the report to which Mrs. Sack is referring. That is, his question is in effect equivalent to the negative assessment *there isn't any evidence that they actually did that, is there?* Agreeing with this assessment would clearly weaken Mrs. Sack's position. Thus, not surprisingly, she displays considerable reluctance to do so: Her dispreferred, face-threatening turn is delayed by three silent beats and a hesitation marker on the fourth. In fact, she does not produce the agreeing token *no*[2] until the floor has reverted to her interlocutor, which conveniently allows it to be overlapped and thereby deleted from the record.

Thus, the rhythmic patterning encountered so far in argumentative sequences would appear to support an account of interactional rhythm based on a face-related notion of preference.

2.2.1. THE CASE OF 'HOT'-NEWS INFORMINGS   Yet there is at least one set of cases that defies attempts to establish a correlation between face-based preference and interactional rhythm: These are receipts of hot-news informings.

Heritage (1984) has described *informings* as actions whereby "tellers propose to be knowledgeable about some matter concerning which, they also propose, recipients are ignorant" (304). Informings are regularly receipted by the token *oh* (freestanding or with additional assessment components), which displays that the recipient is now informed, and/or by other newsmarks and tags such as *really?* or *you did?*, which request or invite the teller to continue the informing (Jefferson 1981). By contrast, receipt tokens such as *yes* or *mhm* following informings may avoid or defer treating the prior turn as informative by implying that the recipient already knows the information imparted. As Heritage (1984) has pointed out, informers are particularly sensitive to the tellability of information (304–5). That is, they orient to the unspoken maxim that one should avoid telling someone something they already know. For this reason, news-informing receipts with *yes* or *mhm* may signal a dispreferred action which threatens teller's face by implying that the maxim of tellability has been breached.

On occasion, tellers undertake informings with the expectation that the information imparted will be particularly informative to the recipient due to its recency and/or its unexpectedness. These events we refer to as hot-news informings. Following is an example:

(14) [Hodge 98]

```
1    S:       apparently;
              according to this chap;
              who's an English doctor;
              the chap in Spandau is
5             / 'not;   /
              / 'Rudolf /
              / 'Hess!  /
     H: →   / ^    (1.2) /
              / ^          /
10            / 'you    /
              / 'wha?
     S:                     it is/    (slower)
              / 'not Rudolf     /
              / 'Hess!
```

In this excerpt the speaker undertakes an informing action with news that has special prosodic marking: Each word in *not Rudolf Hess* (lines 5–7) has a high-falling emphatic pitch and the accented syllables themselves are equally spaced in time. In other words, the phrase is scanned (Müller 1991; and chapter 6, in this volume), a prosodic treatment that suggests that the speaker considers the news particularly newsworthy or 'hot'. Arguably, this kind of affect display calls for a reciprocal display in the next turn. Notice now that Mr. Hodge not only responds with a scanned expression himself, *you wha?*-, but also delays the onset of this response by two silent beats. In this context, the silent beats are heard, along with the scansion, as a mark of heightened affect (see also Selting 1994).

In fact, silent beats and late stresses appear regularly following the delivery of hot news:

(15) [Julie 12]

```
1    A:       my sister was—
              for a week
              was here when I was
              the first week we were here
```

```
 5            and
              she got my mother on this
                        / 'no       /
                        / 'fat      /
                        / 'diet
10            and so it was just like— (.)
                        / 'no-fat   /
                        / 'ice cream?
      J:   →  (0.6)    'oh no::      (late)
      ?:      why bother
15    S:      how can you have no-fat ice cream
```

(16) [Teatime 97]

```
 1    E:      let's face it;
              you can buy
                        / 'food on          /
                        / 'credit now,      /
 5                      /^           if you/
                        / 'want,            /
      P:   →  /^                    (1.4) /
                        /^                  /
                        /^                  /
10                      / 'what?
              (1.4)
      P:      okay;
              if the whole system;
              is a credit system. eh?
```

In (15), Ann is describing the no-fat diet her mother has been put on; her news is that this diet involves *no-fat ice cream* (the existence of which, at the time, was hot news). Note that recipients treat this information as surprising when they respond *oh no::* (line 13) and *why bother* (line 14), *how can you have no-fat ice cream* (line 15). In (16) Ernest is talking about how the custom of buying things on credit has recently spread. His hot news is *you can buy food on credit now* (lines 2–4), which Peter receipts with a display of incredulity (lines 7–10). Not only are silent beats and late stresses regularly produced between a hot-news delivery and its second, we would argue that they are done so preferentially: Rhythmic delay contextualizes the unexpectedness of the news and thereby confirms informers' estimation that the news was indeed hot.

Corroborating evidence for the preferred status of delayed receipts to hot news is found in cases in which prosodically marked news deliveries are not receipted with delay but with rhythmic integration:

(14a) [Hodge 98 (*continued*)]

```
      S:      it is
                        / 'not Rudolf       /
```

Rhythm and Preference Organization in English

```
                    /'Hess!           /
15  H:  →           /'so this guy    /
                    /'says;
            I mean let's take that with a bit of a
            pinch of salt,
```

Notice that Mr. Hodge's response here *so this guy says* is rhythmically integrated with the prior turn, which restates the news *it is not Rudolf Hess* (lines 12–14). Accompanying a remark to the effect that the report is hardly credible, this rhythm is heard as cueing a frame 'nothing to get excited about'. Playing down the 'newsiness' of prosodically marked news is a dispreferred activity (in a face-based understanding of preference), as it suggests that alter has misjudged the situation. But this dispreferred activity is cued here by rhythmic integration. In other words, the routine handling of hot-news informings is diametrically opposed to the rhythmic patterns for preference discussed so far. With hot news, it is rhythmic delay that appears to be the preferred variant and rhythmic integration, the dispreferred variant for next-turn onset. The fact that marked rhythm here does not accompany a face threat to alter constitutes a serious drawback to viewing rhythm generally as a marker of functional preference.

Hot-news informings, with rhythmically delayed but unmarked responses, appear to weaken the claim made in chapter 3 that rhythmic integration is the unmarked alternative for timing next turns within activity sequences. Yet, upon reflection, it can be seen that the unmarked nature of rhythmic delay following hot news can only be appreciated against the background of rhythmic integration as the default option. It is precisely because hot news is not routine that it makes a nonroutinely timed response appropriate. The rhythmic delay of surprised responses to hot news thus only makes sense if we assume that nonsurprised responses are rhythmically integrated.

3. Rhythm as an independent gloss of preference

We have thus reached an impasse: It appears that we must also forgo establishing a systematic correspondence between face-based preference and rhythm. Yet there is one way to reconcile the conflicting evidence. This is to think of interactional rhythm as an independent prosodic dimension of turn shape. Such a position is in many ways compatible with Bilmes's (1988) view of so-called dispreference markers (delays, pauses and prefaces). He argues that these should actually be thought of as *reluctance markers* because they are "expressive of the speaker's reluctance to produce the response which follows" (173). Reluctance markers, Bilmes (1988) argues, may occur with preferred responses without vitiating their preferential status. In fact, in his words, "reluctance marking is a strategic resource available for any speaker to apply at any time for any reason" (176).

The analysis of interactional rhythm presented here suggests that this view is basically correct for delayed rhythm, although the term *reluctance* is clearly too narrow: Witness hot-news informings, where respondents can hardly be said to be 'reluctant' to receipt surprising news. But Bilmes's view needs expanding to account for the phenomenon of syncopated beats and early stresses. All things considered, we believe that interactional rhythm is best regarded as a contextualization cue which is related to, but ultimately independent of, preference distinctions. This implies that preference should not be defined formally but rather as a face-related phenomenon. It is this definition we adopt for the following discussion.

Marked and unmarked rhythm may, accordingly, configure in a fashion which is *congruent* with preference status:

  Preferred status ⟷ Unmarked rhythm
  Dispreferred status ⟷ Marked rhythm

Or, more interestingly, they may configure in a noncongruent fashion:

  Preferred status ⤫ Unmarked rhythm
  Dispreferred status   Marked rhythm

As this diagram suggests, there are two types of noncongruency: One is when marked (i.e., anticipated or delayed) rhythm accompanies a preferred course of action. The other is when unmarked rhythm accompanies dispreferred courses of action.

A combination of the two diagrams above reveals that interactional rhythm is 'free' to be deployed as a strategic resource in preferentially organized conversational sequences:

  Preferred status ⟷⤫ Unmarked rhythm
  Dispreferred status ⟷ Marked rhythm

Consequently, it should be possible to observe different contextualization effects for a given course of action with one and the same preference status depending on the type of rhythm present. To show this, we now examine situations in which the same action (preferred or dispreferred) is susceptible to different glossing when the turn in question has unmarked versus marked rhythm (anticipated or delayed).

3.1. *Preferred actions and marked (vs. unmarked) rhythm*

We begin by considering the case of assessments. Recall that these are regularly seconded with agreeing turns and that integrated rhythm is typical (chapter 3, §1.4, in this volume). When syncopated beats or early rhythmic stresses occur, however, the positive face work that such turns accomplish receives an additional gloss, as examples (9) and (10)—repeated here—demonstrate:

(9) [Hodge 100]

 1 G: I think when you've got a nice name like Richard;
     why they call you Dick—
     I'll never know.

```
      H:    well d'you know—
5           privately;
            I agree entirely with you;
            but when you've been Dick as long as I have;
            because your family started it;
            there's(.) /'no point in 'arguing      /
10                     /'really,                   /
      G: →             /'no-      (syncopated)
                       /'quite.
```

(10) [Hodge 101]

```
1     N:    but she was getting really—
            awkward;
            and— (.)
            and everything.
5     H:    it becomes a /'twenty-           /
                         /'four-'hour        /
                         /'job for           /
                         /'you;[didn't it.
      N:                      [it
10        →              /'was.    (syncopated)
                         /'it 'was.
```

In (9), Mr. Hodge deflects Mrs. Giles's potential criticism of his nickname by invoking his family as being responsible for it and by assessing the situation as inevitable. Mrs. Giles now agrees with this assessment in next turn, a face-saving action by any standard. But by rushing to do so, she displays extra concern to accomplish the action urgently, lending her turn a gloss which may help diminish the negative implications of her prior critical remark. In (10), Nora has just divulged that she has had to put her mother into a home for the elderly, although she hoped she could manage the care herself. When Mr. Hodge now assesses caring for the elderly as a twenty-four-hour job, Nora agrees in next turn. But as in (9), by rushing to agree, she displays a desire to accomplish the action urgently. In this case, glossing her action as urgent may help dispel the suspicion that she has acted in an unjustified manner. By contrast with rhythmic integration in agreeing second assessments, the syncopated rhythm here can be seen as a strategic deployment related to the management of speakers' face.

For an example of delayed rhythm as a gloss, we turn to repair initiation (see also Couper-Kuhlen 1992b). Recall that repair other-initiation for a problem of reference or of understanding is preferentially carried out in next turns with rhythmic delay (see chapter 3, §2.2.3, in this volume). This is congruent with its status as a dispreferred action. In contrast to a problem of understanding, however, a problem of hearing is not routinely considered to be face threatening. Rather it is treated as 'no one's fault'. Mishearings are more likely to be due to extraneous background noise or to some other channel disturbance for which participants cannot be held 'morally' responsible.³ And initiation of repair for a problem of hearing (which is therefore a preferred option) is routinely accomplished with rhythmic integration:

(17) [Brain teaser 119]

```
 1   D:      and Ron Mooney;
             who lives in Wigan.
             hello Ron,
     R:      hello Dave,
 5   D:      how are ya;
     R:      not so bad thanks.
                  /'Golborne 'near /
                  /'Wigan.          /
                  /'yeah,           /
10   D: →         /'pardon?         /
     R:           /'Golborne near   /    (slower)
                  /'Wigan;
     D:     /'that's     (syncopated)
                  /'right;['yes  /       (faster)
15   R:                  ['yeah;
     D:           /'Golborne near /
                  /'Wigan;
```

(18) [Brain teaser 2]

```
 1   J:      and also to Jerry O'Sullivan;
     D:      mhm,
     J:      who's at Securitor.
             at work.
 5   D:      yeah;
             and /'anybody else that/
                 /'knows you.         /
     J: →        /'pardon?
     D:                          and /
10               /'anybody else that/  (early)
                 /'knows you.
     J:                          and /  (slower)
                 /'anybody else that  /
                 /'knows me;
```

In (17), Dave has announced his next caller as living in *Wigan* (line 2). Following the exchange of greetings, Ron now corrects this to *Golborne near Wigan* (lines 7–8), whereupon Dave immediately responds with the token *pardon?* (line 10), standardly understood to mean that some part of the prior turn has not been properly heard. Ron now repeats the corrected version verbatim (lines 11–12), confirming that he has understood Dave to have signaled a problem of hearing, and Dave acknowledges the repair in next turn (lines 13–14). In (18) Joy is finishing up a list of the friends and relations she wishes to say hello to on the air before the call comes to a close (lines 1–4). Dave, with no prompting, now completes the list with *and anybody else that knows you* (lines 6–7). Joy immediately responds to this with the token *pardon?* (line 8), whereupon Dave repeats his turn verbatim (lines 9–11) and Joy acknowledges the repair in next turn (lines 12–14). In both (17) and (18), the repair-initiating turn *pardon* is produced with rhythmic integration.

Yet there is no determinative relation between a repair for a problem of hearing and rhythmic integration. In fact, a turn may be ostensibly designed to signal mishearing but executed with rhythmic delay:

(19) [Brain teaser 120]

```
1    D:     you can find reference in any Latin
            dictionary to a brigade
     C:     is it– / 'honi            /
                   / 'soit–            /
5                  / 'qui 'mal y /
                   / 'pense.
     D: →   (2.0) 'pardon?       (late)
     C:                  / 'honi         /      (slower)
                         / 'soit; qui    /
10                       / 'mal y pense.
     D:     good job Sweeney's not [on the radio,
     C:                            [hh h he. hehe
     D:     with this;
            well— whatever you said,
15          no
     C:     it's the motto of the guards brigade.
     D:     oh it is?
     C:     uh huh,
     D:     ah; well—
20          never being in the guards of course,
            I wouldn't know a thing like this—
            no, it's not that;
```

Here Corinne proffers a French saying *honi soit qui mal y pense* (lines 3–6) as a possible solution to the riddle in lines 1–2. Dave signals in next turn that Corinne's answer has been 'misheard' (see line 7). Corinne now repeats the quote verbatim (lines 8–10), signaling her understanding of Dave's turn as a request for repetition (and not, say, as a request for an explanation or a translation). Yet the noticeable delay with which Dave's *pardon?* is produced arguably frames the repair process as more problematic than routine. The problematic nature of Corinne's quotation becomes manifest when Dave must deal with it as a possible answer to the riddle in question: His first comment, *good job Sweeney's not on the radio, with this*, cleverly evades the question of what the phrase actually means,[4] and his subsequent circumlocution *whatever you said* implies by its vagueness that Dave has not understood it himself. Thus, despite its verbal formatting as repair initiation for a problem of hearing, the delayed rhythm of Dave's *pardon* prosodically indexes the trouble as being more than merely 'acoustic' in nature. The rhythmic cue—delay—is one which, deployed congruently, would be associated with a problem of understanding. In noncongruent use it carries the face-threatening connotation it would not have in congruent contexts.

3.2. *Dispreferred actions and unmarked (vs. marked) rhythm*

We turn now to the noncongruent use of interactional rhythm with dispreferred actions. Take the case of self-denigrating assessments. These, as we have seen, invite disagreements as next courses of action (see [7]). To agree with alter's self-criticism is a face-theatening action *par excellence*. Accordingly, it should be accompanied by the usual reluctance markers. Yet consider the following exchange:

(20) [Hodge 95]

```
 1  H:    hel-/'lo sir.       /
                 /['madam.
     C:         [h-
                 hel-/'lo Dick—     /      (new rhythm)
 5  H:               /'that was a   /
                     /'clanger,
                 /'wasn't it.      (syncopated)
     C:                              it/
  →                  /'was,
10  H:    h hh g(h)o o(h)n dear.
     C:    I just wanted to
     H:    have you forgiven me.
     C:    yes I have.
     H:    oh good.
```

Mr. Hodge here mistakenly addresses his new caller Mrs. Clay with *sir* (line 1) but self-corrects immediately (line 2). When he later self-disparagingly refers to his mistake as *a clanger* (lines 5–6), Mrs. Clay immediately agrees with this negative assessment of his behavior in next turn (lines 8–9). The fact that the two are total strangers makes Mrs. Clay's action seem all the more surprising: Their relationship does not have the intimacy that might render such a threat to face more tolerable. Yet the rhythmic packaging of Mrs. Clay's turn—by virtue of the fact that it conjures up its congruent use in non–face-threatening situations—adds a 'routine, nothing-to-get-excited-about' gloss to her words, casting them in a prosodic cloak which neutralizes their impact. The fact that this apparent conversational incident comes off smoothly, as subsequent talk shows that it does (see lines 10–14), can be seen as achieved in part by its prosodic, and especially its rhythmic handling.

Rhythm and Preference Organization in English

Finally we come to a special case of questioning, but one that nicely demonstrates the glossing function of interactional rhythm. Consider the out-of-the-blue questions about work that are regularly put, primarily to male callers, at the beginning of calls to the brain teaser radio program. These are used by the moderator to establish his callers' social identity, an undertaking all the more delicate due to the fact that social identities are being established publicly, on the air. A case in point is the exchange with Gary McDonald discussed in chapter 3:

(21) [Brain teaser 107]

```
1   D:    couple of callers (.) .h
          er firstly to Bolton and Gary McDonald (.)
          hi Gary
    G:    hi
5   D:    hi how are ya
    G:    not so bad thanks
    D:    good (.)
          /'whereabouts in      /
          /'Bolton do you       /
10        /'work.
    G: → (0.5) 'eh— I    (late)
                /'don't; I'm unem-    /
                /'ployed (-) well a   /
                /'student;            /
15              /'part-time.
    D:    (0.2) a 'student (-) 'uh    (late)
                /'part-time unem-   /
                /'ployed.           /
    G:          /'yeah.
```

Gary's predicament is due in part to the fact that he cannot name an occupation or place of work that would fit the slot opened up by Dave's question. He and numerous others on the program cannot supply the answer this question expects. In this sense their responses are dispreferred, because they impinge negatively upon callers' face. Yet not all callers in this situation handle their answers in a rhythmically marked way:

(22) [Brain teaser 108]

```
1   D:    what d'you /'do in life        /
                     /'John?             /
    J: →             /'uh—               /
                     /'well I'm—         /
5                    /'off ,sick at      /
                     /'present,          /
    D:               /'how long ya ,been off /
                     /'work;             /
```

```
        J:                  /'oh— I been off           /
10                          /.quite a while now,
        D:      have you
```

(23) [Brain teaser 265]

```
 1      DJ:     and our first caller in Stockport.
                that's Mike Summers.
                hi Mike,
        C:      hi Dave;
 5      DJ:     how are you.
        C:      er not so bad,
        DJ:     /'first day back at /
                /'work today?       /
        C:   → /'er unem-           /
10              /'ployed.           /
        DJ:     /'oh.
                so er i it's 'one long 'holiday;
                in a /'way of /
                     /'course,/
15      C:           /'yeah.
        DJ:     yeah [(.) how
        C:           [if ya (???)
        DJ:     /'how long ya been on the /
                /'dole;                   /
20      C:      /'er since last Oc-       /
                /'tober;
        DJ:                              oh/
                /'quite a time eh?        /
        C:      /'yeah.
```

(24) [Brain teaser 248]

```
 1      DJ:     you /'working at the     /
                    /'moment,            /
        C:   →      /'no (.) I'm         /
                    /'not.               /
 5      DJ:         /'ah you're
                /'off for the bank       /    (early)
                /'holiday are you?       /
        C:   → /'no
                h heh heh
10      DJ:     you're /'off (.) all the /
                       /'time
        C:                      yeah I'm a-/
             →         /'fraid=
        DJ:            /'how long you been off   /   (early)
```

```
15                      / 'work;                              /
        C:              / 'mm 'bout three month.
        DJ:     mm, one of the er Nat King Cole (.) group
                eh?
        C:      that's right, (.) yeah;
```

In (22), John preserves the rhythm of ongoing talk in his dispreferred answer *well I'm off sick at present* (lines 3–6)—making adept use of the hedge *uh* to create a rhythmic beat. In (23), Mike deploys *er* as the first rhythmic beat of his (dispreferred) answer *unemployed*. And in (24), the caller's negative answers to Dave's leading questions *you working at the moment* (lines 1–2) and *you're off for the bank holiday* (lines 5–7) are timed isochronously (see lines 3–4, and 8). Even the crucial question *you're off all the time* (lines 10–11) receives a well-timed affirmative response (lines 12–13).

In these cases the unmarked rhythm of callers' responses appears to be glossing them as unproblematic: Just as with preferred responses where rhythm is deployed congruently, there is no outward prosodic sign of anything amiss here. Thus it would seem that participants can deploy unmarked rhythm to work against the face threat their dispreferred answers may be heard as evoking.

We conclude that interactional rhythm is an independent glossing device which takes its primary signaling value from its use in congruence with preference status. Integrated rhythm typically cues the fact that interaction is proceeding as usual. By contrast, nonintegrated rhythm typically cues some impediment to the smooth development of talk, anticipated timing being associated with, for instance, energetic and (self-)defensive actions, delayed timing with, for example, surprise and/ or a face threat. These primary values transfer quasi metaphorically to situations in which preference and rhythm are noncongruent. Thus, when verbal content and sequential context suggest that a response is preferred, marked timing in the onset of this turn may cue an additional gloss calqued on congruent use: With anticipated rhythm, that the response is energetic and/or in self-defense; with delayed rhythm, that the response is in one way or another associated with a face threat. When verbal content and sequential context suggest a dispreferred response, unmarked timing may help gloss the associated face threat as 'routine, nothing to get excited about'—that is, as inconsequential in the long run. Both marked and unmarked rhythm then 'gloss' situated actions—whether preferred or dispreferred—in characteristic ways.

5

Rhythm in Telephone Closings

*An Analysis of Italian
and German Data*

This chapter was written in cooperation with Marcello Panese.

In contrast to prior chapters, this chapter introduces an explicitly contrastive perspective: We discuss the same discourse-contextualizing functions of rhythm and tempo in similar conversational environments, using German and Italian data. The topic is telephone closings, another classic object of study in conversation analysis. As in the case of turn taking and preference organization, the role prosodic parameters play in achieving telephone closings has not been investigated in detail in orthodox CA. We try to show that a purely segmental treatment of telephone closings misses an essential aspect of their structuring.

This chapter proceeds in four steps. It starts with a discussion of the structural (phonological and phonetic) differences between English/German and Italian with respect to rhythm. Section 2 summarizes the most important design features of telephone closings, as they have emerged from conversation-analytic research. We then present in section 3 the main results of our research on rhythm and tempo in German private telephone closings. In the fourth section of this chapter, we carry out a similar analysis for a comparable collection of informal telephone closings in Italian.

1. The rhythmic structure of English and German vs. Italian

For a long time, scholars working on natural language have expressed the intuition that rhythmic structure may differ from one language to the next. The earliest writers on rhythm in modern times, such as Steele (1775) for English or Moritz (1776) for German, had in mind of course the classical languages Greek and Latin, to which they compared their native tongues. In the 20th century, however, impressionistic writing on rhythm has been superseded and rhythmic differences between living languages, particularly those of Europe, have become a respectable topic of research. The phonetic-phonological distinction that has dominated the debate about rhythm since then is that between two types of isochrony which are said to lay the ground for interlanguage rhythm differences: *stress timing* and *syllable timing*.

This is not the place to present in great detail the substantial phonetic and phonological research on isochrony which has accumulated since the 1940s and which, with its technical delicacies, would easily fill a monograph of its own.[1] However, for an interactional approach to rhythm it is important to discuss the feasibility of transferring a set of tools developed for the analysis of rhythm and tempo in English to conversational materials from other languages, which is what we intend to do in this and the following chapters. We need to evaluate the robustness of our notion of rhythm when applied to languages other than English, especially when these languages are known to display different structural features both on the phonetic and phonological level.

Of the languages from which conversational materials are taken for this chapter, one is similar in its rhythmic makeup to English (German) but the other is quite different (Italian). The aim of this chapter, then, is to investigate whether the established phonetic and phonological differences between German (and English) on the one hand, and Italian on the other, affect the conversational uses or usability of rhythm as a contextualization cue.

The modern notion of isochrony was first developed for English in early chronometric work by Classe (1939); it was popularized by Pike (1945) and given its most radical formulation by Abercrombie (1967: 96–7). Pike (1945) states in his *Intonation of American English*:

> The timing of rhythm units produces a rhythmic succession which is an extremely important characteristic of English phonological structure. The units tend to follow one another in such a way that the lapse of time between the beginning of their prominent syllables is somewhat uniform. (35)

This is the notion of rhythm to which we have adhered in prior chapters; Pike's "rhythm units" are roughly equivalent to the phonetic duration from one rhythmically prominent syllable (beat) to the next. (As outlined in chapter 1, §5.1 and in chapter 2, §2, our notion of the rhythmic pulse is more liberal than Pike's—or, for that matter, Abercrombie's—in that we allow stressed syllables to occur between the rhythmic beats; as a consequence, our 'rhythmic interval' is not entirely synonymous with Abercrombie's foot or Pike's rhythm units.) For the perception of English rhythm, it is irrelevant, according to Pike's definition, how many unstressed syllables intervene between the rhythmic beats. To perceive rhythmic structure, it is enough to focus on the stressed syllables and their (regular) occurrence in time. Rhythm (which in the sense of this definition is equivalent to isochrony) is perceived if the durations from one stress to the next are heard as being of approximately equal duration.

In addition to the stress-timed rhythm typical of English, Pike (1945) also distinguishes "a rhythm which is more closely related to the syllable . . . ; in this case it is the syllables, instead of the stresses, which tend to come at more-or-less evenly recurrent intervals" (36). He mentions Spanish as a language which follows this "syllable-timed rhythm." This means that the rhythm of English is not a universal phonetic pattern but, rather, a specific feature of this language. Different languages have their own 'pulse', or in other words their own timing pattern for the regular succession of rhythmic units.

Yet there are not as many rhythm types as there are languages; rather, the distinction between stress timing and syllable timing provides a typological parameter. The most important types of isochrony, according to which the languages of the world may be classified, are therefore (a) isochrony related to intervals between stressed syllables (usually marked by pitch obtrusion and loudness, less frequently by syllable lengthening) (i.e., foot duration) and (b) isochrony related to intervals between syllables (i.e., syllable duration).

If a language is of a particular rhythm type, other phonetic features follow from it. Thus, as already mentioned by Pike, a stress-timed rhythm usually allows for the possibility of some kind of reduction either in the stressed or in the unstressed syllables of a rhythm unit: To make rhythm units of various sizes (in terms of numbers of syllables) fit into the isochronous pattern, it may be necessary to compress (or sometimes to lengthen) the syllables of a polysyllabic foot. This quantitative reduction often implies qualitative reduction as well. Therefore, it is predicted that the duration of syllables in a rhythm unit of a stress-timed language should be a function of the overall number of syllables it contains: The more syllables, the shorter their duration (hypothesis Ia: compression hypothesis). In this way, it is possible for the rhythm unit to remain constant in duration independent of the number of syllables it contains (hypothesis IIa: strict isochrony hypothesis). On the other hand, we would predict that in a syllable-timed language, no compression will take place within the rhythm unit (or foot), because there is no need to make the syllables fit into the rhythmic interval (hypothesis Ib). Instead, the duration of a foot (from one prominent syllable to the next) will increase in an additive way with the number of syllables in the foot. To maintain a syllable-timed rhythm, a language of this rhythm type would instead be expected either to have syllables of more or less identical internal makeup (thereby guaranteeing durational constancy) or to compensate within the syllable for structural differences, so that the duration of the individual syllables will remain approximately even (hypothesis IIb). The first of these alternatives is, for instance, exemplified by a language that has short open syllables only (ideally only words with CVCV . . .); the second alternative is, for instance, exemplified by a language that regulates vowel length as an inverse function of the type and number of syllable-final consonants (ideally CV:: ≈ CV:C ≈ CVCC).

Of the two languages discussed in this chapter, German is said to belong to the stress-timed type (i.e., its typological classification with respect to rhythm is the same as that of English), whereas Italian is often cited as a typical syllable-timed language (i.e., it is grouped with Spanish). In the usual definition of the two rhythm types outlined previously, we would expect the following isochronous patterns in these languages (/   / = intervals of approximately equal duration; the number of structural units within the rhythmic interval—syllables or nuclear segments/ morae[2]—is given beneath each interval):

German

```
              /'Peter       /'raucht     / (= /'Peter        /'smokes/)
syllables:       2              1         (     2                1    )

              /'Fridolin    /'raucht     / (= /'Fridolin     /'smokes/)
syllables:       3              1         (     3                1    )

              /'Fridolin be/'trinkt sich/ (= /'Fridolin gets /'drunk /)
syllables:       4              2         (     4                1    )
```

Italian

```
         /San /dro /fu /ma /        ('Sandro smokes')
morae:    2    1    1   1

         /San /dro /ha /fu /ma /to /        ('Sandro smoked')
morae:    2    1    1   1   1   1

         /A   /les /san /dro /ha /fu /ma /to /     ('Alessandro smoked')
morae:    1    2    2    1    1   1   1   1
```

To achieve isochrony in the first case (German), intervals with many syllables have to be compressed and/or those with few syllables lengthened; in the second case (that of Italian), segments have to be compressed in two-segment intervals and/or lengthened in one-segment intervals.

Although the predictions made by the isochrony model are precise and should be quite easy to test, the phonetic debate about isochrony is far from being closed. This is partly due to methodological difficulties in measuring durations of interstress intervals and in linking acoustic measurements to perceptual rhythms.[3] Yet, phonetic problems of methodology notwithstanding, numerous findings support the idea of clear differences in the temporal organization of German (and other stress-timed languages such as English, Swedish, Portuguese or Dutch) and Italian (and other syllable-timed languages such as Spanish). These differences result more from the overwhelming positive evidence for hypothesis I than for hypothesis II.

With regard to temporal compression, Kohler (1982, 1983) has shown quantitative reduction in German syllables to be a function of foot structure. In contrast, comparable phonetic research for Italian (Marotta 1985; Vayra, Avesani & Fowler 1984; den Os 1988) supports hypothesis Ib: There is little compression and occasionally even lengthening of the stressed syllable if unstressed syllables are added to the foot. On the other hand, there is some evidence for syllable-internal quantity compensation in this language; in particular, the well-known correlation between vowel duration and consonant length in Italian (Vogel & Scalise 1982: 36) (e.g., in words such as *ca:&sa* 'house' vs. *cas&sa* 'box, ticket-office' [a stressed vowel before a short consonant is always lengthened, whereas a long consonant/geminate shortens the preceding vowel]) points in this direction.⁴

Other phonological and phonetic features of the two languages in question support stress timing (and compression) versus syllable timing, respectively, as well. Thus, German, like English, has qualitatively reduced vowels (in particular, a central schwa-vowel) which occur only in nonaccented syllables, whereas (standard) Italian vowels retain nearly the same quality whether stressed or not. Because schwa-vowels may be reduced in duration, they provide an ideal segmental basis for temporal compression. The same is not true for full vowels. Another relevant structural feature is syllable structure, which in German may become quite complex in stressed monosyllabics. Because it is the nucleus of a syllable that is responsible for rhythmic alignment, it is particularly significant that a high number of coda consonants is possible (up to four in simplex words such as *Herbst* 'autumn', up to five in inflected words such as [*du*] *schimpfst* '[you] scold'). In contrast, Italian has only open syllables in native words occurring in prepausal position, and occasional single coda consonants otherwise (e.g., in function words or with apocope, such as *con* 'with' or *San* 'Saint'). Only in loan words are more complex codas permissible (*film*, *sport*, etc.). Statistically, CV (open) syllables are by far more frequent in Italian than in German, both as tokens and as types (den Os 1988:21). In this way, Italian is more predisposed in its structure than German to keep the duration of the syllable constant. Compare the previous segment count in the syllable nuclei, in which the number of two morae per syllable (= two phonemes in the nucleus) is never exceeded.

A further structural feature of German which supports a stress-timed rhythm is the unstable nature of schwa. In allegro speech we observe elision (syncope), which usually leads to more complex syllable onsets (cf. *Batterie* → *Battrie* ['battery'], *gerade* → *grade* ['straight'], [*ich*] *rudere* → [*ich*] *rudre* ['I row']). In diachrony, schwa apocope and syncope often lead to the closure of open syllables (cf. MHG *obez* → NHG *obst* ['fruit']; MHG *hane* → NHG *hahn* ['cock']). The same alternating effect between open and closed syllables is produced synchronically by morphologically conditioned alternations between schwa and zero, such as in *atem* ('breath') ~ (*ich*) *atme* ('I breathe'). The instability of schwa thus leads to an uneven distribution of syllable length and syllable weight. It further increases the durational difference between stressed and unstressed syllables and makes it hard to maintain a syllable-based ischronous rhythm. In Italian, syncope is frequent as well, but it has the opposite effect, namely, that of enhancing CV structure by simplifying sequences of two or more vowels (cf. *la unica* → *l'unica* ['the only one'], *quanto anni* → *quant'anni* ['how many years']), thereby turning phonologically (and therefore potentially also phonetically) dissimilar syllables into similar ones.⁵

Particularly relevant to hypothesis I is the comparative work on English, French, Spanish and German by Delattre (1966, 1969). According to his results, syllable duration is much more variable in English than in Spanish (which, in this respect, may be compared to Italian), whereas German is in between. For instance, the ratio of stressed, final, closed syllables to nonstressed, nonfinal, open syllables is 3.39 for English but only 1.77 in Spanish and 2.73 in German.

With regard to hypothesis II, there is some agreement in the phonetic literature that although a stress-timed language compresses syllables in complex feet as the number of unstressed syllables increases, this compression is not sufficient to achieve equal duration in interstress intervals in the strict, acoustic sense (see, among many others, Lehiste 1973:1230; Faure, Hirst & Chafcouloff 1980). That we are nonetheless able to hear isochronous patterns is due to the following factors:

a. Human rhythm perception is not very exact, and it is highly likely that differences in rhythmic intervals below a threshold of 60 msec (for German, according to Hoequist, Kohler & Schäfer-Vincent 1986) are irrelevant. (This is roughly a tenth of the average rhythmic interval.) When English interactional material is used, Couper-Kuhlen (1993) finds a tolerance of 20% and more (see chapter 2, §6.1, in this volume).
b. The human ear seems to align stressed syllables in a way which has not yet been explored in enough detail but leads to a systematic distortion between perceived rhythm and acoustic measurements (when the latter align syllables throughout with respect to the onset or peak of (quasi-) periodicity or with respect to the beginning of the first noise burst of the syllable onset).[6]
c. In perception, rhythm is not necessarily identical with a succession of equally spaced stresses, as has been taken for granted in the phonetic literature; there is, instead, a more ambiguous relationship between rhythmic beats and stresses (see chapter 2, §2).

Given the fact that hypothesis IIa does not hold even for English, a stress-timed language *par excellence*, but that we nonetheless perceive regular rhythms in this language, the finding that the same hypothesis IIa does not hold for Italian either[7] comes as little surprise and does not prove much. The important question is rather whether the fact that no syllable compression takes place in Italian is *per se* crucial evidence against (perceptual) stress-based isochrony in this language (i.e., against the kind of rhythm with which we have worked in the previous chapters of this book).

A few simple considerations make it clear that this is not the case: The duration of rhythmic intervals can be kept constant even when no syllable compression takes place. Among the alternatives for doing this are the following: (a) every rhythmic interval can be made to contain the same (or a similar) number of syllables of equal (or mutually compensated) duration/structure by adjusting lexical and/or morphological structure; (b) too great a number of syllables within one interval can be adapted to that of the neighboring intervals by deletion (instead of compression) of nonbeat syllables; (c) intervals can adapt to each other durationally through variation in pause structure; and (d) the duration of stress intervals can be kept constant if the realization of strong phonetic prominences is variable with respect to underlying lexical primary accents. Thus, the alternation between strong and weak (or more weakly stressed) syllables on the phonetic surface may be kept in balance by the 'destressing' of lexical bearers of primary accents adjacent or quasi adjacent to other primary accents on the one hand, and by adding phonetic stresses in place of lexically unaccented or secondarily accented ones to resolve overlong sequences of syllables between beats on the other hand.[8]

All four alternatives seem to be used in Italian. Alternatives (a), (b) and (d) result from features of phonological structure specific to Italian as compared to English or German. They make it obvious that although there is no objection on principle to stress-based isochrony in Italian, such a rhythm, if it exists, must look different in detail from what it is like in English or German because the means by which equal durations between rhythmic beats are achieved are different. In particular, given the comparatively uniform structure of Italian syllables, and given the traditional (Camilli 1965) and more recent empirical (Müller 1989a) finding that the number of syllables per foot varies less in Italian than, for example, in English, we hypothesize that rhythmic intervals may be kept (approximately) constant in Italian by *keeping the number of syllables within an interval relatively constant*. We call this type of isochronous rhythmization *isometric*.

Distinctive structural traits permit Italian to use this solution. Italian words are on the average longer than those of English (and, as far as noncompounds are concerned, also longer than those of German). They contain, in addition to the one primary accent, a varying number of secondary accents which are in part lexically determined (Vogel & Scalise 1982) and in part variable (Camilli 1965: 270–1). Each of these may be realized phonetically, if rhythm demands it. Given this strong reliance on secondary prominences as potential rhythmic beats, an utterance such as *Lei ri'corda con 'tanta ˌnostal'gia il ˌsuo pa'ese Caˌsale ˌMonfer'rato* ('you remember with so much nostalgia your native village Casale Monferrato'), which contains relatively long sequences of syllables between the primary lexical accents *-cor-, tan-* and *-gia* as well as *-es-* and *-ra-*, but also secondary lexical accents on *nos-, suo, -sa-* and *Mon-*, may display quite a balanced rhythmic structure in actual performance (rendering it in fact isochronous and almost isometric), as primary and secondary lexical accents are both made use of to achieve a nicely alternating rhythm with bisyllabic and trisyllabic feet:

```
(1)  [Attested example]           No. of syllables

  1   G:    lei ri-
            /'corda con /              3
            /'tanta     /              2
            /ˌnostal-   /              2
  5         /'gia il    /              3
            /ˌsuo pa-   /              3
            /'ese Ca-   /              3
            /ˌsale      /              2
            /ˌMonfer-   /              2
 10         /'rato      /              2
```

To achieve this rhythm, the speaker makes use of secondary lexical accents—indeed, *every* primary or secondary lexical accent is turned into a rhythmic beat.

German, which also has long words, has secondary accents which may be turned into rhythmic beats mainly in compounds and in its lexical periphery (i.e., in relatively recent loans and latinized vocabulary; see the various possible stress positions in words such as *'absolut—abso'lut, 'defensiv—defen'siv*, etc.). In a German rendition of (1)—*sie erinnert sich mit vielen nostalgischen Gefühlen an ihren Heimatort Castrop-Rauxel*—the speaker would therefore be forced to include more material in each rhythmic unit (in addition to using pause structure), and also to compress syllables to achieve an isochronous rhythm[9]:

(1a) [Hypothetical example]   *No. of syllables*

```
1     sie er-
      /'innert sich mit /          4
      /'vielen no-      /          3
      /'stalgischen Ge- /          4
5     /'fühlen an ihren /          5
      /'Heimatort (.)   /          3
      /'Castrop (.)     /          2
      /'Rauxel
```

In conclusion, the occurrence of rhythms in Italian comparable to those found for English in prior chapters cannot be excluded on principle, based on our knowledge of Italian phonetics and phonology. Yet these rhythms will have a different structural basis. By keeping the number of off-beat syllables approximately even (and by adding rhythmic pauses where necessary), Italian can also achieve stress-timed isochronous rhythm.

It should be remembered at this point in our discussion that the existing research on isochrony and rhythm in Italian is exclusively laboratory based. It is not clear that these results can be transferred without restriction to spontaneous, conversational language. In fact, we believe that an interactionally relevant, perceptual rhythm based on *syllabic* isochrony (syllable timing) is hard to imagine, given the short duration of syllabic intervals. If, in a stretch of talk such as example (1), rhythm was based not on isometric/isochronous feet but on isochronous syllables, how could such a passage be distinguished from a nonisochronous one? Differences in syllable duration would surely often remain below the threshold of perception. It is highly unlikely therefore that interactionally relevant rhythm will be based on the recurrence of syllables of equal duration. We conclude that the distinction between stress-timed and syllable-timed languages, well-founded as it may be in phonetic and acoustic terms, cannot have a direct correspondence in interaction. Rather, interactionally relevant rhythms have to be based on the regular recurrence of accent-based beats both in so-called syllable-timed and so-called stress-timed languages. Italian and German are both structurally disposed to achieve rhythmic structures in speech. Whether this disposition is made use of—whether rhythm is actually used as a contextualization cue in either of these languages (or rather, speech communities)—remains to be seen. It is this question we investigate in the present and in subsequent chapters.

2. Telephone closing in German and Italian

The structure of telephone closings is one of the central discoveries of CA. Although the ritual aspects of leave taking were given extensive treatment and received a face-related interpretation in the work of Goffman (see Goffman 1971), it was not until the appearance of Schegloff and Sack's seminal paper on telephone closings (1973) that the structural details of the orderly suspension of conversational turn taking were recognized. Schegloff and Sack's contribution is rightfully considered a classic in CA: It is one of the most convincing proofs available that small-scale technical details in the sequential development of conversation are highly relevant for co-participants' orderly conduct in bringing an interactional episode to its termination.

The basic argument is well-known. Schegloff and Sacks argue that it is not the hanging up of the receiver that closes a telephone call or the exchange of farewells that usually precedes it but, rather, a trajectory of conversational activities within a so-called closing sequence. This sequence is initiated when participants, having jointly brought to conclusion a conversational topic, exchange 'preclosing' tokens such as *all right* or *okay*. With these turns, they signal to each other that no further topical talk is intended. The closing sequence lasts from the exchange of the preclosing tokens until the termination of the call, which, in its simplest canonical form, consists of a pair of farewells (or substitutes for them). The relationship of these farewells to each other is that of an adjacency pair: the production of the first farewell by one speaker makes the adjacent production of a second farewell by the other speaker conditionally relevant. The minimal canonical structure of a telephone closing is therefore:

A: preclosing token
B: preclosing token
A: final farewell token
B: final farewell token

This minimal canonical sequence has been called "pervasive" (Button 1987:101) in American and British English conversations. We have occasionally found it in German phone calls as well:

(2) [6–9.5]

M is giving instructions on how to put his child to bed.[10]

1 M: wenn ihr ins bett gehn (dued) (na er soll) au ins bett
when you go to bed he should go to bed too

F: ja:
yeah

M: gell?
you know?

F: guet;
all right

5	→	oke:
		okay
M:	→	o[ke:
		okay
F:	→	[tschüß
		bye
M:	→	ade:
		bye

However, the minimal sequence is rare in our German corpus of predominantly private calls. For Italian, we have no examples at all for such a minimal closing in our collection; yet, it is intuitively acceptable.

Versions of phone closings lacking one of the sequential components of the minimal canonical version have a marked status which usually coincides with other features of the phone call, making this deviation from the canonical structure accountable as an instance of 'being in a hurry' or 'being perfunctory'. (A call may be 'perfunctory' if it has preliminary or supportive status in interactional history; for instance, the call may be preparing the imminent meeting of two people.) In such cases, either (one of) the preclosings or (one of) the final farewells, or one of the two pairs may be missing or replaced by (one pair-part of) an appreciation–appreciation sequence (such as *danke–danke*), or an appreciation–response sequence (such as *danke–bitte*), which then take(s) on the status of the farewell(s). Of the many types of such foreshortening, we give just two examples from our German collection, one (3) from an institutional call, and the other (4) from a private call:

(3) [235.2–238.9]

M = caller, F = secretary

1	M:	hinterlassen Sie ihm bitte Herr Braun hätte angerufen=
		please leave him a note that Mr. Braun called
	F:	=ja, mach [ich
		I sure will
	M:	[ich melde mich nochmal=
		I'll call back
	F:	=ja,
		yeah,
5	M:	ich ruf so vierzehn uhr dreißig fünfzehn uhr an;
		I'll call at around fourteen thirty fifteen o'clock
	F:	→ gut, danke=
		okay thank you

M: → =danke, wiedersehn
  thank you good-bye

(4) [203–205.9]

1 F: da kann ich noch schnell einkaufen gehn
  so I can go shopping quickly beforehand

 M: ich bin bis fünf uhr nich da;
  I won't be home until five

 F: mhm,
  mhm,

 M: → servus
  cheers

5 F: → servus mein schatz
  cheers darling

In extract (3), there is no second farewell after the caller's good-bye (line 7), and there is just one preclosing token (line 6, *gut*).[11] The main closing job is done by an exchange of appreciations (*danke–danke*, lines 6–7).[12] The foreshortening of the sequence takes place in a phone call to the secretary of the person to whom M wanted to talk. It reflects the perfunctory and highly formal character of the interaction. In extract (4), the exchange of final farewell tokens in lines 4–5 is not preceded by any preclosing formulae. Leaving out essential parts of the canonical sequential format in this case reflects both the preliminary character of leave taking (participants have arranged to meet again within a short period of time) and the hurry that F announces she is in to get her shopping done (line 1).

Yet the unmarked and by far most frequent form of the closing sequence, both in the German and Italian data, is neither the minimal canonical form nor its foreshortened version but an extended version of the canonical sequence. The extension may be done in a number of ways, but the following (or a combination of them) appear to be most frequent: (a) more than two final farewells may be produced;[13] (b) more than two preclosings may be produced; (c) appreciations and responses/counterappreciations may be added; (d) references to future encounters may be made (these arrangements having been fixed earlier)—that is, participants may anticipate the future development of their interactional history (a formulaic reference to future meetings is also possible, such as German *bis dann* or Italian *ci sentiamo* 'see you'); (e) wishes may be added (in particular, formulaic ones such as German *mach's gut* or Italian *auguri*); (f) greetings to third persons may be added. In addition, names and endearment terms may be attached to any of these activities. Typical examples of phone closings in our data are therefore extracts (5) and (6) for German, and (7) and (8) for Italian, rather than (2):

Rhythm in Telephone Closings

(5) [0–5]

1	F:	aso ich sag ims gell?	(preclosing +
		okay I'll tell him right?	topic closure)
	M:	sagsch im pscheid?	
		you'll tell him?	
	F:	jo (-) jo	
		yeah (-) yeah	
	M:	alles klar? =	(preclosing)
		all right?	
5	F:	=gell?	
		right?	
	M:	machs [guet	(good wishes)
		all the best	
	F:	[gue:t; jo; dank [e	(preclosing +
		all right yeah thanks	appreciation)
	M:	[dankschö [:n	(appreciation)
		thank you	
	F:	[h h	
10	M:	wieder [hörn	(farewell)
		good-bye	
	F:	[a:de [:	(farewell)
		cheers	
	M:	[a:de	(farewell)
		cheers	

(6) [29b: 207–220.7]

1	M:	du kannst ja mal anrufen oder: (-)	(arrangements)
		you can call her or (-)	
		oder die ruft dich an (.)	
		or she will call you	
		beides (.) [ne?	
		both (.) no?	
	F:	[oke (-)	(confirmation)
		okay (-)	
5	M:	tschüüß (.)	(farewell)
		byebye	

		[schönen grüß an mammi	[und an Anselm=	(greetings to
		greetings to mom	*and to Anselm*	third parties)
	F:	[álso (.) bis	[morgen	(preclosing+
		okay (.) till	*tomorrow*	arrangement)
		=mhm (-)		(acknowledgement)
		=*mhm* (-)		
		tschüüß		(farewell)
		bye-bye		
10	M:	tschüüß		(farewell)
		bye-bye		

(7) [8: 247]

1	G:	quindi la sera è facile che sono libera	(topic closure)
		so in the evening it's likely I'm free	
	S:	mhm (-) va bene.=	(acknowledgement +
		mhm (-) okay.	preclosing)
	G:	=va bene?	(preclosing)
		okay?	
	S:	okey	(acknowledgement)
		okay	
5	G:	ci sentiamo	(routine
		we'll hear from each other	arrangement)
	S:	ciao Gianna=	(farewell +
		bye Gianna	address term)
	G:	=ciao (.) ciao	(farewell +
		bye (.) bye	farewell)

(8) [6: 181]

1	S:	mi prendo ste stoffe e: e vado hai capito?	(topic closure)
		I'll take these fabrics a:nd and I'll go you see?	
		(1.1)	
	F:	ho capito va b[ene	(acknowledgement +
		I see all right	preclosing)
	S:	[poi le telefono. (-) okey,	(topic closure, cont'd.)
		afterward I'll ring her up. (-) okay?	
5	F:	mhm	(acknowledgement)
		mhm	

S:	ti saluto		(farewell)
	greetings to you		
F:	okey=		(preclosing or acknowledgement)
	okay		
S:	=ciao=		(farewell)
	bye		
F:	=a dopo ciao		(routine arrangement + farewell)
	see you bye		

In extended closing sections, a multitude of usually very short turn-constructional units is produced, the sequential status of which is not always easy to reconstruct unambiguously. In particular, the tokens used for preclosings (such as German *gut, o.k., alles klar, also* or Italian *va bene, okey*) can serve other functions in addition to preclosing a conversation (as in extract 8, where *okey* is first used to elicit agreement in line 4 and later in line 7 either as an acknowledgement of the previous farewell or as a preclosing). The sequential structure of such extended closings also shows that the relationship between first and second preclosings cannot be that of an adjacency pair: Not only are there sequences of more than two preclosings (as in extract 5), but preclosings are not necessarily produced adjacently either. (In fact, although preclosings are sequentially implicative, they may not be typically used to prestructure the immediately following conversational slot in a unique way. Rather, they seem to leave a number of alternatives for the second speaker to choose from.) Also note that although the inventory of forms used as farewells is relatively restricted in Italian and English, German uses a variety of forms (which are hard to render in English translation): Those documented in extracts (5) and (6)—*wiederhörn, ade, tschüß, servus*—are just a selection.

In addition to extended closing sequences of this type, cases are frequent in which participants, after agreeing to open up closing by producing preclosing tokens, introduce further topical material relating, for instance, to the 'reason for call' (for instance, in the format of a summary or a 'formulation'), or to making an arrangement (rather than simply repeating it). Extensions that add topical material in this way typically require longer turns or exchanges. The sequential implicativeness of these preclosings is thus attenuated; often, another exchange of preclosings takes place in such cases before the conversation comes to an end (see [9] and [10]).

(9) [3: 77]

1   S: si si adesso c'ho tutto qua.
         yeah yeah now I have everything here.

    F: mhm [{p}va bene.
         mhm all right.

	S:		[ho preso due copie (0.2)
			I took two copies
			va bene. allora ci sentiamo domani cosi
			all right. so I'll see you tomorrow or so
5	F:		{p} mhm [va bene
			mhm all right
	S:	→	[tu stasera che fai? (-) al cineforum ci vai?
			and this evening what are you doing? (-) are you going to the cineforum?
	F:		non lo so (-) non so proprio devo: (-) bo devo vedere
			I don't know (-) I really don't know (-) I have to see
	S:		va be in caso ci sentiamo
			okay. in case you do go we'll hear from each other
	F:		ci sentiamo più tardi=
			We'll hear from each other later on
10	S:		=si
			yeah
	F:		va bene?
			okay?
	S:		d'accordo
			all right
	F:		okey
			okay
	S:		[ciao Silvana
			bye Silvana
15	F:		[ciao Giuglia ciao
			bye Giuglia bye

After a first exchange of preclosings (lines 2, 4), Giuglia reintroduces the topic of making arrangements for a future meeting in line 4, a topic already dealt with in previous turns. A meeting for the evening is indirectly suggested by a presequence about Silvana's plans (see arrow). After Silvana's negative reply, a further triple sequence of preclosings (lines 11–13) leads into the termination of the conversation.

(10) [Radio Genova][14]

	1	C:	e allora poi sto fuori sto fuori poco;=e
			so now I go out go out seldom;
		DJ:	mi raccomando [e? giudizio,
			I beg you be careful.

Rhythm in Telephone Closings

```
    C:                  [(vado vado; vado e vengo)=
                         (I go I go; I come and I go)

    DJ:    =hm giudizio; e?=
           hm be careful; okay?

5   C:   → =comunque Luisa mi fa piacere sentirti; un po parlare un po con te,
           anyway Luisa it's a pleasure to hear your voice a little to talk to you a little,

    DJ:    e s [i:, e di,
           oh yes, come on,

    C:         [ti faccio sempre i complimenti per la tua trasmissione,
                I must always compliment you on your program,

    DJ:    grazie,
           thanks

    C:     e: voglio fare un saluto a tutto l'ascolto;
           and I would like to greet everyone who is listening in;

10  DJ:    si,
           yes,

    C:     e a voi festeggiati ti facciamo tanti auguri;
           and to you, congratulate yourself, congratulations to you from us;

    DJ:    si,
           yes,

    C:     (-) e io ti saluto caramente;
           (-) and I send you my kindest regards;

    DJ: → e io ti contraccambio il saluto;=
           and I send you back my regards;

15  C:     =ecco. (-) e ti sentiremo;
           right. (-) and we'll hear from you;

    DJ:    ciao (-) c [erca di star bene,
           bye (-) try to take care

    C:   →           [tan
                      bes

           tanti saluti da Silvana;
           best wishes from Silvana;

    DJ:    a: anch'io la saluto tanto;
           oh my very best wishes to her too;

20  C:     hm me lo dice sempre se senti Luisa salutamela;=
           hm she always tells me if you see Luisa greet her for me;

    DJ:    =benissimo; (-) [dille che venga in gita con noi a
           very well; (-)   tell her she should come with us on

    C:                     [(      )
```

DJ:		Toirano il diciannove mi raccomando e?
		our trip to Toirano on the 19th won't you?
C:		può anche darsi,=
		maybe she will,
25 DJ:		=ecco; dille che mi chiami; perchè io ho bisogno
		fine; tell her to call me; because I need to know
		di sapere i nominativi, (-) [hm?
		the names, (-) o.k.?
C:		[si glielo dico; (-) subito=
		yes I'll tell her; (-) immediately=
DJ:	→	=bene;
		fine;
C:		(-) ciao Luisa;
		(-) bye Luisa;
30 DJ:		ciao ( ) [auguri;
		bye ( ) congratulations;
C:		[saluti; [ciao ciao [(ciao)
		best wishes; bye-bye (bye)
DJ:		[ciao ciao [ciao
		bye-bye bye

This very elaborate closing section is introduced by the caller's *comunque* (line 5, first arrow), which precloses the conversation and is followed by a series of compliments, good wishes and congratulations to the DJ, addressing, among other things, her institutional role, as well as by good wishes to the audience (line 9). The last activity in this series of activities, each of which is initiated by C (the caller), is an exchange of good wishes (lines 13 and 14, see second arrow), via which participants approach the final exchange of farewells. But only one such farewell is actually produced by the DJ (line 16), while C makes use of this final sequential opportunity to confer good wishes from a third party to DJ (*tanti saluti da Silvana*, line 17f, third arrow). These good wishes, although a routine component of extended closings, on this particular occasion lead to an expansion of the closing section with topical talk (about Silvana's participation in a future trip to Toirano). Finally, DJ produces a preclosing herself (line 28, fourth arrow). This preclosing, although quite far removed from the first preclosing by C in line 5, may be seen as a response to it. C immediately resumes the final farewell sequence, which again includes many extensions and additions, such as *auguri* and *saluti*, and no less than four expressions of farewell by each participant (lines 29–32). Even more marked versions of closings occur when co-participants move back into topical talk completely ("moving out of closings," as Button 1987 puts it).

In conclusion, when compared to turn taking within a phone call, closing sequences in the moderately extended version (without resumption of topical talk) in both the German and the Italian data display some interesting characteristics which, in combination, are rare in the middle parts of the conversation. First of all, the turn-constructional components used are typically very short. Second, in many cases, the same activity type is used in a sequence of two activities: farewell–farewell, preclosing–preclosing, good wishes–good wishes, recognition–recognition. Often the same tokens are used as well. Third, sequences of more than two activities of the same type are also frequent (such as exchanges of more than two preclosings or more than two farewells). Fourth, many activities are produced in overlap or simultaneously: There are few silences. Given the amount of simultaneous talk, it is not always obvious that participants are still orienting to a one-speaker-at-a-time rule (see, for example, the final farewells in [9] and [10]). Fifth, in the majority of cases—in particular in private phone calls—closing sections do not follow the minimal canonical format given at the beginning of this section but are considerably more elaborate. Because the minimal canonical form would be sufficient to do the job that Schegloff & Sacks (1973) assign to it (i.e., to achieve the orderly suspension of the turn-taking machinery), it may be asked why closing sequences exhibit these features.

3. The rhythm and tempo of German phone closings

Having summarized the most important characteristics of telephone closings as they emerge from a sequential treatment within the limits of orthodox CA, we now invite readers to disregard for a moment the level of activities or moves carried out by participants in these closings, as well as that of the topics they discuss or the rituals they perform, and to imagine instead a frequent situation in everyday life. It is the situation of unintentionally overhearing a telephone conversation going on next door, when one is too far away to understand the words produced by the speaker, but close enough to perceive their prosodic shape.

Often in such a situation, we are able to foretell the imminent termination of the phone call by listening to the way in which the syllables and words are produced, even though the segmental basis of speech is not available to us. Working only on the prosodic information in what we perceive, we can nonetheless make interactional sense of it. The reason is that the prosodic contextualization of the final part of a phone call is as a rule sufficiently different from that of ordinary in-conversation talk to signal that termination will be reached soon. What is this prosodic contextualization like? We claim that rhythm and tempo play a crucial role in it.[15]

First, the prosodic shape of the exchanges in a telephone conversation that is approaching termination is as a rule different from usual in-conversation talk because the exchanges consist of a succession of short intonational phrases (prosodic contours), often containing one foot only.[16] For instance, the final part of the telephone conversation of (1) contains seven intonational phrases (marked by | | in [2a]), each with a pitch accent of its own. None of them has more than two syllables, however:

(2a) F: | ja:|
      M: | gell?|
      F: | guet|
           | oke:|
      M: | oke:|
      F: | tschüß|
      M: | ade:|

Note in passing that the prosodic structure of many of the small tokens exchanged in farewells or preclosings is a peculiar one compared to the prosodic structure of German words in the 'native' core vocabulary in general (the reason being, of course, that they are by and large loans). Although words in the core vocabulary may be monosyllabic, if they contain more than one syllable, (at least one of) the nonstressed syllable(s) is usually a schwa syllable (i.e., there is a nonstressable nucleus) (cf. (3): *hinterlassen Sie ihm bitte Herr Braun hätte angerufen*, with the following lexical stress patterns in the polysyllabics—lexically stressed syllables are marked with ' for primary and ˌ for secondary stress, schwa syllables are underlined: ˌhint__er__'lass__en__, 'bitt__e__, 'hätt__e__, 'ange__ˌ__ruf__en__). Apart from the formal (*auf*) *wiedersehen*/(*auf*) *wiederhören*, rarely used in private phone calls, the usual tokens in the final farewells of our corpus, which has a southern German bias,[17] and the usual tokens for preclosing a telephone conversation are either monosyllabic (*tschüß, ciao; gut*) or bisyllabic ('tschü̞ˌüß, 'ciaoˌciao, 'servus, 'ade, ad'e, 'ada; 'oke:, 'also) but do not contain schwa syllables. The frequent bisyllabic rendition of the originally monosyllabic *tschüß*[18]—by far the most frequent farewell token in private German phone calls—and the reduplication of *ciao* indicate a certain preference for trochees without schwa.

Therefore, the prosodic shape of the utterances typically produced in succession in closing sequences is a first important reason why these passages are perceived as different from in-conversation talk even when the words cannot be understood. We hear a succession of short outbursts of speech, either within one speaker's turn or, more usually, in alternation with the other speaker (provided we are able to overhear both parties). The shortness and marked structure of the intonation phrases which make up a high proportion of the utterances in closings—particularly as the termination of the call approaches—are used and usable as contextualization cues for this part of the telephone conversation.

However, other features are involved as well. One is rhythm. We regularly observe in the data that the final portion of a telephone conversation is produced with an isochronous rhythm to which both participants contribute[19]:

(2a)

1   M: wenn 'ihr ins 'bett gehn (dued) (na er
          soll) 'au ins bett

          when you go to bed he should go to bed too

    F: /'ja: /
    M: /'gell?   /

```
5   F:     /'guet o-      /
           /'ke
    M:                    o-/
           /['ke
    F:         ['tschüß   /
10  M:     /'ade:
    F:     yeah
    M:     you know?
    F:     all right o-
           kay
    M:     ok [ay
    F:        [bye
    M:     bye
```

(11) [327–333.3]

```
1   M2:   i 'ruef (eventuell) nochemal 'o:
          (maybe) I'll call back later
          / ['gell?
    M1:       ['ja? o-      /
          /'ke: (.)         /
5   M2:   /'ada             /
    M1:   /'ade             /
    M2:   /'ade
    M2:   [right?
    M1:   [yes o-
          kay: (.)
    M2:   bye
    M1:   bye
    M2:   bye
```

The particular structure of the intonation phrases (their shortness) and the fact that isochrony is a regular and prevalent feature of closings are not unrelated, of course. It seems that small tokens and short phrases give participants more leeway to position their contributions such that an isochronous rhythmic pattern will emerge. In extended closings, rhythmic isochrony is likely to be based on longer rhythmic intervals of course, because more syllables have to be integrated into the rhythmic pattern. For this reason, the rhythm is often slower, although it may nonetheless be isochronous:

(12) [6–9.5]

```
1   M:    ich werds g(h)e(h) 'nie(h)ßn
          I'll e(h)nj(h)oy i(h)t

    F:    h h h o'ke: h h h [h h 'h
                     okay:
```

| | M: | | ['also |
| | | | *okay* |

| | F: | 'tschüß mein [ˌschatz |
| | | *bye my   darling* |

```
 5     M:                 /['tschüß 'liebling /
                          /['ade                /
       F:                 /[pf ((kiss)) viel    /
                          /'spaß, [gell         /
       M:                        [ja ich        /
10     F:                 /'lieb dich
                                          ich/
                          /'auch
       M:                        't [schüß
       F:                           ['tschüß
```

M: [*bye darling*
      [*cheers*
F: [*pf((kiss)) have a good*
      time [*won't you*
M: [*yes I*
      love you
F: *I love you too*
M: *b*[*ye*
F: [*bye*

An important prosodic fact about German phone closings then is that even though the passage before the closing sequence may have been anisochronous, participants regularly begin to use an isochronous rhythm, and to integrate their own contributions into this isochronous rhythm, as soon as the closing sequence is initiated by the first preclosing, or shortly thereafter.

In addition to this rhythmic regularity, another contextualization cue is of great importance. Within this isochronous passage, which persists throughout the closing sequence up to the final farewells, may be *tempo* changes. Particularly in more extensive closings, the tempo may accelerate; that is, the rhythmic intervals may become shorter, sometimes even several times. The accelerations can be said to anticipate imminent termination, accompanying, as they do, those steps that take participants closer to termination.

The following examples demonstrate the typical rhythmic structure of a closing section in an informal German telephone call, where rhythm and tempo acceleration go hand in hand:

(13) [221.5–226.4]

M = father, F = daughter

```
 1     M:    'also f ich 'wünsch dir 'viel ver'gnüg [n,
             okay I hope you'll have a lot of fun

       F:                                           [hn,
```

```
       M:    und s=is 'gut daß der mammi was
             'hingeschriebn has
             and you did well to leave a note for mom

5           → da /'freut se sich        /
                /'sehr daß du ˏkurz     /
                /ˏheimgekommen [bist    /
       F:                     ['ja-ˏa,
                /^                      /

       M:    she will be very pleased to hear
             that you dropped in at home
       F:    yeah yeah

10     M:       /['schreib noch 'drunter
            →   /' pappi hat mit mir    /    (new rhythm, faster)
                /' auch gesprochen      /
       F:       /' ja, ˏgu:t            /

       M:    add a note saying dad talked to me as well
       F:    yes okay

       M: →    /'danke  /      (faster)
15              /'tschüß /
       F:       /'tschau /
       M:       /'servus /

       M:    thanks bye
       F:    ciao
       M:    take care
```

This extract starts with an anisochronous passage in which M closes off the previous topic; when he initiates the closing section, however, he uses an isochronous rhythm (line 5, first arrow). F does not pick up this rhythm yet (see the off-beat *ja= a* in line 8); her response creates a syncopated beat within the rhythmic pattern established by M. In *Pappi hat mit mir auch gesprochen* 'dad talked to me as well' (line 11, second arrow), M accelerates his tempo by using slightly shorter isochronous intervals; this time, F joins in as well (line 13, *ja gut*). The final exchange of farewells (lines 14–17, third arrow) again accelerates the tempo, and both participants join in this slightly faster isochronous pattern.

(4a)

```
1      F:    da kann ich noch schnell 'einkaufen gehn
             so I can go shopping quickly beforehand

       M: → ich bin bis /'fünf uhr nich    /
                        /ˏda;
```

```
           F:                                    m- /
5                          / 'hm

        M:    I won't be there until five
        F:    mhm

        M: → / 'servus               /      (early, faster)
        F:    / 'servus mein          /
              / 'schatz

        M:    cheers
        F:    cheers darling
```

In this example, discussed earlier as an abridged version of the minimal closing format, taking prosody into account discloses the rhythmic contextualization of the sequential foreshortening. M marks the somewhat precipitated production of the first farewell (line 6, second arrow) by initiating an acceleration of the already established isochronous tempo; he does so by producing the next stressed syllable (*ser-*, line 6) slightly before the expected next beat. F takes up this accelerando, as her next stressed syllables establish an isochronous rhythm which is shorter than the one in lines 2–5. Thus, M initiates the accelerated rhythm precisely on the turn-constructional unit which foreshortens the closing, and F displays her collaboration by joining in this rhythm.

(14) [192.3–197.8]

```
   1    M:      isch der auf de 'fasnet
                is he away for carnival

        F:      'noi [ (-) 'schulunge
                no      (-) for training

        M:           [ ('sondern?)
                       (but?)

                ('de:s isch oi ˌnarr)
                (he is a fool)

5       F:      hm, (-)

        M: →        / 'also(-) o-              /
                   / 'ke: na bach=mers morge   /
                   / 'früh
                right (-) okay: so let's get it done tomorrow morning

        F:  → / 'jo(-)        /     (early, doubled tempo)
10      M:    / 'dange::(-) /
        F:    / 'bidde: [ :
        M:             [ ˌa- /
```

```
            [/'de
    F:      [/ˌa'de
    F:      yeah (-)
    M:      thank you:: (-)
    F:      you're wel[come
    M:                [good-
            [bye
    F:      [good-bye
```

Here, talk is rhythmical from the first preclosing onward (line 6, first arrow), but F accelerates the tempo when she produces her *jo* before the beat (line 9, second arrow). The new, faster tempo is established by M in his following contribution. He doubles the tempo by reducing the length of the rhythmic intervals from approximately 1 sec. to less than 0.5 sec.

Of course, the passage before the closing section is not necessarily anisochronous in German telephone conversations. If there is rhythm already, speakers can no longer mark the beginning of the closing sequence with isochrony. In this case, it is often acceleration alone which contextualizes the beginning of the closing sequence (see examples [15] and [18]).

Why should faster tempo be used to contextualize the imminent termination of the call? Is this type of contextualization purely arbitrary, a conventional means to mark the closing of a telephone conversation, or does it have some 'natural' basis? We believe that the latter is the case. Because faster tempo optimizes rhythmic gestalts (among other things, by reducing the likelihood of off-beat stresses), increases in tempo can be seen as a way to enhance rhythmicity. Shorter rhythmic intervals are more salient and easier to follow.

Up to now, we have argued that by joining together in a common rhythm participants jointly contextualize the upcoming closing. It is as if the production of preclosing tokens or similar elements typical for the closing section alone were not enough to actually terminate the conversation; rather, the sequential production of these tokens must be regularly structured in time. A number of features in closings support our hypothesis that there is a close link between the initiation and sequential development of a closing sequence on the one hand and its rhythmicity and tempo on the other. A first piece of evidence is this: In many of the phone calls in our data, one of the two participants can easily be identified as the one who takes the initiative, proposing or even urging the termination of the call. This is easy to see on the sequential level. For instance, in (13) M is the participant who takes the lead over F: He produces the first and only preclosing *also* (line 1) and, after a number of extensions also initiated by himself, he moves into the final sequence of farewells (third arrow). F merely responds to these initiatives. In (14), M again produces the first (and only) preclosing (*also*, in line 6), urges the female participant into a sequence of appreciation/acknowledgement (*danke–bitte*) and produces the first of the final farewells.[20] As we have argued before, the rhythmic development of the passage supports this sequential interpretation.

The coincidence between sequential and prosodic development is also plainly visible in the following extract, in which one of the participants' attempts at imposing an accelerated rhythm and at the same time moving the conversation toward its end on the sequential level are less successful than in the examples considered so far:

(15) [134–138.8]

```
1   F:       wir hatten ja / 'ganz starken      /
                            / 'frost bis heut   /
                            / 'nacht, ne        /
    M:                      / 'ja ja

    F:       we had very strong freezing weather until last night you know
    M:       oh yes

5   F:       ja: [ / 'oke:                      /
    M:           [ / 'mhm                       /
    F:             / 'tschüß [kufst heut /
    M:  →                   [ 'alles 'kla:r
    F:             / 'a [bend nochmal       /
10  M:  →             [ 'tschüß
    F:             / 'an [ 'gell?              /
    M:  →               [ 'ja:
    F:           [ / 'tschüß
    M:           [ / 'tschü üß

    F:       yes [okay:
    M:           [mhm
    F:       bye [you call²¹ back again [this evening [all right?
    M:          [fine                   [bye          [ye:s
    F:       [bye
    M:       [bye-bye
```

In this case, F precipitates the closing sequence with a preclosing (*oke:,* line 5) and an immediate farewell (*tschüß,* line 7). Rhythmically, the closing sequence is initiated by a marked acceleration of tempo: Average rhythmic interval duration drops from approximately 0.75 to approximately 0.5 sec. Yet for M, this step seems to come unexpectedly, or he is reluctant to terminate the conversation[22]; in any case, his contributions in the early phase of this closing sequence (marked by arrows) all fail to take up the new rhythm. He misses the beat with *alles klar, tschüß* and *jaa.* Only the final farewell (line 14) is produced on the beat, in strict synchronization with F's final farewell. The point is that the party who initiates the closing on the sequential level also initiates the new, accelerated rhythmic pattern, and the more responsive party may find it difficult to follow the leader prosodically .

Thus a first piece of evidence for our claim that prosody and sequential development are interrelated is that initiating parties in closing sequences are initiative

Rhythm in Telephone Closings

both on the sequential and on the rhythmical level. A second piece of evidence is given by the fact that failure to establish a common rhythm in the closing sequence may have more dramatic consequences than in (15), in that it may hinder participants from closing the conversation 'properly'. If participants' tempos in terminating the conversation diverge considerably, or if one of them follows an isochronous rhythmic pattern while the other does not (and they are therefore 'out of phase'), it may happen that the initiating party closes down the conversation and thereby precludes the other from asking or giving the information he or she wants to ask or give. This is the case in the following exchange between a mother and her son (the mother is the caller):

(16) [110.5–118]

F = mother, M = son

```
1   F:       /'als [o                    in/
    M:            ['jaja
    F:       /'zehn min͵ute simma de-/
             /'hai [m                       /
5   M:            ['jaja(-)'jaja
    F:       /'tschü͵üß
    M:                          'tschü͵üß

    F:       o[kay
    M:        [mhm mhm
    F:       in ten minutes we'll be [home
    M:                               [mhm mhm (-) mhm mhm
    F:       byebye
    M:       byebye

    F(?):    ((hangs up receiver))

    M:  →    'du:
             hey mom:
```

F precloses the conversation with *also* (line 1). M is not able or not yet willing to take up the closing rhythm, however, as signaled by his off-beat *jaja*'s and *tschüüß* (lines 2, 5 and 7). Although the boy seems to collude with his mother on the sequential level, or at least in the joint production of the canonical terminating exchange of farewells, the rhythmic disintegration of this closing foreshadows the possibility of diverging interests. In fact, the boy's attempt to introduce topical material at the last possible moment comes too late: His final contribution is cut off by the interruption of the line.

A third piece of evidence for the interactional relevance of rhythmic integration in the production of smooth telephone closings is that a reversal in the direction of a closing sequence (i.e., a 'moving out' of the closing via topical turns which lead back to in-conversation talk) is often accompanied by a breakdown of isochrony:

(17) [207–220.7]

M = father, F = daughter

```
1  F:       'oke:
            okay:

   M:       ('jo?)
            (yeah?)

   F:       /'also 'bis ˌmor[gen /
   M:                       [bis
5          [/'morgen(-)
   F:      [/'nachmittag        /
   M:      /'tschü[ˌüß

   F:      all right see you tomo[rrow
   M:                            [until [tomorrow (-)
   F:                                   [afternoon
   M:      bye[bye

   F: →          [ich 'ruf dann die 'Susi [nach
                 I will call Susie then         later

   M: →                                         [wie war
10         denn die 'arbeit?    ((conversation continues))
           what was your exam like?
```

(18) [284–301.2]

```
1  M:      /'mach mal /
   F:      /'also du /
           /'auch=

   M:      you do that
   F:      you too=

   M:                              ='tschüß/
5  F:      /'spätzele                      /
   F:      /'tschüßle                      /
   M:      /'tschüßle                      /
   F:      /'tschüßle [(du)
   M: →               [was is=des für en /
10         /'brief (.)            von/
           /'Stollwerck?                  /

   F: → /'äh 'ja

   M:      =bye darling
   F:      bye-bye
```

```
       M:    bye-bye
       F:    bye-bye [(dear)
       M:           [what letter is it (.) from Stollwerck?
       F:    ehm well

       F:    sie hat gsagt von Stollwerck (.) aber
             eh=sie=äh die Fräuln (Edeltraut) kumm(t) 'au
15           erst so um 'siebe rum von de 'stadt
             she said from Stollwerck (.) but ehm=she=ehm Miss (Edeltraut)
             will only be back around seven from town

             ((conversation continues))
```

In (17), F extends the closing with an item typical for this sequential context: an arrangement (line 8, first arrow). Occasioned by this extension, M adds a turn initiating a new topic, which is then dealt with at length in the ensuing part of the conversation (lines 9–10, second arrow). In (18), M reinitiates talk about a topic mentioned earlier in the conversation (lines 9–10, first arrow); this moving out of closing is first done in a rhythmically integrated fashion (lines 9–12). In F's response (line 13), however, the moderately paced rhythm is abandoned and the turn becomes anisochronous. In both cases, a participant uses a very late slot in the closing sequence as a last chance to reopen the conversation. Isochrony breaks down, which contextualizes the sudden breakoff of the closing sequence before the call has been terminated.

4. The rhythm and tempo of Italian phone closings

Having established that isochronous rhythms and accelerandos have important contextualizing value for telephone closings in German, a stress-timed language, we move on to discuss whether a language such as Italian, which according to linguistic and phonetic evidence has a different kind of rhythmical structure, also uses isochrony (or, rather, isometric isochrony) and tempo for the same interactional function. This is indeed the case, as the following rhythmic extracts demonstrate (the number of weak vs. strong syllables per rhythmic interval—or light syllables with one mora vs. heavy syllables with more than one mora—is added in parentheses):

```
(7a)
   1   G:    quindi la 'sera e 'facile che sono 'libera
             so in the evening it's likely I'm free
       S:    m / 'hm (0.2) va              /           (2w?)
             / 'bene.=
       G:                  =va 'bene?=
```

```
 5  S:                              =o-      /           (6w)
            /'key
    G:                          ci sen-/                 (1w, 2s)
    S:   mhm (-) okay.=
    G:   =okay?
    S:   okay
    G:   we'll
    G:         /'tiamo      /      (much faster)         (2w)
    S:         /'ciao       /                            (1s)
10            /'Gianna=     /                            (1w, 1s)
    G:         /='ciao (.) /                             (1s)
            /'ciao                (early)
    G:   hear from each other
    S:   bye Gianna=
    G:   =bye (.) bye
```

(8a)

```
 1  S:   mi 'prendo ste 'stoffe e: e 'vado hai
         ca'pito?
         I'll take these fabrics a:nd and I'll go you see?
         (1.1)
    F:   ho ca'pito va 'b[ene
         I see        all  right
 5  S:                   [poi le te'lefono.(-)o-
                         afterward I'll ring her up.(-)o-
            /'key
    F:               m-/                                 (1w, 1s)
            /'hm
    S:                ti sa-/                            (3w)
10          /'luto
    F:               o-/                                 (3w)
            /'key=
    S:           ='ciao=
    F:               =a 'dopo /                          (3w, 2s)
15          /'ciao
    S:   kay?
    F:   mhm
    S:   greetings to you
    F:   okay=
    S:   =bye=
    F:   =see you bye
```

Rhythm in Telephone Closings

(9a)

(Final part only, preceding section is not isochronous.)

```
 1  S:    va 'be in 'caso ci sen'tiamo
          okay. in case you do go we'll hear from each other

    F:    ci sen'tiamo più
          we'll hear from each other

                   /'tardi=
    S:                     ='si
 5  F:                         ˛va/                      (3w, 1s)
                   /'bene?
    S:                         d'ac-/                    (2w, 1s)

    F:    later on=
    S:    =yeah
    F:    okay?
    S:    all=

    S:    /'cordo        /    ((double time))            (1w, 1s)
    F:    /˛o'key        /                               (1w, 1s)
10  S:    /['ciao Sil-                                   (2s)
    F:        ['ciao    /                                (1s)
    S:    / ['vana
    F:        ['Giuglia

    S:    =right
    F:    okay
    S:    [bye Silvana
    F:    [bye Giuglia
```

(19) [13: 379]

```
 1  G:    c'e comunque qualcuno se:(-)se arriviamo dopo
          le tre e mezzo(-)le quat     [tro
          but somebody is going to be at home if (-)
          if we arrive after half past three (-) at f[our

    M:                                 [si. si si si
                                        yes. yes yes yes

    G:    a va bene {p}allora=
          fine {p}so=

 5  M:    =si(-)comunque poi ci sen-
          =yes (-) anyway later we'll see

                 /'tiamo
    G:                   per-/                           (2w, 1s)
                 /'fetto                                 (2w, 1s)
```

	M.	m-/	
10		/'hm(-) /	(?)
		/'ciao Gino /	(2w, 1s)
	G:	[( )	
	M:	/ ['grazie	

M:	each other
G:	very good.
M:	mhm (-) bye Gino
G:	[( )
M:	[thanks

(20) [20: 202]

After initiating the closing sequence, J gives M her phone number, which she now repeats.

1	M:	va /'bene ‚trenta /	(3w, 1s)
		/'nove ‚quaran- /	(3w, 1s)
		/'totto ‚dicias-/	(2w, 2s)
		/'sette	

okay. thirty-nine forty-eight seventeen

5	J:	si d'ac /'cor [do /	(1w, 1s)
	M:	[‚o'key	
	J:	/‚ci ve- /	(2w)
		/'diamo /	(2w)
	M:	/'si /	(1w)
10	J:	/'ciao /	(1s)
	M:	/'ciao /	(1s)
		/'grazie /	(2w)
		/'Jana /	(2w)
	J:	/'ciao	

J:	yes all ri [ght
M:	[okay
J:	we'll see each other
M:	yes
J:	bye
M:	bye thanks Jana
J:	bye

In these data, both rhythm and tempo develop in a way that can easily be compared to the German data. Toward the end of the conversations, a neatly integrated and isochronous rhythm emerges, to which both participants contribute, although not always to the same degree. As the syllable counts in each rhythmic interval indicate, the final rhythms are quite fast, usually containing no more than one to three syllables. With only a few exceptions (such as the first two intervals in lines

Rhythm in Telephone Closings 147

2–7 of [7a] and the interval in lines 12–14 of [8a]), the number of syllables is relatively even. But even if weak and strong syllables are assumed to have different lengths,[23] the rhythms perceived as isochronous certainly cannot be said to be isometric in the strict sense: Given the small number of syllables within a rhythmic interval, even variability by ±1 syllable per beat is indicative of some compensation. This is probably achieved primarily by pause structure between prosodic phrases across and within speakers' turns. For instance, the extraordinary high number of syllables in the next to last interval of (8a) is compensated for by latching between speakers' contributions, and the extraordinary isometric misfit between the first and second interval in (7) does not disturb rhythm because of the pause of approximately 0.2 sec. in S's turn.

Yet the number of fully integrated telephone closings is much smaller in the Italian than the German data, and only occasionally does the absence of rhythmic integration in the Italian data seem to indicate urging, impatience, unwillingness to finish or other interactional trouble, which it regularly does in the German data. One of the occasions on which it does is the following:

(21) [9: 254]

Massimo, the caller, has been looking for Gianna's husband, who is at his office.

```
1    M:     'pronto?
            yes?

     G:     'si, 'Massimo
            yes, Massimo

     M:     'oh; 'scusami
            oh sorry

     G:     ah hai richia'mato?
            ah you're calling again?

5           (1.1)

     M:     'si, ho richia'mato
            yes, I'm calling again

     G:     'ah; [va 'bene
            ah    all right

     M:          [ah pen'savo di aver 'fatto il 'numero
            dello 'studio
            ah I thought I had dialed the office number

10   G:     eh ma 'tanto è 'presto a quest' 'ora eh, più
            'tardi chiama
            well it's too early at this time you know, call later

     M:     m / 'hm (-) va /
                 / 'bene       /
```

	G:	/'ciao
	M:	*mhm (-) all right*
	G:	*bye*
15	M:	'ciao, 'ciao, 'scusami 'ciao {p}(Gianna)
		bye, bye, sorry, bye (Gianna)

In this phone call, almost everything goes wrong: Massimo has previously spoken to Gianna to inquire when and where he can reach her husband. He now has erroneously dialed the same number again, instead of that of the office of Gianna's husband, where he hopes to find him. The beginning of the present conversation therefore develops in a highly irregular, noncanonical way: The caller (instead of the called party, as is usual in Italian and English telephone conversations) speaks after the machine summons and opens the line with his *pronto?* (line 1). The called party then other-identifies the caller in the second sequential position (instead of the usual self-identification of the caller; see line 2). The following lines are remedial, but in line 10 Gianna brings up a further face-threatening issue: Not only has Massimo erroneously dialed the wrong number, thereby troubling her again, he has also chosen the wrong time to reach her husband anyway. Massimo now initiates the closing sequence (line 12–13), which is foreshortened by Gianna's sequential leap into final farewells (line 14) (skipping the second preclosing). There is a short phase of isochrony in this part of the conversation—where, on the basis of the previously discussed isochronous examples, one would indeed expect it most. However, this rhythm is not taken up by Massimo in his final series of farewells (plus apology, line 15). The lack of isochrony in this extract may be attributed to the face-threatening nature of the whole conversation. The *faux pas* are doubtless on Massimo's side, and it agrees with this state of affairs that only Gianna creates a short spate of isochrony with her *ciao*, placed just in time to be combined with the two previous prominences produced by Massimo—((m)hm, (va) be(ne))—into one rhythmic gestalt, while Massimo indicates his predicament and, indeed, embarrassment by subsequent anisochronous rhythm.

Yet many closings in the Italian data are *not* found to be rhythmical, although nothing in their sequential structure or interactional development seems responsible for, or contextualized by, this lack of rhythmic integration. Take, for instance, the following three cases:

(22) [1: 12]

1	A:	non sarebbe pos['sibile
		it wouldn't be possible
	S:	[si in'fatti
		yes indeed
	A:	mah
		well
	S:	va 'bene Anna ti 'faccio sa'pere
		all right Anna I'll let you know

```
5   A:      o'key [buon pome'riggio ]
            okay   good afternoon

    S:            [d'ac'cordo        ]
                   fine

            'grazie ['ciao
            thanks   bye

    A:              [ti rin'grazio 'ciao=
                     thank you bye

    S:      = 'ciao
              bye
```

(23) [21: 234]

Marco is promising to bring candles for the birthday cake which Dora is going to prepare for his party.

```
1   D:      se [le pro'curi 'fai un='opera 'buona
            if  you bring them you'd do a good deed

    M:         ['sei un po impe'gnata
                you are a bit busy

            'si si si (-) le pro'cu [ro 'io
            yes yes yes  (-) I will bring them

    D:                              ['non te ne cu'rare 'sai=
                                     don't be cross

5   M:      =h h h

    D:      'ciao bello {p}mio
            bye my dear

    M:      'ciao Dora a do'mani 'ciao
            bye Dora till tomorrow bye
```

(24) [16: 48]

B and G are talking about a bricklayer who used to work at M's house but is now needed by G.

```
1   B:      va 'bene no per'ché: 'no lui si è abitu'ato
            ormai a 'noi non 'sai? (-) ma'gari c'ha un po
            di 'trauma quando: (1.9) non lo
            traumatiz'zate 'troppo

            okay no because: he is now used to working for us
            you know? (-) he might have a little trauma when: (1.9) don't
            traumatize him too much
```

```
                [h h h
 5   G:     [ (     )
            saluti 'pure(-) buona do'menica [ci sen'tiamo
            best wishes (-)      nice Sunday      we'll hear from each other

     B:                                       ['graz si ci
                                               than yes we'll hear

            sen'tiamo=
            from each other

     G:     ='ciao 'ciao
            bye bye

10   B:     'ciao 'ciao Gianni 'ciao
            bye bye Gianni bye
```

In these cases, participants come to a smooth and mutually accepted termination of the telephone conversation, although not even the final exchanges (which, on the sequential and lexical level, are very similar to the rhythmically integrated ones in [7], [8], [9], [19] and [20]) display isochronous rhythm. No participant seems to be particularly eager or particularly unwilling to leave the interaction, and no topical extensions are included which might prepare a moving out of the closing sequence. Therefore, a first difference between the German and Italian data is the prevalence of rhythmic integration in the first, but its only occasional appearance in the second data set.

Further differences support our claim that isochronous rhythm is merely an option in Italian phone closings, whereas it is regularly employed in German, the absence of rhythm prompting certain inferences about the development of interaction. It has been noticed that the isochronous stretches of talk in the Italian closings occur in very short rhythmic intervals only. In the German data, rhythmic intervals in the final exchanges are often very short too, but longer rhythmic intervals (in terms of number of syllables) are observed as well (see extract [12] in this chapter). Also, the German extracts (13), (14), (15) and (18) show that isochrony often sets in earlier than in the Italian data, where it is typically restricted to the very final part of the telephone conversation. (The isochronous passage in [20] is due to the internal rhythm of the telephone number memorized by M.)

5. Conclusion

In this chapter we demonstrated that there is at least one sequential environment in which the use of rhythm and tempo as contextualization cues is not restricted to languages whose phonology is structurally similar to English (or whose rhythmic typology is 'stress timed'). Rather, rhythmicity in phone closings may be a phonology-independent phenomenon governed by the conversational structure of these closings, their function within the larger conversational episode and their particular demands. Rhythmicity is found in German just as in Italian, although it is certainly more prevalent in the German phone closings. In the Italian data, rhythmic nonintegration does not seem to be exceptional or 'marked' (i.e., inferentially rich).

In telephone closings, participants make an increased effort to establish and maintain a common rhythm, disregarding, if necessary, the dispreference for simultaneous talk. Thus, overlaps, simultaneous starts and adjacent production are all possible, but which of them occurs is not merely a question of the preference for 'one speaker at a time' but, often, if not predominantly, a question of rhythmic integration. The possibility for rhythmic integration in closing sections is enhanced by the routine formulae typically produced in this part of the conversation: They are very short, often consisting of one or two syllables only, and each of them carries at least one prosodic prominence. Whereas rhythm in 'ordinary' turns is partly contingent upon matters of syntax and lexical choice, and the tendency to establish or maintain isochrony is often at odds with questions of content, this is hardly the case with these 'small tokens'. They are repeatable, largely independent of each other and have few unstressed syllables to be squeezed in between the rhythmic beats. A promising way to look at these small tokens in phone closings is therefore to see them as doing a job for rhythmic integration. Although the fact of isochrony cannot be derived from their occurrence (i.e., isochrony is not determined by them), they provide the necessary segmental grounding for isochrony. Rhythmic integration in turn enables participants to organize a strictly sychronized exit from this particular type of focused interaction.

How many small tokens are produced (and consequently, how long the closing section becomes) is not only a question of how long participants want to provide a 'last chance' for 'forgotten' topical material but also of how much rhythmic integration participants consider to be necessary before leave taking. This, in turn, is a matter of the amount of face work felt to be appropriate. As a consequence, closing sections tend to be longer, and rhythm more integrated, if it is intimates who are taking leave of one another and they do not expect to meet again soon, whereas closing sections tend to be shorter in more perfunctory interactive episodes between near strangers or between persons who know they will be meeting again soon. It is as if rhythmic integration signals a state of heightened interpersonal involvement, a state of being particularly close to (or 'with') the co-participant before the interactional episode is dissolved.

Because these interactional considerations hold equally well for German and Italian telephone conversations, and because in both linguistic cultures, tokens of a similar phonetic makeup are used (in German, as argued earlier, they are not typical of core phonology), there is little reason to expect major differences between conversational closings in the two languages. Nonetheless, we have seen that rhythm and tempo are used less frequently and less extensively in the Italian data for contextualizing imminent closing. This alludes to the possibility of more far-reaching differences between Italian and the two other languages being investigated here when Italian in-conversation speech is studied in detail. It is to this problem we turn in the following chapters.

6

Rhythm in Turn Construction

Scansions in Italian Conversation

Moving from turn transition—the dominant topic of the preceding chapters—to turn construction implies a shift of analytic focus. Although every contribution by a conversationalist, no matter how extended, is subject to the basic regularities of turn taking, the construction of some types of extended turn requires additional techniques and skills which are part of what we wish to call the *rhetorics* of everyday language. These skills are not available to the same degree to every speaker, as is reflected in the fact that a speaker's performance in the construction of an extended turn such as telling a story or a joke, presenting a point of view convincingly in an argument or engaging in some other oral genre may be assessed by other participants in terms of its quality. In humorous modalities one token of appreciation may be prompt and shared laughter, as in the informal multiparty dinner conversations among friends from which we take the material discussed in this chapter. Rhetorically successful performance in oral genres implies a number of cultural specifics. This is not a subject we can treat here in detail, but at least in some of the performances discussed here, the reader will notice the cultural *spiritus loci* of our data, which is that of southern Italy, the birthplace of (formal) rhetorics.

Among the many rhetorical strategies that can be used for successful everyday performance, we focus on a particular usage of rhythm which appears most often in co-occurrence with other verbal strategies. For this particular type of rhythm we use the traditional term *scansion*, taken from the analysis of literary metrics. As noted in chapter 2 (in this volume), when listening closely to determine the rhythm of an utterance, it can be useful to coordinate some kinetic or kinesthetic activity like tapping or nodding. Traditional terms for the description of metrical rhythm reflect this kinesthetic origin in their etymology by referring to bodily rhythms in walking and dancing. In Greek metrics *arsis* and *thesis* (off-beat and beat, Ger. *Hebung* and *Senkung*) are derived from the lifting of the foot (or some other object) and its setting down. The affirmative part of the motion, the setting down of the foot in marking time, provided the name for the strong time, *thesis*, and was used to refer to the accented syllable; *arsis*, the lifting of the foot, marks the weak time. Latin metrics later reversed the Greek use of these notions. This is still evident from the development of the Latin verb *scandere*, 'to climb': It is the term derived from the lifting of the foot, which has provided the word for the activity of scanning a verse by strongly marking its rhythm.[1] To scan a verse is, as defined in the *Shorter Oxford English Dictionary*, "to recite (it) with metrical emphasis."

We use 'scanning' and 'scansion' to refer to particularly marked rhythmical sequences in oral conversational discourse. These are produced in a highly salient, rhythmically regular pattern—for instance, by lining up a number of phonetically strongly marked primary lexical stresses in a continued series of isochronously recurring beats. They appear as ordered and marked stretches of speech within the construction of what is (usually) an extended turn.

Set in the more general framework of research on contextualization,[2] the line of reasoning we want to pursue is the following: Contextualization cues such as rhythm, speech rate and loudness, as well as the gestural and facial symbolism that accompanies and helps to interpret utterances, do not have fixed signaling values we can list or look up in a dictionary. Although they have at their base an iconic value, they are usually employed as indexical signs that gain their signaling value and their context-creating force only as situated occurrences.[3] Indexical signs, as has been argued repeatedly and convincingly within the ethnomethodological tradition,[4] display a special kind of reflexivity: They co-interpret each other, attributing meaning to each other in a joint and reciprocal manner. For instance, to determine the meaning of a gesture and its contribution to contextualization in an ongoing face-to-face conversation, one must look at the verbal utterance the gesture accompanies, of which or for which it projects an interpretation (see Schegloff 1984; Goodwin & Goodwin 1986). But given the co-interpreting aid of the contextualizing gesture, a speaker can afford to foreshorten the segmental or verbal part of the utterance. To determine its local meaning the recipient must look at the gesture and the interpretation it projects of or for the upcoming verbal part of the utterance. It is only within and through this interplay, which is coordinated and finely tuned in sequential and temporal order, that the several 'channels' of the 'multi-channeled system' (Goodwin & Goodwin 1986) of spoken discourse gain their indexical meaning values and mutually create contexts, each for the interpretation of the other.

Given the reflexive and flexible nature of the phenomena involved in contextualization, it follows that a cue such as rhythmicity should also be considered in its interaction with verbal content and other cues. The heuristic strategy followed for the research presented in this chapter is therefore the following: (a) to locate salient occurrences of scansions in the data, (b) to analyze the specific interactional context (i.e., the conversational and sequential *loci* where they occur), (c) to derive insights into the contextualizing value of rhythmicity from this analysis of situated performance, and (d) to analyze and describe the compositional elements and properties of scansions. A detailed discussion of specific cases is carried out to gain a more general understanding of scansions as a recurrent pattern in oral speech performance.

1. Scansions: A first approximation

The data in which we looked for scansions is a corpus of naturally occurring conversations (approximately three hours altogether) recorded in Lecce in southern Italy. It contains mostly multiparty constellations (three to seven participants) of speakers well acquainted with one another.[5] The conversations were recorded in kitchens and living rooms, while participants were cooking, eating or just chatting. Often there were many participants eager to speak and 'crowding' the floor. At times, this results in dramatic crescendos of loudness and speech rate with much simultaneous talk and few pauses. There is some evidence, discussed in more detail later, that scanning a sequence and providing it with a regular and neatly discernible rhythmic pattern may, among other things, be a 'survival strategy' fitted to the specific conditions of a crowded floor.

Our first examples of Italian scansion are taken from storytelling. As a foregrounding strategy, scanning is exceptional rather than ordinary in conversation, and the example in (1) is even more exceptional in that it contains two scanned sequences fairly close together. Both are situated at salient points within the sequential unfolding of the story. Preceding talk has been about the rights and obligations of landlords vis-à-vis their tenants. The main speaker (P), who is also the narrator of the story, asserts that landlords in town (Lecce) do not respect the privacy of their tenants and make unrightful use of their keys to enter their tenants' flats without warning. The same landlords, furthermore, are said to refuse their tenants the right to pass their keys on to relatives and friends, as this would cause too much of a 'mess' (*casino*) in their houses. The narrative occurs within an argument and, at the point where it occurs, it is a case of 'instantiating'.[6] It provides an 'account'—a particularized, dramatized and detailed account in story format that is designed to give empirical and personally documented support to the speaker's political and moral stance against the town's landlords.

Extract (1) reproduces the last part of P's narrative and begins at the moment when P quotes the report of a figure in the story (*la signora*), who is a witness and a source for the point the narrator wants to make.

(1) [La Denuncia (Lecce II/2: 180–193)]

    1   P: disse la signora capito perchè io pago l'affitto (.)
              said the lady that's clear because it's me who pays the rent (.)

              quella è casa mia
              this is my flat

```
        S:      hm

        P:  → /ˈeːntra   /
 5            /ˈesso     /
              /ˈquando   /
              /ˈcazzo    /
              /ˈvoglio   /
              /ˈchi chi  /
10            /ˈvuole    /
              /ˈdo le    /
              /ˈchiavi   /
              /ˌa chi    /
              /ˈvoglio   /
15            /ˈquesti   /
              /ˈchiavi   /
              /ˈson' le  /
              /ˈchiavi   /
              /ˈmiei     /
```

anybody can enter whenever the fuck I want it who whoever
I give the keys to whoever I want
these keys are my keys

20   (? capito ?) .hhh (0.5) dico se c'è mai stato
        (? o.k. ?) .hhh (0.5) I say if there's ever been

        S: sì {f}infatti
             yes that's true

        P: casino no (0.5) perchè casino no be: ca facìa la festa
             a mess (0.5) why a mess it's not because one has parties

             addai (.) a parte che=è piccina la casa (.) quindi che
             there (.) not to mention the fact that the flat is very small (.) so

             quando mi dice che c'è casino (.) vabbeh posso anche
             when I'm told that there's a mess (.) alright I can accept

25   accettarlo come discorso (.)
             this as a way of speaking (.)

        S: sì
             yes

```
        P:  → /ˈproprio  /
              /ˈquando   /
              /ˈio       /
30            /ˈtrasu e  /
              /ˈbessu    /
              /ˈquando   /
              /ˈvoiu     /
              /ˈentra ed /
```

```
35          / 'esce chi  /
            / 'vuole a   /
            / 'casa      /
            / 'mia       /
            / 'proprio   /
40          / 'non ad-   /
            / 'aggiu     /
            / 'dà        /
            / 'cuntu     /
            / ˌa ni-     /
45          / 'sciunu    /
```

only if I can go in and out whenever I want to
if whoever wants can enter and leave my house
surely I do not have to give an account to anybody

(2.0)

The two scanned sequences occur at salient points in the narrative: as the reported direct speech of a witness in the first case and as a final statement, completed by an idiomatic expression which summarizes the point of the story, in the second (*non ad- aggiu dà cuntu a nisciunu*). As is apparent from a comparison of the two sequences—see the many parallels in the propositional content as well as in the wording—both are used to formulate the main point of the story, which is to insist on the legitimate claims of tenants vis-à-vis their landlords. In the second and story-final sequence—presented, like the first, in the first person—the first-person markings now refer to the storyteller, who affiliates with the point of view of the *signora* quoted before and endorses it as his own. In closing this way the narrator firmly establishes the main point of the story. Furthermore, not only does the closing refer back to the first instance given as a quote, but at the same time it ties the whole of the story back to the storyteller's preceding argument. He thus documents the story's function of providing detailed empirical support for the general argument about landlords and tenants.

Although the two scanned sequences are not literally identical, in both cases similar rhythmic patterns appear and are marked to the point of being articulatory and prosodic *tours de force*. This aligns the two sequences prosodically and clearly distinguishes them from the rest of the argument and from the story.

Some comments on compositional aspects, in particular on those that make the scansions prosodically salient *tours de force*, are now in order:

(a) *Intonation and grouping*. Despite syntactic breaks and repairs, each of the two sequences is produced as one long intonation phrase. The phrase, however, does not have one culminative pitch peak but, rather, a series of successive high peaks. The stressed syllables, except for the last ones, all appear to be distributed fairly evenly on approximately the same pitch level. The sequences are produced without internal pausing but are followed by pauses. At the end of the first sequence and before the pause (see line 20 in the linear transcript), the speaker stops for a long and audible in-breath. Each sequence is produced with fast tempo, and the impression created in both sequences is that of a fast *staccato*.

(b) *Rhythmic intervals and meter.* The impression of staccato is enhanced by the shortness and regularity of the rhythmic intervals.[7] As argued elsewhere, short rhythmic intervals, with few stressed syllables that intervene between the stresses or beats which constitute the regular pulse of the rhythmic pattern, "enhance the impression of tight rhythmic integration" (Couper-Kuhlen & Auer 1991). With only a few exceptions—the presence of a superfluous (i.e., nonelided) syllable in *esce chi* (line 35) and the lack of an unstressed syllable between two stressed syllables with a resulting 'clash' in *dà cuntu* (line 42f)—the intervals contain one stressed and one unstressed syllable only.

The rhythmic patterns as a whole thus tend strongly toward an isometric structure.[8] Both are composed primarily of trochaic words. This unusual regularity may be considered an 'extreme case': In everyday speech usually only a subset of stressed syllables are evenly spaced in time and constitute the rhythmic beats of a regular pattern. In the case of these scansions, all the stressed syllables are involved. That is, the class of phonetic prominences is coextensive with the class of lexical stresses. Our scansions are thus extreme cases in the sense that the speaker makes a 'maximalist' use of stressing and exhausts its potential.

In several instances the speaker goes even further and, as often happens in metered poetry, gives additional stress to syllables that would not usually carry stress at all except in very selective contrastive surroundings: See the nonclitic realization of the prepositions in *a chi voglio* (line 13f) and *a nisciunu* (line 44f), and the two repairs, which secure integration with the ongoing rhythmic pattern. (In *chi chi* [line 9], only the first of the two tokens is stressed; in *ad-aggiu* [lines 40–44] it is the second.) In this way the repairs are made to fit into the preestablished pattern and prolong it. Instances of this kind, in which lexically 'unstressable' syllables become stressed constituents of an ongoing rhythmic pattern, are good indicators of the integrative and regularizing force of a gestalt-like prosodic pattern and the impact it may create in spontaneous oral discourse. (It hardly need be mentioned here that oral conversational discourse does not permit the time-consuming aesthetic and stylistic processes of written metered text.)

(c) *Segmental composition.* It is tempting to speculate on the constraints imposed by rhythmic integration on the lexical makeup of speech. As noted earlier, scanning a sequence in conversation means foregrounding its rhythm. In these cases, then, rhythm is not a marginal aspect merely implied by other linguistic choices. Once the rhythmic pattern is set, the speaker has to be selective in choosing the next items if he or she wants, for instance, to continue the regularly alternating trochaic mode as in our examples. In this case he or she is well advised to avoid polysyllabics or a series of polysyllabics. In fact the speaker in our examples uses only mono-

and bisyllabic lexical units (exception: *nisciunu*, lines 44–45). The beat therefore recurrently falls on the first syllable of words, where it is reinforced through phonemic recurrences: See the frequent alliteration between immediately or closely adjacent items as in *entra esso* in line 4; *entra ed esce* in lines 34–35; the /k/-series, sustained throughout the first scansion in *quando . . . cazzo . . . chi . . . chiavi . . . questi . . . chiavi* in lines 6–19 and continued in *quando . . . casa . . . cuntu* in lines 28–43.

(d) *Length of the pattern.* Clearly in conversational prose there is no prefigured verse-line or frame such as pentameter or endecasyllable, no abstract scheme organizing a limited array of strong and weak positions that could guide expectations as to the continuation of a rhythm and tell us at each moment in the development "where we are in the line" (Attridge 1989).[9] Neither is there in our scansions a projectable end point of the 'line' or any other structural measure by which to judge its length. However, given the regularity of the prosodic pattern, in particular the shortness of rhythmic intervals and the lack of pauses across syntactic breaks and repairs, the length—fifteen trochaic feet in the first, nineteen in the second sequence—certainly constitutes one of its most striking features, clearly contributing to its gestalt-like prominence and establishing it as a mode of continuation or even of 'perseveration'.[10]

(e) *Contextualization value.* The degree of perseveration may indicate most clearly the contextualizing function that scanning has in the particular narrative at hand. As indicated earlier, the two sequences are exposed *loci* in the narrative's sequential structure, where the speaker formulates the legitimate rights of the tenants as the main point in his story and argument. The perseveration within one and the same rhythmic pattern contextualizes the firmness and 'unfaltering' commitment of the speaker to the propositional content and the argumentative point formulated. Such a mode of presenting and prosodically underscoring an utterance should be considered part of the rhetorics of everyday speech.

2. Scansions and their role in the performance of speech activities

2.1. Rhythm as an 'affirmative' gesture: Scansions as 'extreme case formulations'

Perseveration, when the beat goes on and on, may hint at a more general and more elementary meaning potential which can be associated naturally and iconically with the isochronous recurrence of beats in marked instances; it may be a prosodic metaphor of the unfailing reliability and predictability of next events in time. For this reason it is a particularly appropriate contextualization cue for 'thetic' acts (i.e., affirming, insisting on a point and ensuring the credibility and reliability of statements).

Even though the scanned sequence is brief, a scansion with a similar 'affirmative' contextualization value is evident in extract (2). The interaction occurs after about one hour's talk in this constellation. At this point all five co-participants have been active, though not with the same enthusiasm as speaker A, the youngest in the group, who has introduced a number of 'big topics', told several stories, initiated guessing games, and so on. A starts another turn (line 2) after a six-second pause, making the pause 'accountable' and taking it as an occasion to 'formulate'[11] an aspect of the conversation. He does this at first with a boisterous and ironically exaggerated invective against the lack of participation of the other speakers, who are said not to have talked at all and who, at first, do not seem to grasp A's irony; he then (line 13) proceeds to express hyperbolic self-praise, exaggerating his participation and presenting himself as the unique and only worthwhile active speaker who 'stays on the scene' and 'holds the bank'. (The idiomatic expression *tenere banco* in line 15–18 here means to be the 'banker'—that is, to be a participant in the game on whom one can 'bank'.)

(2) Tenere banco [Lecce I/2: 720–721]

```
1             (6.0) ((E starts humming a tune))
    A:       {ff}però questi ragazzi che registrano però voi non
             even though these boys are recording but you
             avete detto una parola e:
             have not said a word yet
    E:       come [no h h h
             what  do you mean
5   A:            [{ff}fate schifo
                  you're disgusting
             (1.0)
    C:       h h [h
    D:           [come no
                 what do you mean
    E:           [h h
10  B:       si [si
    A:          [{ff}Angelo manco
                Angelo hasn't either
    D:      h  [h h
    A:         [{ff}e: va io (praticamente) sto al [palco (.)
                well it's me (practically) who is     on the scene
    E:                                              [e poi mi stai
                                                    and then you keep on
15  A: → /'io          /
         /'tengo       /
         /'ban-        /
```

```
                /'co
                I hold the bank
         E:     a parlare di queste cose che=
                talking about these things that=
20       D:     =e:
         A:     mercante in fiera
                salesman at the fair
                (0.7)
```

The scanned sequence constitutes the apex of this episode, not only in rhythm but also in loudness and pitch. This may be due to the overlap situation in which it is produced. The metrical emphasis provided through scansion is further supported synaesthetically, by nonverbal sound and gesture: The speaker marks the last two beats of the pattern by knocking on the table. The knocking is synchronized with the articulation of the last two syllables (*ban-co*), which are produced with similar pitch and stress prominence: *banco* thus has a 'clash' of two adjacent main accents. Other structures, in particular the hyperbolic and formulaic quality of the idiomatic expression used, also contribute to the salience of this passage.

Considering the *tour de force* qualities of the scansions seen so far, and reconsidering them in their interactive setting, scanning may be said to be a prosodic means of contextualizing formulations as 'extreme case formulations' (see Pomerantz 1986). In extreme-case formulations, speakers use linguistic hyperbole to legitimize claims and do 'credibility work' in anticipation of nonsympathetic hearings. In such formulations (e.g., 'completely innocent', 'no time', 'forever', 'every time', 'everyone') the strongest case is asserted, here to legitimize a complaint. Part of the activity of complaining involves portraying the objectionable situation in such a way as to warrant the associated complaint; a speaker may portray an offense by magnifying, upgrading and intensifying terms to ensure that it is in proportion and cannot be dismissed as minor. As Drew and Holt (1990), also working on complaints, have shown, the upgrading means can also be 'idioms', which is their cover term for set expressions, metaphors, proverbs, generic sentences and maxims. The scanned sequences considered so far contain lexical intensifiers (e.g., *quando cazzo voglio* in [1]:6–8), hyperbolic universal quantifiers (e.g., *nisciunu* in [1]:44–45), and also idiomatic expressions (e.g., *dà cuntu a nisciunu* in [1]:42–45, *tengo banco* in [2]:16–18). Rhythmic scansion applied to these formulations may be a further, prosodic means of achieving extreme case formulation and doing the 'credibility work' of speakers in legitimizing claims, making strong assertions, and so on.

2.2. Competitive overlap

The next examples, again taken from narratives, corroborate this hypothesis. Excerpt (3) depicts a conversational situation of some delicacy. A participant and guest (Jean François), a friend of F, has just left the constellation. Talk is initiated about this interesting guest soon after he leaves and F, with her brief narrative in (3), initiates the activity of 'bringing things up till today' (Sacks 1971) for the remaining participants, who have no prior knowledge of the guest. This 'bringing things up till today' is initiated in the canonical way described by Sacks: F takes up the last meeting with her friend and makes this the first point of a news telling. She then however tries to reframe what has started as a news telling into a more dramatic narrative. It is here that she uses rhythmic scansion (see lines 10–12). The scansion is produced in continued overlap with D's turns in lines 9 and 13.

(3) [Certi elementi (Lecce I/1: 398–399)]

```
1   F:    perché io l'ultima volta che l'avevo visto a Roma
          because I the last time I had seen him in Rome

          mi aveva spiegato una complicata situazione in
          he explained to me a complicated situation in

          cui (.) lúi stava con una donna léi aveva il suo
          which (.) he lived with a woman she had her

          amante lúi aveva i suoi amanti=
          lover he had his lovers

5   ?:    ={p}hh

    D:    guarda certi [tipi
          look certain  types

    F:                 [e ognuno stava per cazzi suoi
                       and everybody had it his own way

          (1.0)

    S:    a:h

    D:    io- voi reputatevi (.)
          I- consider yourselves

          [fortunate (.) che io ho
          lucky       that I

10  F: → [{ff}il/'tutto gri-       /
                /'dando nell'      /
                /'autobus          /
                /'pieno di         /
                / ['gente a        /

15  D:            [avuto la giusta
                  had the right

    F: →          / ['Roma la      /

    D:            [reazione
                  reaction

    F: →          / ['faccia a     /
```

| D: | [con le persone (.) |
| | *with persons* |

20 F: → /'terra

shouting out all of this in the bus crowded with people in Rome with my face to the ground

| D: | che presentano certi elementi all' improvviso |
| | *who show some peculiarities without forewarning* |

F's report comes to a first possible closing with the completion of the last element of a three-part list structure in line 4, which is taken as a completion and possible transition point by speakers "?" in line 5, and D in line 6. D starts a turn next but is interrupted by the 'real' closing formulation of F in line 7, signaled as such by several characteristic marks: It is a résumé that summarizes the preceding list, it uses an idiomatic expression (*stava per cazzi suoi*),[12] and the speaker leaves the floor afterward (see the following pause). In line 9, D starts another turn and is again interrupted by F with the scanned utterance. The scansion is thus produced as an afterthought or addendum to the previous report, which was clearly marked as closed; it is also produced as a second interruption of the same speaker (D) and in overlap with his turn.

From a sequential point of view, the utterance in question is clearly misplaced; the same holds from a narrative point of view. The afterthought—although specifying the setting and the modalities of the action to be narrated and thus being more properly part of an 'orientation' (Labov & Waletzky 1967) which precedes rather than follows the main body of the narrative—nonetheless contains an important point: Most of the lexical components of the scanned sequence are later expanded and developed into more detailed narrative sequences (see the beginning of the dramatized version at the end of extract [4]). Though not an 'extreme case formulation' in the sense outlined earlier, the scansion occurs under rather unusual conditions—in view of its sequential as well as its narrative status: The speaker has something important to say, but she says it at a point in the course of interaction which is improperly chosen. For this reason an 'extreme' or at least unusual marking is called for.

The scanned sequence is produced in overlap, and the rhythmic markedness co-occurs here with two prosodic features described as typical for 'directly competitive turn incomings' (French & Local 1983): higher pitch and increased loudness.[13] Compared to F's previous talk—the preceding report—the sequence also appears to involve a clear decrease in speech rate.

As a rhythmic pattern, the scansion in (3) is similar to the previous ones in several respects: It is produced without a caesura, within one long intonational phrase lacking a culminating pitch peak but characterized instead by a series of equally high-pitched prominences which recur at short intervals, and with a regular (isometric) alternation of stressed and unstressed syllables. Extract (3) contains eight dactylic feet. It is an 'extreme case' in the prosodic sense given previously:

Rhythm in Turn Construction

Each stressable syllable is actually stressed. Rhythmic scansion in this case constitutes a strategy for 'surviving' overlap: Rhythmic markedness in combination with increased loudness and heightened pitch upgrades F's formulation in the sense that it stands out effectively in simultaneous talk and remains clearly understandable.

2.3. Verbal dueling

Our next example is from a subsequent episode with the same constellation of speakers. After the episode in extract (3), talk continues about the French guest who has left, and an argument arises between F and her boyfriend, D. The interactive exchange is thus an example of quarreling between a couple, acted out in public. Throughout the sequence about the absent French guest, F defends him and takes his side while D tries to ridicule him. The argument is acted out in the form of sustained verbal dueling (seven minutes long) between F and D, while the other two participants—S and E—take over the role of evaluating audience. The duelists propose and oppose verbal descriptions of Jean François, D imitating and ridiculing his words and ways of speaking, his effeminate appearance and behavior, F praising his nonconformist attitudes. The verbal dueling here has a number of interactive features in common with the speech event of 'sounding' (Labov 1972), in particular the overt and immediate evaluation of each 'sound'—a blow or *battuta* in our duel—by the audience. The primary indication of positive evaluation is laughter.[14] At the onset of our extract (4), D has 'won' several *battute* in a row—to judge by the criterion of laughter—and is just winning another one (see lines 1–2). Extract (4) shows an effective *contro-battuta* by F (see lines 4–6), which is forceful in the lexical means employed and in the prosodic cues that contextualize it, including sustained loudness on a par with or even beyond that of the preceding laughter, and rhythmic scanning with metrical emphasis. Sequentially, the scansion is effective not only as a local *battuta*: It also serves as a floor-getting device to launch the following longer narrative, the dramatized version of the news told seven minutes earlier and depicted in extract (3). (Only the beginning of this narrative is contained in [4]. The narrative ends the verbal dueling and introduces a more serious key in the talk about the guest's homosexuality.)

(4) [Certi Elementi (Lecce I/a: 398–399)]

```
1    D:      =e:h vabbeh ma non me le fare o tu te pensi che io
             =well all right but don't tell me or do you think I
             so' fesso (.)  [oppure (      )
             am stupid (.)  [or (          )

     S,E:                   [{ff} h h h h h h

     F:  → {ff} / ˌti sta  /
5               / ˌcoglio- /
                / 'nando
             he is screwing you
```

```
                    ma  [tu
                    but  you

     D:                 [ no::

     S, E:              [h h h h h

10   F:  →    / 'non ti           /
              / 'rendi            /
              / 'conto            /
              / 'Jean Fran-       /
              / 'çois cogli-      /
15            / 'ona              /
              / 'tutti            /
              / 'quanti
              don't realize it Jean Francois screws them all

     S:    h h h =

     F:    Jean François cogliona tutti quanti
           Jean François screws them all

20         =cioè (.) quando si è messo a raccontarmi di quella
           =that is to say (.) when he started to talk to me about
           cosa (.) stava coglionando un autobus intero perchè
           this matter (.) he was screwing a whole bus because
           l'ha detto con un volume proprio megafonico=
           he really said it with the loudness of a megaphone=

     D:    =quale=
           =what kind of=

     F:    =un autobus pieno a Roma così (.) pieno di gente
           =a crowded bus in Rome like that (.) crowded with people
```

The sequence in lines 7–17 is scanned as trochaic meter (with two elements—*ma tu*—metrically not clearly discernible due to overlap with D's *no* in line 8). The scansion contains, as onset and 'spearhead' for F's *contro-battuta*, the slang term *coglionare* (lines 5–6), which receives three main stresses including the pronoun (/ ˌti sta / ˌcoglio/ 'nando).

It was argued previously that foregrounded rhythmic patterns, in particular isometric ones, impose constraints on the selection of lexical items to make them fit into an already established and ongoing pattern. In the present case, the argument may be reversed: The trochaic pattern is called forth by, and aligns with, the use of a heavily stressed slang term, which is expanded into three strong isochronous beats that establish the rhythmic pattern. This pattern is then continued by a second generalized and hyperbolic use of the same slang term again, *cogliona tutti quanti* (lines 14–17), which appears within the ongoing pattern now in its alternate form (*cogli'ona*) as a *parola piana* with middle stress. (The third occurrence of the term in line 19, where it is 'explained', introduces the following narrative and connects it with the *contro-battuta.*) The trochaic pattern here seems to strengthen the effect of the slang term: Main stress on this term together with metrical emphasis 'expose' it (Jefferson 1986) and affirm the adequacy of its selection at this particular point in the interaction. In our case it also makes it an offensive tool in the verbal dueling: The slang term *coglionare* has an obscene literal meaning which may, however, remain in the background when the form is used in its 'normal' or unmarked (i.e., metaphorical) sense. Exposing it prosodically tends to reactivate its literal, nonmetaphorical meaning and make it more offensive.

2.4. Highlighting an aphoristic 'last' line

Further examples, taken from several different speech activities, corroborate some of the hypotheses developed so far, in particular the frequent association of rhythmic scansion with the prosodic cues of increased (relative) loudness and slow tempo. Speech is usually perceived as 'emphatic' when many stressed syllables occur per given unit of time.[15] Clearly this correlates well with the 'maximalist' exploitation of stressability in scansions.

Extract (5), instantiating this triadic constellation of prosodic cues, is a case in point. In prior discourse speaker F has described his (marginal) involvement in a traffic accident. On this occasion he also talked to a lawyer. The lawyer now wants him to pay 300,000 lire for the consultation.

(5) [Avvocato Pompelmo (Lecce I/1: 500–501)]

```
1   F:    ho detto io al telefono ma lei scherza con molto
          I said on the telephone but you are joking to an extreme

          (     ) (.) perché io non s sono pronto a
          (     ) (.) because I am not ready to

          pagare queste (.) trecentomila lire=
          pay these (.) three hundred thousand lira

    D:    =massimo trentamila
          at most thirty thousand

5   F:    dato il fatto che io non c'entravo per niente in
          given the fact that I didn't come in for much in

          questo questa: (.) massimo che cosa=
          that that (.) at most what

    D:    =trentamila
          thirty thousand

          (0.5)

    C:    no nemmeno (.) perché [concilia
          no not even (.) because  it would be conciliatory

10  D:                          [paga (.) tre tremila lire allora=
                                [pay (.) thr three thousand then
```

E:	=h h h=
	=l'uno per cento
	 one percent
	in proporzione paga=
	pay in proportion

D:	= l'uno per cento=
	=*one percent*

15	F:	=no ma mi sembra un [affare
		=*no but it seems an affair*

E:	 [no nulla (.) non pagare niente
		                      no nothing (.) pay nothing at all

S:	no figu [rati
	no ima gine

F:	 [no: (.) se fosse trentamila lire (.) casomai=
		        no: (.) if it were thirty thousand (.) maybe=

D:	={ff}senno (.)
	= *if not* (.)

20	→ /'trovati l'avvo- /
	/'cato che ti di- /
	/'fende dal tuo avvo- /
	/'cato
	find you a lawyer who will defend you against your lawyer

Several:	h h h [h h h h h

F:	 [ecco (.) ecco (.) ecco
		      indeed (.) indeed (.) indeed

When F has finished explaining his state of affairs in lines 1–6 he readily obtains comments and (cost-free) advice from several participants. Looking briefly at the sequential order of the advice, a pattern of organization interactively achieved through common work by the participants is recognizable. Lacking an appropriate term in conversational theory, we use the rhetorical notion of *comparatio*. The notion of *comparatio* is applied to describe a particular type of successive gradation in enumerations: "[It] corresponds to a *locus a minore ad maius* and is a schema for 'upping' the stakes by outbidding an *exemplum* which is already an extreme case" (Lausberg 1967:37, our translation).

In quantitative terms (and for obvious reasons in our case), the usual order *a minore ad maius* is reversed: The first piece of advice (see lines 4 and 7) lowers the fee of 300,000 lire to 30,000. From there it goes down to 3,000 in line 10, or 1% in lines 12 and 14, and from there to nothing at all (line 16). At this point, beyond which further advice can hardly be expected, F shows readiness to return to the first 30,000 (line 18). It is then that D comes up with an inventive southern Italian proposal that shows how to go beyond the dead end (lines 20–23). D's aphoristic formulation, presented with a clear increase in loudness compared to all previous turns in the 'consultation' episode, has rhythmic scansion.

Rhythmic scansion serves again to stage an 'extreme case formulation', a hyperbolic last step in the 'outbidding'. As a rhythmic pattern it is not extreme, however, as it does not maximally exploit all available stressable positions. Only a subset of the stressable syllables is used to constitute the pattern. The pattern seems to be structured mainly around the occurrences of the polysyllabic *avvocato* at the end of the two syntactic constituents. Their main accents, the highest peaks in the pitch contours of the two intonational phrases, are in second and fourth position in the rhythmic pattern and are separated by one beat, but they are aligned to constitute the two most salient of the four recurrent beats in the pattern. Isochrony and lexical recurrence are nicely balanced and give the aphorism a formal symmetry that is well suited to ensure a rhetorically effective takeup.

Formulaic expressions and generic sentences that contain a potential 'lesson reading' (Sacks 1971) carry closing implications (Sacks 1971; Drew & Holt 1990). The aphoristic formula of lines 20–23, presented in the genre of a maxim and using the generic imperative, is interactively effective in precisely this way: After the laughter the statement provokes, the 'consultation' sequence comes to an end. The scanned form thus forms the end of a longer sequence. Sequentially and prosodically, it is artfully brought about and clearly appreciated by the participants as a *bon mot*. More generally, the sequence supports Pomerantz's notion that 'extreme case formulations' may be 'last' formulations, where 'last' is to be defined in terms of successive steps in a sequentially developing interaction.

2.5. Formulating an interdiction

A scanned formulation which stands as the 'last word' on a topic also appears in excerpt (6). It is sequentially much less elaborate, but the three prosodic cues—rhythmic scansion, increased loudness and decreased speech rate—clearly do co-occur. In previous discourse, speaker A has told a story about leaving a fairly new car parked for several days and nights at an ill-famed place, the Porto di Milazzo in Palermo, to get it stolen. When C asks whether the car was locked (line 2), B, her friend, boastingly claims that he could open her car with any key. C apparently takes this boast as a threat and vigorously rejects it (see lines 5–14).

(6) [Macchine rotte (Lecce I/1: 243–244)]

```
1   A:    e beh non [è che
          well not    that

    C:              [e beh la serratura?
                     and the lock?

    B:    io ti apro la Panda tua con quale chiave vuoi (.) a
          I will open your Panda for you with any key you want (.)
```

           scomessa
           I bet you
5   C: {ff}no:
           no
      → / 'lassa   /
        / 'stare la   /
        / 'macchina   /
        / 'mia   /
10   / ^(.)   /
        / 'non la   /
        / 'devi ne-   /
        / 'anche guar-   /
        / 'dare
        leave my car alone do not even look at it

C's rejection, an emphatic imperative, is articulated in two intonational phrases of fairly equal length. Both contain a series of high pitch peaks but no culminative highest peak. Each phrase has four heavily stressed beats evenly spaced in time. In its syllabic constitution, with either one or two unstressed syllables between the stressed ones, the pattern in excerpt (6) is not isometric. Yet in the exaggerated prominence of the stressed syllables and in the mechanical way it is produced, the scansion of the imperative, which is almost shouted and, impressionistically, sounds very aggressive, resembles a 'schoolboy's scansion'.[16]

Why should a prosodic pattern as in excerpt (6) cue an imperative? Note that it is a maximal scansion, where the whole array of grammatically possible stress positions is actually used and where all the stressed syllables are aligned in a continuous isochronous pattern. Further, the rhythmic pattern contains only main stresses, which is tantamount to saying that each lexical word receives a strong stress. Reinforced and supported through isochronous spacing, this introduces a prosodic mode of production one might call 'emphatic spelling' or 'itemization'. Each lexical term is exposed, implicating literalness of meaning and claiming appropriateness of selection for each term, item per item, high pitch peak for high pitch peak and beat for beat, even though the terms co-occur and are bound within one coherent syntactic and semantic structure.[17]

2.6. Rhythm as part of the rhetorics of complaining

A scansion within yet a different activity, complaining, appears in excerpt (7). In the preceding discourse, A told a story about a traffic accident he witnessed in Milan which caused a number of wrecked cars. C uses the current topic to remind A of his (A's) own history of car wrecking (line 1). A admits to having wrecked one of C's cars, and this provokes C's (mockingly?) dramatic complaint, where she enumerates in a list A's past car mishaps (lines 4–15).

Rhythm in Turn Construction

(7) [Macchine rotte (Lecce I/1: 243–244)]

```
1    C:     a:h già (.) tu mi sai che significa le macchine
            a:h talking about this (.) you well know what wrecked
            rotte
            cars mean

     A:     a:h là (.) scusa è perchè te ne ho rotta u:na
            a:h well (.) excuse me it's because I have wrecked one of yours

     C:     no u:na (.)
            not one (.)
5         → {ff} /'ci:nque              /
                  /'sei    [ru-          /
     A:                    [(     )
     C:               /'ba:te             /
                      /'rotte             /
10                    /^              (.) /
                      /['fonde il mo-     /
     A:                [(    )
     C:               /'tore              /
                      /'basta che le      /
15                    /'guarda
```

five six taken away wrecked (-) the engine melts down
he only needs to look at them

e la batteria si scarica
and the battery discharges

All: h h h h

To make the complaint substantial, the list goes to extremes and even accumulates idiomatic (Drew & Holt 1990) and hyperbolic expressions, sequentially arranged following an order of successive gradation *a minore ad maius*, in content as well as in length of constituents. It is produced with a clear increase in loudness, even before the onset of simultaneous talk. As above, the scansion 'survives' overlap, remaining clearly understandable.

List structure is adapted here to serve the complaint. To be effective, the list of grievances in a complaint must be long. On the other hand, lists usually have only a three-part structure.[18] At first glance, the present list seems to go beyond a three-part structure, given the number of items it contains. Yet there are clearly three recognizable sections, each of which consists of two parallel units. The first has two adjacent counting terms, *ci:nque, sei*. (It may be no accident that it is the counting, an isochronous symbolic activity *par excellence*, which triggers the isochronous pattern of recurrent beats in this case.) The second has two parallel lexical items, both deverbal past participles, accentuated by alliteration and assonance (*ruba:te, rotte*). And the third has two final elements of increasing length in the form of sentential units (*fonde il motore; basta che le guarda e la batteria si scarica*).

Thus, there is homogeneity within the pairs, but a structural heterogeneity across them that is fairly unusual: List elements in this case do not co-select by word–class properties. Given this structural heterogeneity, prosodic cues—and in particular integration into a regular rhythmic pattern already initiated at this point—become a means to read across the constructional diversity of the constituents and ensure the gestalt-like unity of the list by showing that the items are co-selected to stand together.

The three-times-two structure of the list has both a rhetorical and an interactive aspect. It lengthens the list and enhances the complaint with a display that spreads out the array of grievances. The isochronous recurrence of beats contributes to the same effect: After the first four lexical terms, each with one main stress and each listing one of the mishaps, the 'counting' continues in the same rhythm, signaling an uninterrupted series of complainable mishaps as long as the continuing series of recurring beats.

3. Conclusion

Scansions are a recurrent 'ethnopoetic' pattern in oral speech performance. They are marked prototypically by a configuration of prosodic means—strongly marked rhythmicity accompanied by the use of a voice that dramatizes through intensity, intonation and speech rate. Scansions have been found in several speech activities: storytelling embedded in argumentation, ironic 'formulations' of a stage in the conversation, verbal dueling, aphoristic *bon mots*, interdictions and complaints. From a sequential analysis of the *loci* where scansions occur and from their analysis as situated performances, it has been argued that scansions are used to 'stage' utterances as 'extreme case formulations' (Pomerantz 1986).

The 'extremity' of these formulations has a sequential and an interactional interpretation. Participants can be observed to use the pattern to formulate 'last positions', which are manifestly intended to exclude any doubt about the speaker's commitment and are displayed as not being available for further modification, attenuation or other negotiation in continued verbal interaction. A sequential warrant for such use can be seen in the fact that, in the cases observed, recipients actually do not attempt to go further, do not try to pursue interaction on the question at hand, thus letting the speaker's formulation in fact stand as his or her 'last words' on the matter.

For obvious reasons the scansion pattern described previously can be used effectively to impose a claim in argument or to attempt to cut short further negotiation. Seen in this way, it is a highly appropriate vocal and prosodic means which fits into the larger ensemble of everyday rhetorical strategies described as 'interactive forcing' (Ger. *Forcieren*; Kallmeyer & Schmitt 1996) or 'battening down the hatches' (Ger. *Perspektivenabschottung*; Keim 1996), strategies whereby speakers try to impose their interests in interaction by refusing to consider any further objections from opposing parties.

Yet as has been described previously, scansions may also occur in different interactive modalities, in verbal play, in mock-heroic aggression, in irony and teasing, and the same prosodic pattern may thus have differently shaded and nuanced contextual values according to the specific speech activity where it occurs.

In terms of prosody, scansions also appear to be extreme: One of their defining features is the exhaustive, 'maximalist' use of available virtual stress positions for actual stress placement. This leads to an itemized 'stressed-syllable-by-stressed-syllable', 'beat-by-beat' mode of projecting the utterance. As the analysis of our collection of scansions shows, other prosodic cues frequently co-occur with rhythm and 'maximalist' stress placement. This is true in particular for increased (relative) loudness, decreased (relative) speech rate and high pitch obtrusion on the stressed syllables—features described as distinctive for 'emphatic' speech (Selting 1994).

7

Rhythm and Performance

An Analysis of an Italian Radio Phone-in Program

This chapter analyzes Italian data from a particular oral genre, the radio phone-in program. The data consist of dialogues between a moderator and various callers from the elaborate Italian radio program *Radiodue 3131*.[1] Our focus continues to be on rhythm as both a conversational and a rhetorical strategy. (Perhaps one may speak here of 'radio rhetorics'.[2]) We start (§1) with a brief consideration of the specific importance temporality has gained with and through the radio as a medium. As the phone-in analyzed has a fairly elaborate structure, we then provide a brief descriptive overview of the program (§2).

To cope with the polymorphic character of rhythmicity as an indexical sign, different aspects of the material have been selected for analysis. Rhythmic patterns are described in the sequential context of openings and topic nomination (§3). A global hypothesis is formulated to explain the finding that rhythmicity is strongly and persistently present at the boundaries (openings/closings) of calls, where rhythmically integrated transitions across three speakers are found (§4). Next we focus on formulaic paradigms, where rhythmicity accompanies grammatical parallelism and lexicosyntactic configurations, notably in contrastive pair sets and in lists (§5). A specific task for callers involves the construction of extended turns (§6). Observing closely the completion points of such turns, which are frequently marked by the use of formulaic paradigms, we argue that rhythmicity, in co-occurrence with other verbal and sequential features, may also take on a delimitative value and contextualize the 'exit' from extended turns.

1. Temporal and other aspects of radio phone-in programs

Mozart and Bach seem to have miraculously composed their works with the format of radio programs in mind. The long symphony comes to an end just in time to leave the roughly twenty seconds necessary for a brief pause, a postannouncement with the name of the symphony and its performers, another brief pause which marks a boundary to the following program and a preannouncement that news will follow next at the full hour. Small events such as pauses, post- and preannouncements are clearly easier to tailor according to available time slots than big ones like a symphony. But for all events, big and small, radio situates and in many ways designs its events according to a schedule which is strictly organized by the clock. This is done so perfectly and pervasively that the temporal extension of events no longer appears as a necessity contrived and imposed by the constraints of a program schedule but, rather, as a natural quality inherent in the events themselves.

Clock-time tailoring is also found in talk events on the radio. By miracle or by nature, and with a little help from the moderator, participants seem to coordinate their talk activity in such a way that the event comes to a 'natural' end at the scheduled moment in clock time. Clearly, talking space on a phone-in program is not, as in everyday conversation, 'self-administered' by members (Sacks, Schegloff & Jefferson 1974). It is not open-ended but an objectively limited resource. This limitation can be expected to have interactional consequences. Because the moderator knows that next callers are already waiting on line, for example, and that the expansion of one call will reduce time for one or more of the following calls, whether to continue an interaction gains particular significance. The negotiation between moderator and caller of limited talking space thus becomes an interesting locus for the analysis of interaction. One can observe the moderator's techniques of initiating closing, thereby bounding the talk of a call, as well as when and how such initiations are negotiated.

In addition to clock-time design, the medium imposes other constraints. For instance, as interaction is exposed to an overhearing audience (in our case, that of a national radio station), it can be expected that closings will be executed smoothly and politely. Yet, as becomes evident in our analysis, initiating the closing of the 'macro turn' of a call is not only a specific task requiring specific verbal skills; it is also a resource. Initiating the closing offers the moderator specific rhetorical possibilities which he does not have elsewhere in the sequential and temporal structure of the phone-in program.

The basic interactive tasks of the moderator include ushering the callers in and out (i.e., making one caller 'stop' and the next one 'start' talking). In contrast to everyday conversation, however, the work of bringing about this 'stop' and 'go' is a frequently repeated, routine event that recurs as an element in a series.[3] Moreover, it is brought to the air and to the ears not only of an 'overhearing audience' (Heritage 1985) but also of those callers who are waiting on the call-stacking mechanism to be summoned onto the public 'stage' of the program. For these callers, who are at once audience and candidates for the role of next speaker within the program, the closing of a call is an important cue: It signals an upcoming transition relevance point, where they may be summoned onto the program as participants. Upcoming closings thus occasion a particularly attentive monitoring of conversational work and, more generally, create a context of 'attentional involvement' (Couper-Kuhlen 1990:182), which creates pressure to be on cue when the summons finally arrives.

Clearly it is not only the limitation in time that distinguishes radio phone-in conversation from informal 'mundane' telephone conversation.[4] The mutuality of co-constructive processes on a phone-in program is constrained and in many ways preempted by technical and radio-institutional conditions. Participants (i.e., moderator and callers) have widely differing rights, obligations and responsibilities. The moderator is in charge of and responsible for the macrostructural organization of the event, including the management of openings and closings, both of the program as a whole and of the constituent calls, as well as many other aspects of the interaction.[5]

Also prominent among the distinctive features of radio phone-ins are the 'two faces' of radio conversation: The moderator must address a particular caller and at the same time the radio audience. His or her contributions are meant for two parties: the caller and the audience. This double recipiency, including the rhetorical *mise en scène* of the conversation for the benefit of a large radio audience, is given special attention in our analysis of the program.[6] As shown, the rhetorical strategies involved in the *mise en scène* also include the use of isochronous rhythmic patterns.

2. A descriptive overview of the program

The program chosen for analysis is the popular Italian series *Radiodue 3131*, directed and moderated by Corrado Guerzoni. The recordings considered here were made in March 1990. 'Dottor Guerzoni', as he is addressed by some of his callers, is a 'radio personality' in the sense of Goffman (1981). Guerzoni manages to give his programs an unmistakable personal style. He is well-known in Italy as a poet; his personal style as a radio moderator includes frequent quotations and references to literary authors and texts.

The program is produced by the national chain RAI and broadcast five days a week from 10:30 to 12:00 A.M. with a break in the middle. Obviously, the morning broadcasting time exerts an influence on the selection of callers and on the audience. In the program analyzed here, twelve of the thirteen callers are women.

Although the following analysis is restricted to the data transcribed, it may not be superfluous to mention the mass media dimension: *Radiodue 3131* receives an average of 150 calls per program. As the station's six to ten telephone lines quickly become blocked, the number of calls actually received is but a small subset of the number of people trying to get through.[7] The ten to seventeen callers typically admitted to the program often have tried in vain many times before. Being admitted to the program is thus an exceptional event, one that is commented on accordingly by several of the callers.

In the first part of the program, a topic is set for would-be callers. Because topics in a radio program of this kind cannot be developed through the common work of co-present participants, as in everyday conversation, this elicitation has an important function in generating a set of mentionables (Maynard 1980). In the broadcast analyzed here, the topic is the autobiographic past (*il passato*)[8]: how people remember and keep in touch with their past, for instance by visiting friends and familiar places from their childhood or by leaving it behind in favour of the present, etc. The moderator aligns his callers according to two broad membership categories: the *ancients*, callers who prefer to stay in close touch with memories of the past, reactivating and working through them frequently, and the *moderns*, those who do not believe in indulging in past memories and who prefer to concentrate more on the present.

But the topic setting goes beyond instructing potential callers what to talk about. It also sets the 'key' and is meant to stimulate calls. In the present case, a fairly long (six-minute) section follows the first mention of the topic and a call for calls. In this section the moderator recites two poems by Baudelaire—accompanied by background music—and uses a large array of verbal and paraverbal means to create an empassioned framework. This framework is meant to encourage potential callers to adopt a passionate delivery themselves in their autobiographical reports.

The poetics of the elicitation framework prior to the calls also has a more practical purpose. The Baudelaire recitation with its musical background is a precomposed studio production which, while it is on the air, gives the moderator and his assistants in the studio time, for instance, to select a subset of callers to be admitted as participants to the program, to note the names of callers and key words or summary statements of their positions and to negotiate the subtopics the callers may talk about.

When the calls start, the moderator is prepared for each caller.[9] He knows the caller's name and in each case can initiate topical interaction with a 'formulation of gist' (see below), which summarizes the caller's position and sets up a subtopic designed specifically for the individual caller. In their first longer topical turn on the air, callers are asked to explain, detail or elaborate their position. And as closings are almost always initiated formulaically by the moderator, we find summarizing activities at the end of the calls as well.

Evidence of a prearranged order for the calls is apparent in the gender constellation of the callers: The only male caller is reserved for last. A further aspect of the temporal 'orderliness' of the program (total length approximately seventy-three minutes) is seen in the fact that the last call (roughly ten and a half minutes) is approximately twice as long as the other calls (roughly three and a half to five minutes). Paolo, the last caller, is also chosen as the primary recipient of the last autobiographical report on the past, that of the moderator himself.

3. Openings and topic nomination sequences

Isochronous rhythmic patterns, mostly initiated by the moderator, frequently occur at the openings of the calls, particularly during topic nomination sequences, where a topic is formulated and proposed to the incoming caller. To prepare the ground for rhythmic analysis, a brief reconstruction of the sequential context of these patterns is in order.

3.1. Sequential properties and radio-rhetorical design

One of the important tasks of the moderator is to introduce callers onto the program. The topics, which have been previously negotiated in nonpublic interaction, are recipient designed for each individual caller, and, more specifically, they are projected to elicit extended talk from the caller that is likely to fit into the general design of the program.

The topics are designed to be clear to the particular caller as well as to enable a third party (the audience) to situate the upcoming interaction and its contribution to the emerging program. To see how this is accomplished on the sequential level, consider extract (1), which contains the moderator's summons of the caller (line 3), the caller's response (line 4), topic nomination by the moderator (lines 5–6), and the caller's start of extended topical talk (line 7). (A is the moderator.)

(1) [Opening Grazia (22:10–11)]

```
1   A:    h bene grazie tante Luisa      [eh
          h well thanks very much Luisa eh

    L:                                   [prego
                                          you're welcome

    A:    {ff}Grazia

    G:    si pronto
          yes listening

5   A:    lei si è sempre ritenuta fortunata (.) perchè (.) ha (.)
          you have always thought yourself fortunate (.) because (.) you
          ricordato (.) tutto (.) dell'infanzia
          recall (.) everything (.) from your childhood

    G:    si certo cioè diciamo io eh s anche sentendo le signore che
          yes certainly that is let's say I eh l listening to the women
          sono intervenute
          before

          ((caller continues with extended topical talk))
```

The summons of the next caller follows immediately after the end of the preceding call (see the closing sequences in lines 1 and 2).

Summoning the caller is done by the moderator with a recurrent prosodic pattern, including a 'calling intonation' and, in most cases, increased loudness (as if the summons had to carry across a long spatial—nonelectronic—distance). Prototypically, as shown in excerpt (1), addressing the caller, summoning her to the program and situating her as a named person for the audience are done in one utterance.[10] After a response by the caller, indicating that the channel is open, a topic is nominated in third-turn position and proposed to the caller (see lines 5–6).[11] It can be compared to 'headline news', which has been shown to prefigure the interaction in broadcast news interviews as well (cf. Clayman 1991).[12] Topic negotiation thus ensues at the earliest possible moment in (public) interaction with the caller (i.e., immediately after he or she has been identified for the audience and has signaled availability as a talking and listening participant on the program).

But note that the openings of the calls are 'local' openings. They project specific continuations of the program. New callers are aligned in the ongoing program as being *ancients* or *moderns*. 'Labeling' the new callers by immediately assigning them a topic reveals to the audience their 'topically relevant identities' or 'discourse identities' (in [1], clearly that of an *ancient*, see lines 5–6).[13]

At the same time, openings address the task of (and provide the resource for) designing the formulation for the overhearing audience and making it radio-rhetorically effective. Topic nomination may be designed, for instance, as a puzzle, to be solved with the help of the 'knowing' recipient; or as a generic maxim of conduct to be validated by the caller, who has reported an experience in the previous nonpublic interaction which may be summarized in this way; or as the beginning of an activity report which is to be continued and completed by the caller, who is in this case the protagonist of the activity, and so on. These radio-rhetorical formats for presenting the caller and her topic have one structural property in common: The 'news' they announce is displayed as incomplete, as standing in need of completion (modification, confirmation, authorization, correction, etc.). It is this structural property (Button 1987) that makes topic nominations of this kind appropriate formulations for eliciting not just a brief response but extended, autonomously developed talk from the caller.

The elicitation pattern most frequently applied by the moderator is the news inquiry, which takes the shape of a recipient-related 'activity report' or 'progress report' (Button & Casey 1985). The report used for elicitation is designed so that the responsible actor, 'experiencer' or other main protagonist of the report is the recipient (see [1]: *you have always thought yourself fortunate*... in lines 5–6). Formulating such a report projects the relevance of having the recipient, who is in possession of the 'full story', tell the 'full story' herself.[14]

Another strategy, related to the first, is to frame the activity report as 'telling my side' and to indicate explicitly the moderator's 'limited access' (Pomerantz 1980) to the news announced. For an example, see the limited-access marker (*se non ho capito male*, 'if I've understood correctly') introducing topic nomination in example [2], lines 3–4 below. In this way the moderator qualifies his own report as provisional and tentative and solicits an 'authorized' version from the present recipient, who has experienced the reported situation. In fact, topic nomination in (2) illustrates how both strategies—unauthorized 'telling my side' and 'activity report' with the recipient as protagonist—can be combined.

(2) [Opening Anna (26: 12–13)]

1   A: {ff}Anna

     a: buon giorno
            good morning

178   LANGUAGE IN TIME

      A: se non ho capito male lei non ama=affatto il ritorno al
                  if I've understood correctly you don't appreciate at all the return to the
                  passato=
                  past

5   a: =esatto
                  exactly

      A: perchè?
                  why?

      a: .hhh la vostra trasmissione questa mattina mi ha . . .
                  .hhh your program this morning has made me . . .

                  ((*caller continues with extended topical talk*))

Further forms of 'incompleteness', notably those supported by the rhythmicity of topic nomination formulation, are discussed next.

3.2. Rhythmic patterns in topic nomination

In most cases topic nomination in our data occurs with an isochronous rhythmic pattern. This may be continued by the caller in the incipient extended turn:

(2a) [Rhythmic detail from (2) (lines 3–4)]

```
 1   A:     se non ho ca-/
                  /'pito /
                  /'male /
                  /'lei non        /         (new rhythm)
 5                /'ama=af-    /
                  /'fatto il ri-   /         (slower)
                  /'torno al pas-  /
                  /'sato=
     a:                             =e-/
10                /'satto
```

      A: *if I've understood correctly you don't appreciate at all the return*
                  to the past
      a: *exactly*

(3) [Opening Fernanda (33: 6–7)]

```
 1   A:     {ff}Fernanda

     F:     pronto buongiorno
```
                  hello good morning

```
     A:     i ri-/'cordi          /
                  /'sono una      /
```

Rhythm and Performance

```
5                    /'cosa (.) in-    /
                     /'uti-         [le
     F:                             [i-/
                     /'nutile 'sì
     A:   memories are something (.) useless
     F:   useless yes
```

((*caller continues extended topical talk*))

Reassembling elements of the sequential description given above, we may now consider the contextualizing work that rhythmic patterns accomplish in topic nominations. In doing so, we must take into account the public, radio-rhetorical design of the formulations on the one hand and their immediate interactive design to elicit extended topical talk from the caller on the other. As noted previously, to solicit continuation by the caller, the activity reports of the moderator are designed to be selectively incomplete. Considered in terms of rhythm, incompleteness can be contextualized iconically by interrupting the continuation of a locally created regular rhythmic pattern at a specific point in the course of its development. Such a break is evident in the pattern which sustains the moderator's formulation projected to 'launch' the entry of caller Gabriella into topical talk:

(4) [Opening Gabriella II (38: 6–7)]

```
1    A:   {ff}Gabriella

     G:   pronto
          hello

     A:   per tanti 'anni
          /'lei non ha /
5         /'mai sen-   /
          /'tito       /     (gradually slower)
          /,il bi-     /
          /'sogno      /
          /,di         /
10        /,ricor-     /
          /'dare       /
          /,il pas-    /
          /'sato (.)
```

for so many years you did not feel the need to recall the past (.)

{ff}ma poi (0.5) che cosa è successo?
but then (0.5) what happened?

```
15   G:   e:h ma /'poi (.)  /
                 /'natural- /
                 /'mente
```

eh but then naturally

quando si comincia a diventare più vecchi
when one starts to become older

((*caller continues with extended topical talk*))

The point where the break in the rhythmic progression occurs—{*ff*}*ma poi* (line 14)—is additionally marked by a preceding micropause, by increased loudness, by an intonational boundary involving dramatic pitch movement and by a subsequent longish rhetorical, suspense-creating pause. The break occurs at a point where the report is manifestly incomplete and the caller is therefore solicited to continue. This is exactly the point where Gabriella continues, taking up the verbal and prosodic features marking the breaking point. At the beginning of her extended turn, Gabriella also continues the regular rhythm of the moderator from before the break.

Topical talk is elicited here in an artful manner, designed both for the audience and for the specific caller. Considered rhetorically, the incompleteness is a simple narrative device to create suspense. The story is initiated and then saliently interrupted at a turning point where crucial further events can be expected. This creates the well-known "and then?" suspense of traditional detective stories. Breaking up a locally established isochronous rhythmic progression at the 'point of incidence', where the caller is to continue and begin her report, is an effective synaesthetic linguistic means to contextualize this suspense-creating strategy.

Rhythmicity may thus help create suspense for rhetorical effectiveness, but it also functions to help manage the interaction with the new caller. Rhythmicity is part of the professional skill of the moderator, enabling him to display with precision the point where the caller may enter the program. In the continuation of initiated syntactic, lexical and even narrative structures, the point at which to start talk is located and situated as an appropriate next point, appropriate in time and in talk.

In this and several other cases, the callers take up an element positioned last in the moderator's topic nomination and make it the first element of their beginning turn. Analyzed in a more detailed way, a range of diversified relations between moderator and callers appears. The 'handover' in (5), where the incoming caller is labeled a *modern* who thinks that memories are *inutile* ('useless'), is one instantiation. The caller takes up the last word in this utterance as a point to enter into topical talk.

(5) [Opening Fernanda (33: 6–7)]

```
1   A:    {ff}Fernanda

    F:    pronto buongiorno
          hello good morning

    A:    i ri- / 'cordi        /
                / 'sono una     /
5               / 'cosa (.) in- /
```

```
                    / 'uti- [le
    F:                     [i-        /
                    / 'nutile 'sì
```

A: *memories are something (.) useless*
F: *useless yes*

((*caller continues extended topical talk*))

The term positioned last in the moderator's formulation is not given special status by a break in the preceding rhythmic pattern, as in the last example, but by a potentially meaningful delay. Prefaced by a slight pause, but not by any articulatory or phonetic hesitation phenomena, its emergence within the course of the utterance, still incomplete in syntax and intonation, is withheld for a moment. Through the micropause the term *inutile* emerges as noticeably withheld and singled out from the preceding uninterrupted fluency of the utterance. The term is prosodically prominent yet still a constitutent beat of the rhythmic pattern.

The timing and placement of the term come as no surprise to the recipient. It is recognized even before its lexical completion and confirmed by the caller/recipient, who adeptly continues the rhythm just established. The delayed production and early recognition of the term within a rhythmic pattern suggest that the caller identifies the marked term as a quotation of her own words. We may also suppose that the moderator, labeling Fernanda a *modern*, has selected her most 'radical' statement. The caller is thus 'provoked' into argumentative discourse. She is now obliged to legitimize and account for a position that has only been summarized briefly and perhaps with exaggerated poignancy in the topic nomination.

The same feature of withholding may be part of the rhetorical structure of the 'headline', indicating that the matter for discussion in the upcoming call is controversial. Note that in this opening, the topic line is presented without making it explicit that it is the caller's point of view being presented. Rather, the topic line is presented rhetorically as a generic sentence of unrestricted validity, which once more activates its potential for provocation.[15]

This hypothesis can be strengthened by observing how participants treat quoted material on other comparable occasions, as in the opening and the handover in (6). The prototypical pattern of topic assignment is varied here: An explicit quotation of a caller's previous (nonpublic) words is used to elicit aligned topical talk from the caller.

(6) [Opening Fulvia (30: 7–8)]

1   A: buongiorno Fulvia=
           good morning Fulvia

     F: =mi sente?
           do you hear me?

     A: la sento benissimo
           I hear you very well

     F: sono mo:lto emozionata
           I am very very nervous

```
 5    A:      /'bene              /
              /'lei 'dice         /
              /,che=è un          /
              /'tema stu-         /
              /'pendo=
10    F:                  =stu-   /
              /'pendo stu-        /
              /'pendo gu-         /
              /'ardi
```

A: well you say that it is an exciting topic
F: exciting exciting look

F: è: tutta la vita che . . .
     it is the whole of life that . . .

((caller continues with extended turn of topical talk))

Extended talk is elicited here by quoting the caller's enthusiastic evaluation of the ongoing program (*stupendo*, 'exciting'), thereby projecting the relevance of an 'enthusiastic' continuation.[16] The caller acts out the projected enthusiasm in her next turn. She not only takes up and confirms the evaluative term, which is a very strong term in its own right, but also intensifies its force by doubling it.[17] It is evident that an enthusiastically confirming next turn, if it is not to lose its emotional 'key', must not be delayed. It must come on time, 'close' to the conversational object praised.[18] Orienting to the rhythmic pattern in course, as the caller does in (6), may thus be part of a more complex 'recognitional' reaction. The caller recognizes and confirms the quotation, reacts to its projected relevance by intensifying it in degree and comes in on time with extended topical talk.

In cases such as (5) and (6), where a quoted lexical term comes up a second time in conversation, callers quickly recognize their own words in the moderator's topic-setting formulations. This strategy leads to an interactive 'last-in, first-out' coherence. But even on other occasions, where this condition does not apply, 'first-outs' tend to be rhythmically integrated continuations.

Returning to the 'well-timed delay' observed in the pattern of (5) and more generally to the role of micropausing[19] in the constitution of rhythmic patterns, it was argued previously that a preposed micropause may, under certain conditions, be a sufficient cue to 'bracket' the use of a term (e.g., to switch from use to mention, or quotation). In the present data, we found the moderator frequently using micropauses at other loci as well. Consider once more example (1):

(1a) [Rhythmic detail from (1) (lines 3–4)]

```
1    A:      /'lei si 'è          /
             /'sempre rite-       /
             /'nuta fortu-        /
             /'nata (.) per-      /
5            /'ché (.)            /
```

```
          /'ha  (.) ricor-       /
          /'dato (.)             /
          /'tutto (.) dell' in-  /
          /'fanzia               /
     G:   /'sì cio'è (0.5)
```

A: *you have always thought yourself fortunate (.) because (.) you recall (.) everything (.) from your childhood*
G: *yes certainly that is* (0.5)

Clearly, it is not possible to assume that every minute pause in the utterance is a cue with specific and significant value (e.g., indicating a change of 'footing' of some kind or other). Nevertheless the distribution of pauses in a rhythmic pattern as earlier suggests a coordinated and holistic orderliness. By repeatedly suspending continuation and by introducing or augmenting space between the stressed syllables, the micropauses achieve an emphatic 'partitioning' of the utterance.[20] With the exception of the first line, all lexical words are stressed, entailing a high density of accents, and the main lexical accents are aligned in an isochronous rhythmic pattern with short rhythmic intervals. The lexical items involved constitute 'focal points' or 'rhythmic landmarks'.[21] The global effect of repeated micropausing is not only to lengthen but also to regularize the space between the main stresses to make the resulting structure isochronous.

In a pattern such as (1a), the 'headline' of the upcoming call is 'spelled out' for the caller and for the audience. Projecting it in this way is a prosodic means of attracting attention and claiming the importance of detail. The use of lexical intensifiers (*sempre, tutto*) is concomitant with such a presentation.

4. Transitions: From one caller to the next

In the tight serial structure of the phone-in program, the closing of one call is immediately followed by the opening of a next one, as stated above. Surprisingly, it is often at these transitions from one 'macroturn' of the program to the next that a common rhythm is established. This rhythm encompasses the last part of a closing and the first part of an opening across three speakers: the moderator, the caller who is 'leaving' and the caller who is newly 'arriving'. As noted in chapter 5 (in this volume), rhythmically integrated transitions, although they do occur, are not the unmarked option in Italian conversation. Why then is rhythmicity such a persistent feature here at the transitions between the calls?

To answer this question, consider example (7), which sets in at the point at which the moderator formulates the 'gist' of the caller's contribution in the preceding call (lines 1–6). *Ipso facto*, he is at the same time proposing to bound further topical talk and to initiate the closing. The excerpt ends at the point at which the next caller has been introduced and has successfully launched into extended topical talk (see the beginning of such a turn in line 22). The rhythmic transcript begins at the end of the moderator's 'formulation of gist'.

184   LANGUAGE IN TIME

(7) [Transition closing Mariuccia/opening Bruna]

1   A: ecco mi pare quindi Mariuccia che per lei (.) il passato (.)
            well it seems to me then Mariuccia that for you (.) the past (.)

            diciamo così (.) è una sorta di terreno fertile
            let's put it this way (.) is a sort of ground that is fertile

    M: fertile
            fertile

    A: sul quale (.) costruisce una pianta a- che ragionatamente
            on which (.) you cultivate a plant to- which is logically

5   A: è colle-/'gata alle   /
                   /'sue ra-   /
                   /'dici   /
    M: /'certo   /
                   /(   )   /
10 A: /'grazie   /
                   /'tante Mari-   /
                   /'uccia e: /
    M: /'grazie   /
    A: /{ff}'Bruna   /   (slower)
15 B: /'pronto   /
    A: /ˌbuon'giorno
    B: si   /'sente   /   (faster)
                   /'bene   /
                   /ˌbuon'giorno
20 A: la   /'scelta del ˌmante- / (new rhythm)
                   /'nere 'vivo il pas- /
                   /'sato (.)   /
                   /ˆ   /
                   /'è una   / (faster)
25   /'scelta di co- /
                   /'raggio   /
    B: /'sì

    A: in touch with its roots
    M: certainly
    A: thank you so much Mariuccia
    M: thanks
    A: Bruna
    B: hello
    A: good morning
    B: I can hear you well good morning
    A: the decision to keep the past alive (-) is a courageous decision
    B: yes

Rhythm and Performance

```
         A:     perché
                why?
30       B:     hhh (.) bé perché io al contrario della signora mi sento ...
                hhh (.) well because in contrast to the preceding lady ...
```

((*caller continues with extended topical talk*))

There are several independently motivated reasons for the (co-)constitution of rhythmicity at the transitions between these calls. For one, (mundane) telephone closings have been shown to be a conversational locus at which isochrony is extremely frequent (see chapter 5). This is in part due to the fact that many of the activities there (e.g., farewells, wishes and preclosing formulae) are reciprocal: The same token is used for the first and the second pair-part. The tokens occurring are, moreover, as a rule syntactically independent, small tokens which can easily be moved, or lengthened, and which are prosodically flexible. The same reasoning applies to the first summons/answer and any greeting sequence that may follow it in the ritualized openings of the phone-ins.

A further set of considerations arise when we look at the work of the moderator in managing the 'ushering' of callers into and out of the interaction. The following table presents a schematic view of sequential positions and activities which make up the transitions between the calls in (7):

	Moderator	*Caller*
1.	Formulation of gist (lines 1–7)	
2.		Confirmation/ratification (8)
3.	First pair-part of closing terminals (11–13)	
4.		Second pair-part of closing terminals (14)
5.	Summons of next caller (15)	
6.		Answer to summons (16)
7.	First pair-part of greeting sequence (17–18)	
8.		Second pair-part of greeting sequence (20–21)
9.	Topic-nominating 'headline' (22–29)	
10.		Confirmation/ratification (30)
11.	Demand for an extended account (31–32)	
12.		Start of extended topical turn (34)

The 'boundary work' of 'stopping' and 'starting' the calls is a specific institutionalized task of the moderator. As the schema reveals, transitions of this type contain a whole series of paired turns, where the initiative or first pair-parts are uniquely occupied by the moderator, while the second pair-parts or confirming/ ratifying/answering parts are allotted to the callers. This distribution of roles applies to the rhythmic configuration as well: It is overwhelmingly the moderator who is the temporal 'conductor' of the interaction at transitions. He initiates the rhythm and sets the pace for the caller who is leaving, he maintains the rhythm across the boundary of the closing terminals and he keeps it up in the opening of the next call. Rhythmic integration at transitions between calls can thus be considered an effective means in the moderator's professional repertoire for managing the exits and entries of the callers.

Similar considerations apply to the 'overhearing' audience. Within the program, crossing the boundaries between calls in a smooth, rhythmically integrated way may be a display to the audience of the moderator's professional mastery in managing the callers, renewing each time the evidence that the next call and the next caller are integrated into the program smoothly, without gap, pause, interruption or disfluency. In short, the integrated rhythm counts as a display of radio-professional virtuosity in 'processing' the callers, documenting that callers may change, but the program continues without faltering.

5. Rhythm in formulaic paradigms

This section deals with the intersection of grammatical and rhythmic structures. In following such a line of interest, however, we do not want to confine rhythm to the domain of the sentence. Rhythm in speech is a relational structure that may reach across the boundaries of syntactic units and intonational phrases, across the constructional units of several speakers and also, as discussed previously, across the boundaries of the macroturns of our program (i.e., the calls). Yet at the same time, rhythmic structures may also occur in more narrowly delimited habitats. In formulaic speech, rhythmic patterns may 'ride on' or 'inhabit' the lexicosyntactic or textual configuration of a stretch of talk in such a way that both co-constitute each other: The regular rhythmic pattern 'fits' the formulaic device as a prosodic display which contributes to its salience and the formulaic device and grammatical and/or textual structure on which it is based invite the regular rhythmic pattern, bringing it to the fore and making it salient.

Formulaic speech should not be conceived of as existing prior to or independently of prosody—often it is prosody that constitutes the formulaicness of an utterance (Kallmeyer & Keim 1994:253). One of the defining criteria for formulaicness, recognized in most studies, is the *Mehrgliedrigkeit* of an expression, its articulation in more than one constituent part (Kallmeyer & Keim 1994:6). The present data suggest that the grammatical and/or textual parallelism of the constituent parts, present in many formulas, has a rhythmic counterpart: "Parallel structures serve as particularly fertile ground for isochrony and may actually invite its use" (Couper-Kuhlen 1990:53). Consider excerpt (8), for example:

(8) [Fernanda]

```
1   F:    io ricordo le suore degli insegnamenti delle suore che mi s- io
          I recall the nuns the instructions of the nuns which made me- I

          sbuffavo quando mi dicevano
          steamed when they said to me

          Fer= / 'nanda    /
5              / 'qua Fer- /
               / 'nanda    /
               / 'là
```
Fernanda here Fernanda there

Lining up the four main accents in a regular rhythmic paradigm supports—and is supported by—the structural paradigm of the formula: The pattern of four equidistant beats is a particularly appropriate oral display for the formal regularity of the bipartite (2 × 2) parallel structure and contributes to its integrated re-presentation as one holistic gestalt. As a rule, formulas show a special closure, a *Gestaltschluss* (Kallmeyer & Keim 1994), which sets them off from their surroundings (and which is important for the interactive work that can be done with them in conversation). In the following sections we briefly discuss some of these gestalts.

5.1. Pair-part formulas

Note that the formulaicness resulting from the partitioning and parallelism of the constituent parts is not confined to the production of a single speaker but can also be found in paired turns (e.g., in the 'same token'–parallelism described by Auer [1990].) For instance, in the closing terminal adjacency pair of (9), the second pair-part is realized in a version that is parallel to the first pair-part—both lexically and in length and number of stressed syllabic constituents. This facilitates the continuation of a regular rhythmic pattern.

(9) [Roberta]

```
1   A:    / 'grazie   /
          / 'tante Ro- /
          / 'berta    /
    R:    / 'grazie   /
5         / 'mille a  /
          / 'Lei

    A:    many thanks Roberta
    R:    many thanks to you
```

5.2. Contrastive pairs

Formulaic phenomena notoriously show a great deal of variety, extending from, for example, idiomatic syntactic frames with variable lexical content (*Phraseo-*

schablonen, Fleischer 1982) to fully lexicalized and invariable idioms, proverbs, and so on. In our data, we find recurrent tokens belonging to the first kind, namely, contrastive pairs. Such pairs have the grammatical form of conjuncts as in the following:

	X or	Y
only	X, not	Y
neither	X, nor	Y
the more	X, the more	Y
always	X, never	Y

The following extracts demonstrate some of these patterns in use.[22]

(10) [Gabriella]

```
1   G:   io considero la società di oggi proiettato
         I think that today's society is oriented

         /'solo sul fu-       /
         /'turo               /
         /'non sul pas-       /
5        /'sato .hhh
```

only to the future not toward the past

(11) [Bruna]

```
1   B:   il passato è qualcosa che si rimuove non si capisce perché
         the past is something which is removed one doesn't know why

         si- non- non si ama molto
         one- not- one doesn't like much

         /'ne a 'traman-      /
         /'dare               /
5        /'ne a 'condi-       /
         /'videre con gli     /
         /'altri
```

either to pass it on or to share it with others

(12) [Gabriella II]

```
1   A:   in qualche misura come dice il poeta Montale chi
         in a way as the poet Montale says

         /'più                /
         /'m'a:ma             /
         /'più non mi         /
5        /'tocchi
```

who loves me most will touch me least

Rhythm and Performance

Rhythmic patterning strengthens and supports the formulaic unity of contrastive pairs by stretching across the Xs and Ys, underlining their parallelism and integrating their parts into one paradigm. Recurrently, it is the very prominent syllables that carry and intensify the contrast, like *solo, non, ne* in the preceding paradigms. At the same time, the prominent syllables constitute the 'landmarks' or anchorage points for the rhythmic patterns.

5.3. Line structures

Contrastive pairs can be elaborated and expanded into larger sets of contrasts, leading to 'pervasive parallelism'. Following Jakobson's (1966) description, pervasive parallelism characterizes 'line structures' in poetry. Line structures showing a whole series of contrasts, sustained for the span of a single holistic pattern, also appear in the formulaic paradigms of our data from everyday Italian speech. Examples (13)–(15) document elaborate cases of contrastive pairing in which the two parts have line structure and fit together like the two hemistichs of a verse, entailing a whole set of point-by-point correspondences.[23]

(13) [Anna]

```
1   A:     la vostra trasmissione stamattina mi ha fatto pensare ad un atteggia-
           your program this morning made me think of an orientation
           mento che per me è stato assolutamente istintivo (.)
           which I have been following absolutely by instinct (.)
           il pen- /'sare al pas- /
                   /'sato          /
5                  /'e:h           /
                   /,con modera-   /
                   /'zione mi      /
                   /'piace   (.)   /
                   /^         il/
10                 /,ritor-        /
                   /'nare nel pas-/
                   /'sato    (.)   /
                   /'mai
```

thinking back to the past eh with moderation is nice (-) returning to the past (.) never

Example (13) once more illustrates the use of micropausing for the regularity of the paradigm; micropauses here serve both to mark the syntactic boundaries (setting off the first hemistich from the second) and to 'balance' the regularity of the recurring beats.

The formulaic pattern in (14), an extended *X o Y*–configuration, also has two hemistichs delimited by micropausing. The formal symmetry and *Gestaltschluss* of the pattern are supported here by lexical recurrence as well: An identical item recurs at the end of the first and of the second part, which closes the pattern. (Caller Mirella, who grew up in the north of Italy, followed her husband as a young woman to Naples. The object of her nostalgia is Casale Monferato (Piedmont)).

(14) [Mirella]

```
1   M:    e quindi man mano sento una nostalgia struggente della
          and therefore more and more I feel a burning nostalgia for
          mia città (.) .hh ehm: ho=ancora u:n
          my city (.) .hh ehm: I still have a:

    A:    Mi'rella /ˌnostal-    /
                   /'gia (.)    /
5                  / ^    strug-/
                   /'gente della /
                   /'sua cit-   /
                   /'tà (.)     /
                   /'o nostal-  /
10                 /'gia di     /
                   /'Lei (.)    /
                   /'giovane in /
                   /'quella cit-/
                   /'tà
```

Mirella burning nostalgia (-) for your city (.) or burning nostalgia for yourself (.) being young in that city?

As mentioned, contrastive pairs are a resource for various kinds of interactive work. In (14) the first part is used to reformulate (i.e., to represent and quote) a part of the caller's preceding turn made salient by its 'flashy' word selection (*nostalgia struggente*, 'burning nostalgia'). The second part constructs (and proposes in a questioning mode) a version that is in plain contrast to the caller's version. But it veils the contrast by closely orienting to the details of the caller's original formulation. This orientation can be seen in the fact that the second part is a literal quotation of the first, and that it maintains elements of the first as a frame for the proposed contrasting version. Making the second part a rhythmically well-formed continuation is a prosodic means to display the formal symmetry of the formulation. The second part is presented as a well-balanced counterpart to the first. Clearly, here as on many other occasions in the moderator's speech, rhythmic well-formedness has a persuasive and rhetorical aspect.

In (15) the formulaic paradigm is used in reformulations as well. Here the moderator takes up and 'recycles'[24] a selected part of the preceding turn of the caller, recasting it in the gestalt of a formulaic paradigm. In doing so, he gives the caller's point a linguistic expression which is more poignant and rhetorically superior to the caller's original formulation.

(15) [Grazia]

```
1   G:    il grave è quando questi cambiamenti noi li subiamo
          it becomes serious when we undergo these changes

          perchè veniamo sopraffatti dagli eventi (.) .hhh (.)
          because we are overwhelmed by the events (.) .hhh (.)

          quando cioè non siamo noi a viverli i cambiamenti ma (.)
          that is to say when it is not us who live these changes but (.)

          li accettar li accettiamo  [passivamente .hhh il fatto
          we ac we accept them        passively .hhh the fact

5   A:                               [quindi quando praticamente
                                      that is when practically

          /'non siamo          /
          /'noi chi vivi-      /
          /'amo eh la la       /
          /'vita ma 'è la      /
10        /'vita che 'viv[e    /
    G:                   [e-
    A:       /['noi
    G:         [satto

    A:    when it is not us who live eh our our life but it is our life which lives us
    G:    exactly
```

In his reformulation the moderator uses the rhetorical device of 'metalepsis', where the semantic concept of a 'reversal' is expressed by inverting the use of the grammatical categories of subject and object in the two hemistichs. Although the moderator's reformulation contains 'flaws' of hesitation and repair, the important parts and anchorage points of the paradigm (*noi / vita / vita / noi*) are aligned as regular beats. Again the rhythmic pattern supports the formulaic device in oral performance.

In conjunction with the various other structural determinants of a salient *Gestaltschluss* in the formulaic paradigm, the regular rhythm also projects a precise temporal completion point. The caller comes in with her confirmation (*esatto*, 'precisely', lines 11 and 13) precisely on the last beat and at the completion point of the paradigm. The overlap must be considered 'achieved overlap'[25]: It is a token of fine-tuned and precision-timed agreement. By not waiting for, but slightly anticipating completion and coming in at a point of imminent completion, the caller documents a precise understanding of the formulaic device employed.

5.4. Lists

List structures are the most frequent formulaic paradigm in the present data and in most cases, they are accompanied by rhythmic integration. List structures, furthermore, commonly incorporate grammatical parallelism, "a serial recycling of a given 'turn constructional unit' (word, phrase, sentence, etc.), each unit consisting of or containing an item which is adequately representative of and adequately represented by each other unit's item" (Jefferson 1990:89). The items in a list co-select each other by lexical, morphological and even phonological parallelism. Prosody is seen here as a part-and-parcel feature of lists, organizing their construction and being organized by it.

Examples (16)–(21) contain instances of lists in which the regular rhythm corresponds to one of several forms of grammatical parallelism. As has been shown by, for example, Jefferson (1990), the constructional partitioning of lists usually involves three elements. In many of the lists encountered in our data, the tripartition corresponds to three rhythmic beats:

(16) [From the introduction by the moderator announcing the program]

1   A: ecco ogni tanto vi soffermate a pensare (0.7) ma io (.) chi
every now and then you stop to think (0.7) but I (.) who

```
/ 'so:no (.) che cosa    /
/ 'e:ro  (.) come la pen-/
/ 'sa:vo
```
am I (.) what was I (.) what did I think

(17) [Mirella]

M: le più belle trasmissioni (.) mi creda almeno per me sono
the most beautiful programs (.) believe me at least for me

que:ste (.) così senza (.)
are ones (.) like this without (.)

```
dot= / 'to:ri specia-      /
     / 'li:sti specializ-/
     / 'za:ti
```
doctors specialists specialized people

(18) [Paolo]

A: dunque noi siamo in cam-
```
/ 'mino noi siamo pelle- /
/ 'grini noi siamo vian- /
/ 'danti
```
thus we are on the way we are pilgrims we are passengers

The list format permits the introduction of sets of semantically similar lexical items, co-selected as additions, enlargements, enrichments or modifications of a formulation and not as repairs, where parallel items are produced to 'wipe out' or replace each other. Rhythm plays an important role in signaling the 'orderliness' of this kind of progression in discourse.

Rhythm and Performance

Constructional and rhythmic tripartition need not go together as they do in the previous cases. The prosodic length of a list (i.e., its length in terms of beats) may be longer than the constructional one:

(19) [From the moderator's discourse announcing the program]

```
1   A:    il loro passato
          their past
          ecco lo / 'vivono lo ri-    /
                  / 'cordono26 (.)    /
                  /^         lo ripro-/
5                 / 'pongono qualche  /
                  / 'volta a se       /
                  / 'stessi
```
well they live it they recall it (.) they bring it back sometimes to their mind

It is a recurrent feature of list construction (Müller 1991) that it is the third constructional part which is made the 'strongest' and which is given the most 'weight', also in terms of number and length of its constituents. The last constituent may thus add more than one beat to the rhythmic pattern. To make a list long can be an interactional resource:

(20) [Mirella]

```
1   A:    credo proprio però Mirella che sia (.)
          I rather think however Mirella that it may be (.)
          il ri=/'cordo il rim-    /
                /'pianto l'attacca-/
                /'mento alla       /
5               /'propria giovi-   /
                /'nezza
```
the memory the regret the attachment to your youth

Prefaced by a 'mitigation' (*credo proprio però Mirella*, 'I rather think however Mirella'), the list in (20) is produced while A is in the course of reformulating the caller's position and of raising doubts about it. The listing paradigm is used here as a means to enumerate pieces of evidence and this enumerating is made more substantial by making the list 'longer' in terms of rhythmic beats than it actually is syntactically.

The rhythmically integrated lists and contrastive sets that have been discussed in this and the preceding sections are usually brief. It seems that in everyday oral discourse formulaic sequences of this kind must be so. A highly stylized speech genre results if rhythm is maintained for longer periods. In fact, it is prolonged rhythm which characterizes the moderator's 'emcee'-style of talking, used to advertise the program and its theme at the end of the first part and at the beginning of the second.²⁷ Consider, for example, the 'epilogue' in (21), which is thoroughly rhythmicized, although there are quick and repeated changes of cadence and meter:

(21) [From the moderator's 'epilogue' to the first part of the program]

```
1  A:    fine della prima
         /'parte (.) mol-            /
         /'tissime ancora le 'telefo-/
         /'nate ora le guarde-       /
5        /'remo nella se 'conda      /
         /'parte sa'rete an 'cora    /
         /'voi
```

end of the first part a lot of calls still ahead right now we will look at them in the second part it will be you again

((*music*))

a raccontare di questo passato
who will talk about this past

10 vi pe:sa vi torme:nta
it depresses you it torments you

```
    l'a'vete abando-
         /'na:to l'a'vete igno-/
         /'ra:to lo conser-    /
         /'va:te
```

you have abandoned it you have ignored it you preserve it

```
15       /'è 'posi-   /
         /'tivo       /
         /'è 'nega-   /
         /'tivo       /
         /'è 'produt- /
20       /'tivo
```

it is positive it is negative it is productive

ecco questo è il tema di oggi a fra poco
well this is the topic of today see you soon

((*music*))

Rhythmic patterns here are supported by (and support in turn) numerous other discourse structures: assonances and alliterations; exaggerated and repeated vowel lengthening to further mark the anchorage points of the rhythmic patterns, already marked by assonance; list structures. (The 'poetic closure' of the first part of the program is brought about by a succession of two three-part lists whose rhythmic intervals vary in length.) The rhetorical elaborateness of the moderator's 'epilogue' may well be due to its not being impromptu speech but read off from notes or

Rhythm and Performance

recited, perhaps even rehearsed and perhaps prerecorded in the studio (see the blending in of music).

In the formulaic paradigms treated in this section, we found rhythmic structures associated with parallel structures. Parallelism, a hallmark of poetic structure, creates "networks of multifarious compelling affinities" (Jakobson 1966:428–429) between the constituents involved. We need not regard formulaic paradigms in everyday speech as poetry. But they are rhetorically well-formed creations which show a fine-grained co-selection of the elements constituting the gestalt-like pattern. This co-selection goes far beyond grammatical well-formedness.

6. *Rhythmic patterns in the construction of extended turns*

As outlined in §3, the moderator elicits extended turns from the callers at an early point subsequent to their joining the program. Extract (22) is an example of a caller's extended turn. Its multiunit nature is evident: Several transitional relevance points (arrowed) are passed over before the moderator finally makes use of one (line 21). As is also evident from the transcript, this extended turn must be developed 'autonomously' by the caller: The usual collaborative recipiency work done with continuers, confirmations, and so on is withheld. This is true even at points where the caller can be heard to 'ask' for it, as, for example, in line 11, when the completion of the caller's point is signalled by a three-part list.

(22) [Grazia]

1 A: {ff}Grazia

    G: sì pronto
           yes hello

    A: lei si è sempre ritenuta fortunata (.) perchè (.) ha (.)
           you always thought yourself fortunate (.) because (.) you (.)

          ricordato tutto (.) dell'infanzia
           recall everything (.) from your childhood

5 G: sì certo cioè: diciamo io eh s anche sentendo le signore
           yes certainly that is let's say I eh l listening to the ladies

          che sono intervenute non mi sono resa conto che la mia
           who intervened I was not aware that my

          impressione (0.7) che gli altri: non rifiutassero ma tendessero
           impression (0.7) that the others might not refuse but might tend

          (.) a rifiutare a dimenticare (.) quello ch' erano stati
           (.) to refuse to forget (.) what they had been

          e:h le cose non tanto le cose le persone ma
           eh the things not so much the things the people but

10   sopratutto come erano stati loro come avevano vissuto loro (.)
            especially how they themselves had lived through

     →   l'infanzia la giovinezza la vita (.) no? (1.0)
            (.) childhood youth life (.) no? (1.0)

            eh (.) mentre io invece io ricordavo tutto cioè (.)
            eh (.) whereas I instead I recalled everything that is (.)

            mh mi dava un senso di: (1.0) cioè mi sentivo fortunata (.)
            mh it gave me a sense (1.0) well I felt lucky (.)

     →   .hhh dicevo io non mi sono persa niente (1.0)
            .hhh I said I have not lost myself (1.0)

15   eh:m (.) e questo (.) per me è stato un grandissimo aiuto
            eh:m (.) and this (.) was an immense help for me

            perchè non mi sono rifugiata nel passato non è che io ripercorro
            because I did not take refuge in the past it is not the case that I

            il passato (.) come rifugio (.) .hhh ma (.) mi è servito per
            use the past (.) as a refuge (.) .hhh but (.) it served me to

     →   affrontare il presente (1.0) cioè (.) eh ricordando continuamente
            confront the present (1.0) that is (.) eh recalling continually to

            a me stessa le cose che avevo vissuto come le avevo vissute
            myself the things I had experienced as I had experienced them

20   (1.0) m il ricordare mi ha dato (.) la chiave (.) per (.)
            (1.0) m recalling gave me (.) the key (.) for (.)

     →   vivere il presente
            living the present

     A: ecco in che modo Grazia . . .
            well in what way Grazia . . .

The 'autonomous' development of extended turns[28] imposes specific tasks on the callers, namely to design their talk with respect to 'turn exit techniques' (Sacks, Schegloff & Jefferson 1974). In other words, they must provide signals for those instances in which long stretches of talk, 'paragraphs' of narrative, argumentative or other kinds of discourse are intended to be complete. There is evidence that rhythm, in co-occurrence with other cues, is such a 'turn exit technique'.

In the present instance, such a point of completion is marked before A's intervention in line 22 by the co-occurrence of (a) a categorical, generic statement (the movement to a generic statement can be a display [see Maynard 1980] that a topic has been exhaustively treated); (b) back-tying to the eliciting question (cf. A's *ricordato tutto* in line 4 and G's *ricordare* [. . .] *per* (.) *vivere il presente* in lines 20–21; the generic statement marks the turn developed so far as a 'complete answer' to the eliciting question and thus bounds it[29]); (c) prosodic marking as emphatic speech, including rhythmic 'scansion' (see chapter 6), as can be seen in the following rhythmic detail:

Rhythm and Performance

(22a) [Rhythmic detail of (22) (lines 20–24)]

```
G:      il ricordare mi ha dato (.)
        la / 'chiave  (.) /
            / ˌper  (.)         /
            / 'vivere           /
            / ˌil pre-          /
            / 'sente
```
recalling gave me (.) the key (.) for (.) living the present

A similar instance of an exit technique at the end of an extended turn (which is approximately 65 sec. in length) is given in (23). Again, a generic sentence, a maxim of what the caller has learned from the past, indicates the completion of the turn. It is marked by a similar configuration of prosodic cues, notably locally increased loudness and 'extreme' rhythmicity, exhaustively using all the grammatically available stress positions. A pause—temporally, syntactically and rhetorically well-placed—is inserted in mid-position.

(23) [Mariuccia]

Last part of an extended turn

```
1   M:    ma io penso che questo ehm: (.) questo modo mi è servito
          but I think that this ehm: (.) this mode has served me
          proprio a: (.)
          really to (.)
          a go- / 'dere        /
                / 'sempre (.) /
5               / ˆ        di/
                / 'cio che    /
                / 'ho
```
to always enjoy (-) what I have

Extremely marked instances such as the previous ones are exceptional in the data. It is recurrently observed, however, that rhythm is used as a display to mark the overall importance of a statement for the current turn or beyond. Extract (24) is a further example of an extended turn, again 'autonomously' developed by the caller and containing several transitional relevance places which are passed over by the moderator (see, e.g., line 16):

(24) [Paolo]

```
1   A:    quindi mi pare Paolo di capire una sorta di estrema labilità di
          well it seems to me Paolo I see a sort of an extreme insecurity at
          confini .hhh
          the borders hh
```

P: esatto ed ora: ho l'impressione .hhh di essere immerso
exactly and now I have the impression .hhh that I am immersed

in un mistero profondo (.) e tutte le certezze che mi vengono
in a deep mystery (.) and all the certainties that I have

5 dalle letture (.) dalle esperienze passate (.) no:n mi danno (.)
from reading (.) from past experiences (.) do not give me (.)

delle vere certezze (.) e sono: come delle sensazioni
real security (.) and are like feelings

come una ricerca .hhh di certezza ma che (.) alla fine e:h
like a quest .hhh for security but which are (.) which finally

si trasformano in incertezze (.) non so la religione
transform themselves into insecurity (.) I don't know religion

stessa io ho cercato tantissime volte attraverso la religione h
itself I tried very many times through religion h

10 delle certezze e mi sono ritrovato invece nella massima
to find security and I found myself again instead in the greatest

incertezza (.).hhh e: la scienza stessa ho letto tantissimi libri h
insecurity (.) .hhh and science itself I have read many books h

e: (.) ehm ehm quando poi alla fine penso alle cose essenziali
and (.) ehm ehm when I finally come to the most essential things

della vita eh mi rendo conto che
in life eh I become aware that

```
         la sci-/'enza          /
15              /'non dà cer-/
    →           /'tezze
```
science does not give security

si ferisce (.) a una realtà: parziale momentanea h del vivere del
it refers (.) to a partial momentary reality h of living in the

presente o di un passato .hhh più o meno lontano al presente ma
present or in a past .hhh more or less far away from the present

```
         delle /'vere cer-      /
20              /'tezze          /
                /'non ce ne     /
    →           /'dà
```
but it does not give real security

A: ecco ma Paolo ...
well but Paolo ...

The only two isochronous rhythmic patterns in the extended turn illustrate the association of regular rhythm with generic sentences. The same statement appears twice in this association, once at a candidate position for turn completion and once at the position actually used by the moderator to take over the floor.

Rhythm and Performance

If we look at the boundaries of these turns, we can observe that the formulaic devices described in the previous section occur in many cases as last-positioned formulations. The contrastive structure in (11), repeated from §5, for instance, serves as a last-positioned generic formulation of the caller's opinion.

(11) [Bruna]

Last part of an extended turn

```
1   B:      quindi è questo che trovo: (.) il passato è qualcosa che
            well then that is what I think (.) the past is something which

            si rimuove non si capisce perchè si non
            is kept away one doesn't know why not

            / 'non si ama        /
            / 'molto             /
5           / 'ne 'traman-       /
            / 'dare              /
            / 'ne ˌcondi-        /
            / 'videre con gli    /
            / 'altri             /
10  A:      / 'ecco ma           /
            / 'questo . . .

    B:      one does not much like either to pass it on or to share it with others
    A:      well but this . . .
```

In the same way, list constructions are frequently part and parcel of 'exits' from extended turns. For instance, extract (25) with its generic sentence has an elaborate list construction: The first three-part list contains a second list as its last and 'strongest' constructional element. In the second list, again the third constructional—and turn-final—element is elaborated into the most substantial and 'strongest' part, prolonging the regular rhythm across an even longer span:

(25) [Grazia]

Last part of an extended turn

```
1   G:      ecco il fatto di sapere sempre chi si è .hhh è legato a questo fatto
            well the fact of always knowing who one is .hhh is tied to this fact

            al ricordo al ricordare (.)
            to memory to recalling (.)

            le / 'cose le per-   /
               / 'sone ma sopra- /
5              / 'tutto come     /
               / 'noi abbi-      /
               / 'amo vis-       /
               / 'suto           /
    A:         / 'ecco           /
```

10   /'Grazia . . .
    G: *the things the people but especially the way we have lived*
    A: *right Grazia but in what way . . .*

Turns that have clearly marked rhythmic endings, such as (11) and (25), often entail rhythmically integrated continuations (see the moderator's *ecco* on the next beat in both cases). Yet the rhythmic continuations by the moderator, who is much more an 'initiator' than a 'continuer' of rhythmic patterns, involve here as in most cases only the first few syllables of his next turn.

To conclude, the loci for rhythmicity in this radio phone-in are as diverse as speakers' rhetorical strategies. When deployed by the moderator in the management of topic nomination and macroturns, rhythmic patterns mark places in time when callers' turns can begin and set the pace of their talk. But they also document to a wider radio audience the moderator's professional skill in managing his program. On a much smaller scale, rhythmic structures help to organize formulaic paradigms such as contrastive pairs and lists in the speech of moderator and callers by providing a display of partition and at the same time integration. Finally, when deployed by callers in 'autonomously' constructed extended turns, rhythmic patterns—at times in conjunction with formulaic devices—serve as a means of marking potential closure in long stretches of talk.

8

A Summary and Some Conclusions

In contrast to the dominant tradition within linguistics, which decontextualizes and at the same time detemporalizes language into 'langue' or 'competence', we have advocated a thoroughly pragmatic, contextual and dynamic approach to language in this book, in which structure and usage are not separate but are seen as complementing each other. We have argued that the retemporalization of language requires a break with a number of metalinguistic presuppositions in Western thinking about language—lay and professional—particularly a break with its referential/representational bias. By this we mean the focus on grammar as a 'tool' for communication combined with a focus on the (allegedly) stable representational functions of language as grammar. The latter implies the equation of grammar with repeatable and therefore time-neutral (detemporalizable and detemporalized) *signum/denotatum* or *signifiant/signifié* relationships, a bias that dates back to when linguistics dealt exclusively with written texts and the 'frozen' temporality of signs objectified on a printed page. Such a view does not take into account the processual and dynamic qualities of spoken discourse, of its emergence as "something produced over time, incrementally achieved, rather than born naturally whole out of the speaker's forehead, the delivery of a cognitive plan" (Schegloff 1982:73). Nor is it possible with the detemporalized view to envisage, as an object for description and explication, the sociosequential organization of participation in conversation. In our view, the temporal and rhythmic modalities and the patterning they introduce into spoken discourse are a contingent *vocal achievement* of the parties involved and an essential quality of spoken discourse which cannot be abstracted away from as a *quantité négligeable*.

The temporal parameters of language, we argue, must move to center stage in linguistic thinking and analysis. One of the foremost aspects of temporal patterning—dealt with at length in this book—is rhythm, a perceptual gestalt which imposes isochronous patterns on speech within and across turns at talk. Its relevance for interaction is seen as that of a 'contextualization cue'.

Because the study of conversational rhythm is a new field of research, the methods for identifying and verifying rhythmic structure in recorded materials are not readily available. In chapter 2 we demonstrated that, folk linguistic assumptions to the contrary, hearing conversational rhythm does not depend on musical talent or training but on careful and repeated listening to spoken data following a number of analytic steps. We presented a notational system able to capture the most important facets of (isochronous) rhythmicity and tempo.

Chapters 3, 4 and 5 address some of the most central fields of 'classical' conversational analysis (turn taking, preference organization and telephone closings) and aim at developing an improved (and partly reinterpreted) account of these regularities taking prosodic, time-related features into consideration.

Coordinated turn taking is surely one of the phenomena of human interaction most intimately linked to rhythm. It seems natural that the question of 'when' to become a ratified speaker is tied to the question of appropriate timing for a next speaker's utterance. When the instruments of rhythmic analysis are applied to turn transitions in English conversation, a large number of cases are found in which an isochronous sequence spans the floor switch. That is, current speaker establishes a clear rhythmic pattern (with at least two prosodically salient syllables creating an appropriate interval) just prior to a transition relevance place and next speaker prolongs this rhythm by placing the first prosodic prominence of the new turn on the next projected rhythmic pulse. Transitions of this sort we have called rhythmically *integrated*. They represent a cooperative achievement by current speaker and next, one that ensures a smooth transition from one floor holder to another. Rhythmically integrated transitions appear to represent the unmarked case for turn transitions in everyday English conversation. When they occur, interaction is to all appearances proceeding as usual; there is no sign of anything amiss in the flow of conversation. Unproblematic turn taking therefore is not simply a matter of the absence of overlapped (simultaneous) talk and/or 'gaps' but, rather, depends on a sense of rhythmicity which makes it possible to predict when the first stressed syllable of a next speaker's turn is due.

Given the previously mentioned preference for rhythmic integration at turn transition, a number of transition timing phenomena which have otherwise defied explanation are easily accounted for. For instance, when there are *many* nonprominent syllables between the prominent syllables to be aligned in a rhythmic pattern and when the tempo is moderate to fast, next speakers may find it necessary to minimally impinge upon current speaker's territory for rhythmic purposes. Alternatively, when there are *few* or *no* nonprominent syllables to fill out the interval between prominent ones in a rhythmic pattern and the tempo is moderate

A Summary and Some Conclusions

to slow, next speakers may have to insert a (micro)pause to come in on time. Minimal overlaps and micropauses such as these, if recorded in conversational transcripts without any reference to their rhythmic origin, may give the false impression of being turn-taking 'hitches' when actually they result quite naturally and unavoidably from the premium on rhythmic integration at turn transitions.

Yet with rhythmic analysis, not only what counts as smooth transition appears in a new light; the assumption that current speaker's rhythm and tempo just prior to a transition relevance place provide a metric for next speaker's entry also leads to a new view of nonsmooth or problematic turn transitions. For instance, if a next speaker's first prosodic prominence comes *before* the next projected rhythmic pulse, the turn onset is heard as 'early' (independent of whether an actual overlap occurs), leading either to a complete breakdown of rhythmic integration or to a momentary syncopation in the overall rhythm.

Another important case of nonsmooth or rhythmically marked turn transition occurs if a next speaker's first prosodic prominence comes *after* the next projected rhythmic pulse. There are two options here. According to the first, it may miss the first pulse but hit a second or third, creating one or several silent beats. Speakers routinely hear a *silent beat* like this as a noticeable (and interpretable) pause. Alternatively, the missed beat may cause the rhythmic pattern to break down altogether. In the local development of the conversations investigated, recipient responses tend to be more explicitly occupied with redressing the interactional balance following a nonrhythmic late incoming and thereby provide evidence for participants' orientation to rhythmically 'marked' events.

The conversation-analytic notion of preference can be thought of in two ways. In one case a second pair-part or potential response in an action chain can be said to be preferred or dispreferred based on its *formal* characteristics. If it has a complex structure (consisting of the response and an account, excuse or explanation) and is accompanied by delays, fillers and/or pauses, it is considered to be dispreferred. A turn that lacks these features is in this view said to be preferred. On the other hand, preference can be thought of as a *content-oriented* notion, one in which an individual's 'face' plays a crucial role. In this case, it is the activity a speaker is carrying out in a given turn which is said to be preferrred or dispreferred.

For the majority of conversational sequence types, we have shown that the preferred response is expected to set in with smooth (rhythmically integrated) timing. Rhythmically unmarked transitions in, for instance, question, greeting, advice, assertion, assessment and compliment sequences do not appear to make any additional inferencing necessary. On the other hand, turns said to be dispreferred on *formal* grounds are late (in one of the senses outlined above), when interpreted on the basis of a rhythmic metric for transition timing.

However, there are also cases in which the preferred response type is routinely accompanied by rhythmic delay and/or nonintegration in the unmarked case. This applies, in particular, to news informings: for 'hot news', the expected or preferred timing for a next response is a rhythmic delay. Rhythmic integration in this case cues a routine, nothing-to-get-excited-about reaction, clearly dispreferred following an announcement of something alter considers hot news.

If preference is viewed as a *content*-oriented notion, on the other hand, more interesting claims can be made concerning the contribution of rhythm to preferred and, in particular, to dispreferred activities. In the case of nonrhythmic (nonintegrated) transitions into dispreferred activities, for instance, speakers can be said to actively disappoint alter's expectation of rhythmic integration and, in doing so, to contextualize the face threat involved in a dispreferred activity as a conversational incident. On the other hand, when speakers rhythmically integrate turns which are carrying out dispreferred activities involving a face threat, they can be said to mitigate the potential face threat of their activity by actively working to camouflage it temporally: With rhythmic integration, face-threatening turns become part of the background.

Whereas in the first four chapters of this book we dealt with English conversational materials exclusively, the second half of the book introduced a comparative perspective, in which Italian and German data were analyzed. In our analysis of telephone closings in chapter 5, the same discursive-contextualizing function of rhythm and tempo in the same conversational environment was discussed, using both Italian and German data.

In conversational speech, Italian (a 'syllable-timed language') was generally found to be less isochronous than English. On the other hand, we do find isochrony in Italian (although in less extended stretches of talk and possibly also with restricted functions) in conjunction with 'isometry', where the number of syllables within a rhythmic unit remains constant. In the specific conversational environment of telephone closings, both languages were found to make use of rhythm and tempo in the following ways (although less frequently and less extensively in Italian than in German): Even if the passage before the closing sequence was anisochronous, participants were regularly found to begin to use an isochronous rhythm, and to integrate their contributions into this isochronous rhythm, as soon as the closing sequence is initiated in the first preclosing, or shortly thereafter. Within this isochronous passage, which persists throughout the closing sequence up to the final farewells, there may be tempo changes. Particularly in more extensive closings, tempo was found to accelerate several times, these accelerandos coinciding with participants' approaching the actual termination of the call. The accelerations can be said to anticipate the imminent termination, accompanying, as they do, those steps that take participants closer toward the end of the call. On the other hand, activities within the closing sequence by which participants move out of closings were found to be accompanied and announced by a slower tempo, or even a temporary abandoning of rhythmic isochrony.

We conclude that the rhythmic structure found in the German telephone data is not restricted to those languages whose phonology is of a type structurally similar to English (e.g., 'stress-timed'). Rather, rhythmicity in phone closings seems to be a functional, possibly phonology-independent phenomenon governed by the conversational structure of closings, its function within the larger conversational episode, and its particular demands.

Because faster tempo optimizes rhythmic gestalts (among other things by reducing the likelihood of off-beat stresses), increases in tempo can be seen as a way of enhancing rhythmicity. We have argued that by 'coming together' in a common rhythm, participants jointly contextualize the upcoming closing. This interpretation is supported by the fact that nonrhythmic closing sections are often not accompanied by an actual termination of the call but rather by some kind of expansion or reinitiation of the closing section during which the lack of rhythmic integration is repaired.

Chapters 3–5 deal with well-established topics of conversation-analytic research and show how a rhythmic and temporal analysis can shed new light on them, whereas Chapters 6 and 7 address topics about which much less is known. Moving from turn transition to turn construction, and, in particular, to the construction of complex and extended 'big package' turns, we have had to shift our analytic focus slightly. For although every contribution by a conversationalist, no matter how extended, is subject to the basic regularities of turn taking (and as such must achieve the specific suspension of transition relevance typical for 'big packages'), the construction of complex speaker contributions requires additional techniques and skills located on the level of what we have called the *rhetorics* of everyday language. These skills are not available to the same degree to every speaker. This is reflected in the fact that a speaker's performance in the construction of an extended turn such a personal storytelling, a joke, or some other oral genre may be assessed by other participants in terms of its quality, the latter being defined with respect to its local or general function (e.g., 'entertainment' in the informal, multiparty dinner conversations among friends which we discuss in chapter 6).

Among the many rhetorical strategies linked to rhythm that can be used for successful everyday performance, we have focused here on a particular usage of rhythm which may appear on its own or in co-occurrence with other verbal rhetorical patterns. For this particular type of rhythm, we introduced the traditional term *scansion*. On occasion speakers were observed to 'scan' their everyday utterances (i.e., to produce them in a highly salient, rhythmically regular pattern) by lining up a number of phonetically strongly marked main lexical stresses in a continued series of isochronously recurring beats. In scansions, speakers go to extremes and tend to exploit the grammatically and prosodically possible positions of stressability in an exhaustive and maximalist way. Rhythm may even be imposed by speakers as a *tour de force* on linguistic structures which would otherwise not invite this kind of rhythmicity. Within an extended turn construction, these rhythmic patterns take over a well-delineated function and thereby contribute to successful performance.

As our analysis of scansions has shown, other prosodic cues frequently co-occur with this particular kind of rhythmicity, in particular increased (relative) loudness, decreased (relative) speech rate and high-pitch obtrusions on the stressed syllables—features which have been described as distinctive of "emphatic speech." Scansions may therefore be thought of as one particular kind of emphasis. This analysis is corroborated by concomitant lexical cues—for instance, the use of intensifiers—and by a sequential analysis of the conversational and textual loci where scansions occur. We have been able to show that scansions are used to set off and 'stage' formulations as 'extreme case formulations' (Pomerantz 1986), where this 'staging' receives an interpretation to be specified by the speech activity in which it occurs: It may mark the punchline or climax of a story, display a claim as particularly consequential and urgent to a speaker in argumentation, expose the face threat of an act to make it more striking and offensive in verbal dueling or make a complaint more substantial.

Our approach takes into account the importance of sequential structure, both in the current interactive sense and in a more specific temporal one, by paying close attention to the details of the unfolding and the trajectory of emergent utterances in real time. As in the previous chapters on conversational structure (of the more orthodox sort), the notions of indexicality and contextualization play a decisive role: Rhythmicity is seen as a prosodic cue which gains—and reveals to the observer—its specific sign value only in its natural speech context, when it is analyzed as a performance that is both situated and has an impact on situating/contextualizing the utterance.

In the final empirical chapter, rhythm was analyzed as part of verbal performance in a set of Italian data different from the previous everyday conversational one: radio phone-in conversations between the moderator and a caller on a well-known Italian radio program (Radiodue 3131). Yet, the analytic interest continues to be focused on rhythm as a rhetorical strategy in the management of larger units of talks. We have been particularly interested in the moderator of the show, Dottor Corrado Guerzoni, a well-known 'radio personality' who manages to give his programs an unmistakable personal style. His stylistic skills, and his poetic performances, are of central importance for the success of the show. We demonstrated that rhythmic performance on this show is to be seen in the context of the moderator's dual task: to conduct the interaction with the caller and at the same time to stage it for the audience.

Clearly, talking space on a phone-in program is not self-administered by members as in everyday conversational turn taking: It is not an open-ended resource but an objectively limited one. This limitation was shown to have interactional consequences. It is the duty of the moderator to make the interactions with the individual callers 'fit' not only into the topical but also into the temporal framework of the program. He must introduce the callers to the audience in the openings, nominate a topic for them and elicit extended turns, formulate the gist or cumulative import of a call and initiate the closing, all in the appropriate amount of time so that a specific number of callers will be given approximately the same length of time at talk and can be dealt with in the overall temporal setting of the show. In addition, there must be enough of the floor available to Guerzoni himself, who must put his own literary performance on stage in appropriate ways. All these temporal constraints need to be dealt with in delicate ways, because radio interaction is exposed to the grand public audience of a national radio station, where 'rude' ways of imposing structure are sanctioned.

Given this setting and the sequential organization of the verbal activities that are part of it, we have identified a number of rhetorical tasks for which rhythmic cues are used. In the analysis of the beginnings and the closings of extended turns (which may contain stories, argumentation, or other activities), we found rhythmicity in co-occurrence with certain verbal patterns (e.g., generic sentences, maxims, formulaic paradigms, list structures with syntactic and lexical parallelisms). Here it takes on a demarcative value and contextualizes entrance into, or a point-laden exit from, extended turns. Rhythmicity was especially noticeable in the moderator's formulations summarizing the gist of a following or a preceding call. At the same time, Guerzoni's 'first' or 'last words' to the caller are an occasion and a resource for formulating 'big words' to the audience. Rhythmicity in these formulations thus has both a demarcative and a radio-rhetorical value, the latter consisting of a display of achieved eloquence to the audience.

Another rhetorical task for the moderator, which we analyzed in detail, is to initiate closing in an institutionalized situation involving unequal status among participants and unequal access to the floor. Not surprisingly, the moderator of the radio show takes the lead in determining not only the timing but also the quality of the closing sections. This applies to sequential development as well as to rhythmic structure. As to the latter, it was found that, in contrast to the informal data, transitions into the closing section coincide with a rhythmic *rallentando* on the thematic summary, which the moderator produces as a topic-exit (and closure-initiating) device (often establishing a textual link to the initial formulation of the caller's point of view). Given the highly metaphorical and indeed poetic character of his thematic summaries (which are his interpretations of the preceding interaction), it seems safe to conclude that the moderator is maximizing the weight of his statements through this rhetorical technique.

A third important task for the moderator (linked to the issue of closings) concerns transitions between calls. At the transitions between the macroturns in the tight serial structure of the phone-in program—where the closing of one call is immediately followed by the opening of a next one—Dr. Guerzoni was found to establish and maintain rhythm *across* two calls. The new caller is thus integrated into the program without gap, interruption or disfluency in the emergent course and trajectory of the radio program provided she takes up the rhythmic pace set by Guerzoni. Rhythmicity at the transition between calls can thus be considered an effective means in the moderator's *professional* repertoire to manage exits and entries with and for callers. It additionally displays to the audience Guerzoni's professional virtuosity in handling the callers, documenting that although callers come and go, the program continues without missing a beat.

NOTES

CHAPTER 1

1. See Auer (1993); Müller (1993).
2. Not all writers of the time evaded the danger of using their texts, once more or less carefully edited from the manuscripts, as a mere quarry for examples.
3. As a somewhat delayed follow-up to this tradition, *Sprachtheorie* (Bühler 1934) should be mentioned; Bühler devotes a section (§17) to the *stoffbedingte Gestaltung des Lautstroms der Rede* ('the materially conditioned formation of the chain of speech'). Traces of this integrative view can even be found in the work of Bally (1965, particularly pp. 201ff).
4. "Immer zwar bewegt sich die Rede linear, die Vorstellungen folgen aufeinander. ... Aber es ist keine gleichmässige, gerade Linie, auch keine ununterbrochene. Jetzt zeigen Modulationen der Laut- und Tonbildung Verstärkungen, Höhepunkte, schroffe oder weiche Formen der verschiedensten Art; jetzt deutet der Rhythmus, ob schnell oder langsam, ob fliessend oder abgebrochen, deuten längere oder kürzere Pausen an, in welchem Masse die Redeglieder miteinander zu verknüpfen oder voneinander zu trennen seien."
5. See *Die Sprache*, (vol. 2, pt. II, 1912).
6. The attempt to derive metrical and rhythmic structure from syntax is in fact much older. As early as 1776, Karl Philipp Moritz conceived of "prosody" as a syntax-based *Verteilungslehre* ('science of distribution'), in which "the prosodic rules of our grammar simply have to be drawn from grammar, insofar as the latter teaches us the manner of the

individual parts of speech, their subordination, according to the weight of their meaning" (1973: 246, our translation).

7. See Zollna (1994) for details.

8. On the link between technological innovations and linguistic praxis at this time, see Auer (1993).

9. And indeed in the 'sound' of language as a real-time event in general. It is one of the peculiarities of generative phonology that this approach is 'soundless', mute (see Tedlock 1981). Phonological theories such as Natural Phonology and, more recently, Articulatory Phonology, in which the basic units are "physical events ... affected by physical processes occurring during the act of talking" (Browman & Goldstein 1992:160), are, strangely enough, still the exception rather than the rule.

10. A similar strategy to eliminate those areas from linguistics that are difficult or impossible to capture with the apparatus of structuralism (here: phonology) may be observed in Trubetzkoy's *Grundzüge* (1956); with Bühler, he distinguishes the 'representational' function of phonology (which he calls *Darstellungsphonologie*) from one called *Kundgabe* 'expressive' and one called *Appell* 'appellative', just to attribute these latter functions to a separate "branch of science," which he calls *Lautstilistik* (see 28) and which is explicitly treated as external to linguistics.

11. de Saussure's choice of the term *rapports associatifs* as well as his way of writing about these relationships suggests that he is leaning toward a psychological approach to language, which therefore is not purely abstract but partially equivalent (if not identical) to a mental activity. In fact, *rapports syntagmatiques et rapports associatifs* are introduced as corresponding to *deux formes de notre activité mentale* ('two forms of our mental activity') (1972:170).

12. de Saussure was aware of this problem and addressed it explicitly (1972:172–3). Despite the previously mentioned indications to the contrary, he states that the syntagm should be regarded as part of *langue*: Because the individual speaker has to adhere to syntactic rules which represent 'generalized types' of sentences, all syntactic (in addition to morphological and phonological) groupings belong to grammar. At the same time he remains conscious of the weakness of this point of view, which implies a separation of those parts of the linearity of language that are 'regular' from those that are 'at the speaker's will': *il faut reconnaître que dans le domaine du syntagme il n'y a pas de limite tranchée entre le fait de langage, marque de l'usage collectif, et le fait de parole, qui dépend de la liberté individuelle. Dans une foule de cas, il est difficile de classer une combinaison d'unités* ('it must be recognized that in the domain of the syntagm there is no clear-cut boundary between facts of *langage*, the mark of collective usage, and facts of *parole*, which depend on individual freedom. In a great number of cases it is difficult to classify a combination of units') (1972:173).

13. For a summary, see Goldsmith (1992).

14. See note 9. It may be noted that in particular on the sentence or utterance level, a disproportionate amount of intellectual energy has been spent on the very few and peripheral cases in which prosody is in fact relevant to representational meaning; as, for instance, the segmentally homonymous pairs *take Grey to London/take Greater London* or *old (men and women)/(old men) and women*. This may be compared to tentative and hesitant remarks on other, "rhetorical" functions of rhythm, as in Abercrombie (1971).

15. A critical discussion of Metrical Phonology and of its relationship to the notion of rhythm used in this monograph can be found in Couper-Kuhlen (1993) and will not be repeated here.

16. An exception is Brazil's work on British intonation (cf. Brazil 1978).

17. See Couper-Kuhlen & Selting (1996) for such an evaluation.

18. See §5.1, as well as chapters 2 and 5 (in this volume) for a discussion of isochrony and how the notion is used in our approach.

19. It is for the same reason that rhythmic structures are sometimes denied interactional relevance at all on the grounds that they are hard to bring to consciousness and hearing them needs some auditory training; here, the preference for segmental, referential and relatively presupposing links between text and context leads to the complete neglect of those links that lack all three features. But note that changing the first feature already demonstrates the untenability of such a restriction: No sociolinguist or phonetician would deny the potential of aspiration in a phonemically nonaspirating language (i.e., a nonreferential, nonpresupposing but segmental feature) to be a carrier (index) of social and/or interactional meaning—despite the fact that it is hard to hear for untrained ears.

20. A more detailed discussion of the relevance of gestalt psychology to the analysis of conversational rhythms may be found in Couper-Kuhlen (1993).

21. This ties in with later results on time perception which report optimalization of interval judgment at around 600–800 msec. At intervals of 6,000 msec or more, interval judgments become about three times less correct than at this tempo (Woodrow 1951:1224f).

22. Cf. Stern's (1900:115) *natürliches Tempo* ('natural tempo'). As an example for culture-bound differences of natural tempos, he cites Neapolitan and Frisian fishermen; further comments on the issue may be found in Müller (1988).

23. See Lehiste (1977); Allen (1975); Hoequist, Kohler & Schäfer-Vincent (1986). For a discussion of time thresholds for the perception of rhythm, see also Couper-Kuhlen (1993:24–36).

24. See note 37.

25. A summary of some of this research is found in Pelose (1987).

26. See, however, the well-founded methodological critique of this chronography in Goodwin (1981).

27. Kendon (1990:101).

28. See Rosenfeld (1981) for a similar critique of Condon's approach to temporal synchronization.

29. Thus Kempton (1980) says: "The synchronized points of change are not at all equally spaced" (71).

30. We would follow Scollon (1992:341–2) here, who argues that the difference between rhythm research in the tradition of Chapple and his own work boils down to an interest in relaxation oscillators versus harmonic oscillators, respectively, as the basis of rhythmic alternations. (For these, see Chapple 1980.) The same applies to our work.

31. See, among others, Cutler & Foss (1977).

32. See Edwards & Sienkewicz (1990). An application of this theory to present-day discourse structure is K. Müller (1992).

33. We were fortunate enough to have Erickson with us in Konstanz as a visiting scholar in 1990 and to have a chance to work through—or literally, walk through—the original transcript of the *Counselor as Gatekeeper*, from which a section is reproduced here (figure 4.2. in Erickson & Shultz 1982). We also had an opportunity to watch Erickson, a trained musician, 'conduct' various videotapes when he demonstrated his rhythmic analysis. The following discussion, highlighting some notable differences between his procedure and ours, is partly based on this experience.

34. It is not entirely clear from the text if this one-second interval is seen as the preferred tempo throughout the data or only for this particular interaction.

35. Erickson also claims that body movements co-occur with phonetic emphases. Figures 4.1. and 4.2. in Erickson & Shultz (1982:90–91) show, however, that this is not necessarily the case in the data.

36. Erickson does not mark phonetic emphasis apart from duration here.

37. Recent phonetic research on so-called P-centers (perceptual centers) has shown that physically isochronous patterns of verbal stimuli (mostly nonsense syllables) are not perceived as such; instead, the 'peg' in a syllable on which we base our perception of isochrony varies according to the structure of this syllable (see Morton, Marcus & Frankish 1976; Fowler 1979; Tuller & Fowler 1980; Pompino-Marschall 1989). For a full analysis of the relationship between perceived and physical rhythmic patterns in everyday language, it is likely that many more regularities of this kind will need to be found, of which we know little up to now.

38. The link with prestructuralist European tradition is obvious: Voloshinov (1976) and Voßler (1904), to give just two prominent examples, present similar arguments; however, they did not develop a theoretical apparatus for the actual interpretation of prosodic phenomena in discourse, as Gumperz has done.

39. See Uhmann 1992.

40. In other conversational contexts the two parameters may be combined in different ways, of course.

41. Strictly speaking, these figures relate to 'articulation rate' and not to 'talking rate' (see Goldman-Eisler 1961).

42. Because allegro rules may reduce or eliminate underlying syllables, surface counts can differ slightly. Our count therefore starts from the assumption that syllable structure adjustments due to higher speech rate are perceived as such and should not result in a lower value for the parameter. This example is reproduced from Barden (1991). The meaning of + + and * * is explained in the following text.

43. As measurements were only carried out at the level of intonational contours and not at that of smaller prosodic units, this perceived change of speed is not reflected in the figures.

CHAPTER 2

1. They are taken from an empirical study of speech rhythm in standard British and American everyday conversation, including both face-to-face and telephone interaction (Couper-Kuhlen 1993).

2. That is, it has no pitch obtrusion or extra loudness and is only minimally longer than the first syllable *re-*.

3. *Ceteris paribus*, the lax vowel /ʌ/ as in *bub-* should be shorter than the diphthong /ei/ as in *break*, but in this utterance it is slightly longer (see table 2.1).

4. The syllable *em-* is louder, although not longer than *-phy-*; *-tween* is longer and somewhat louder than *be-* (see figure 2.2 and table 2.1).

5. We do not mean to suggest that hearers necessarily proceed this way (see chapter 1, §5.1) but that analysts can profitably do so.

6. Our notion of isochrony is thus a perceptually based one and may involve a certain amount of regularization of acoustic durations; see the tapping experiments of Donovan and Darwin (1979).

7. The same holds in (3) for the timing of *tons and*, where the syllables have a ratio of 2:1, as compared to *teeny*, where the ratio is 1:1.

8. Of course it would be possible to achieve isochrony with rhythmic intervals of three and one syllables, respectively: /'anti=vac-/'cine /'stuff. But this would presumably require more work to achieve.

9. See the discussion in Couper-Kuhlen (1993:34–36).

10. The words *didn't even* are realized as /dɪn iːn/ and have therefore been counted as monosyllables.

11. Sudden tempo switches, by contrast, are heard as new rhythms.

12. Our concept of a silent beat is thus more restricted than that of Abercrombie (1971).

13. All intervals in the English rhythmic patterns were measured from vowel onset to vowel onset of the prosodic prominences in question.

14. This is true despite the fact that (2) is isometric but (12) is not.

15. Voiceless plosives and fricatives are, for instance, regularly longer than their voiced counterparts in English stressed monosyllables (Docherty 1992).

16. This figure was calculated with respect to the interval prior to the syncopation.

CHAPTER 3

1. *Place* in this context can be thought of as a spatial metaphor for time.

2. It is of course possible for focused conversation to have multiple floors and for temporal coordination to take place across these multiple floors (Erickson 1981; Komter 1983). When this happens, each single floor has its own clock but there is one 'super' clock to guide overall coordination.

3. Excerpt (4) in chapter 2 was a case in point: /'mucus and /'junk and in/'fections.

4. When two speakers jointly create a single rhythmic interval, each speaker's contribution is notated on a different line. Any intervening pause is assigned to the second speaker.

5. In this and all following examples, those portions of the transcript which have not undergone rhythmic analysis are in the same font as the running text. A different, non-proportional font is used for parts which have been analyzed rhythmically.

6. The partial list is later jointly completed with a more generic third member: *and that sort of thing* (lines 7–8). See also Jefferson (1990).

7. Notice the stress shift on *'absolutely*, whose stress pattern in other environments is *abso'lutely*.

8. See §1.3 (in this chapter) and chapter 5 for more discussion on the role of rhythm in interactional closings.

9. Chapter 7 discusses similar opening sequences in an Italian radio phone-in program.

10. Note how the replicate is cleverly repaired so as to achieve synchronization with the ongoing pulse (lines 11–12).

11. Whether the rhythmic 'well-formedness' constraint on openings is specific to (radio) telephone talk cannot be determined with the current data base. Chapter 7 discusses some of the constraints operating on openings in Italian radio talk.

12. In special cases, for example, where the first assessment is complimentary of another interlocutor or is self-derogatory of the speaker, other expectations will be seen to hold (Pomerantz 1978 and chapter 4).

13. Note that two different types of assessment are involved here. Whereas Mrs. Giles's turn assesses an object outside the discourse, Mr. Hodge's turn assesses what she has just said. In terms of rhythmic configuration, however, the distinction does not appear to be relevant.

14. As we shall see below, syncopated and early beats in turn onsets also occasion extra inferencing and for this reason should be considered marked as well. We look at these marked cases in more detail in the following sections.

15. Although rhythmic integration at such transitions is impossible, rough judgments of whether timing is 'off' or not can nevertheless still be made, presumably on the basis of so-called *natural rhythm*. Natural rhythm, or natural tempo (chapter 1, note 27), is defined as the personal rate at which an individual spontaneously times a voluntary repetitive activity such as tapping a finger on the table. Rather than displaying unlimited vari-

ability, natural rhythms tend to cluster around a median duration of approximately 600 msec. per interval (Fraisse 1982; see also the discussion in Couper-Kuhlen 1993:132).

16. See also the discussion of mishearings in chapter 4.

17. We return to preference structure in argumentation in chapter 4.

18. And closings; see chapter 5 (in this volume).

19. Notice that Mrs. Giles is quick to recover her equilibrium, however, reestablishing the prior rhythm following one silent and one filled beat (line 22). And with her repartee *I'm a childless widow, I'd be chewing it all week* (lines 26 and 28), she even manages to score a point herself.

20. Alternatively the 0.7 sec. pause can be heard as creating a silent beat, with the stress on *people* continuing the rhythmic pattern. On this hearing the rhythmic delay would be less disruptive but would hardly account for the gravity of the conversational incident.

21. Interestingly, although Mr. Hodge verbally attributes the responsibility to himself, he indirectly implicates June's lexical stressing by embedding a correction of her pronunciation in the repair acknowledgement: cf. June's *kerb 'crawlers* (lines 5–6) versus Mr. Hodge's "*kerb 'crawlers* (lines 14–15). See also Jefferson (1987).

CHAPTER 4

1. *Bottle* is a slang term in this dialect for 'courage'.

2. *No* can be heard to do the job of agreeing to the (implied) statement 'There isn't any evidence that they actually did that, is there?'.

3. Even if a particular mishearing *is* attributable to some personal shortcoming, such as speaking too softly or having a hearing impairment, members do not routinely treat it as fault implicative.

4. In one possible reading of Dave's comment, it is treating the caller's French phrase as an innuendo, Sweeney being known for off-color remarks.

CHAPTER 5

1. Interested readers are referred to the following surveys: Lehiste (1970, 1977); Dauer (1983); Auer & Uhmann (1988); Pompino-Marschall (1989); Bertinetto (1989); Auer (in press).

2. More technically, only those segments are counted for rhythmic purposes that have mora status; in the usual definition of the mora, syllable initial phonemes are neglected (see Auer 1991).

3. See the so-called P-center effects discussed, for example, in Pompino-Marschall (1989).

4. However, measurements over all types of syllables do not confirm a syllable-timed rhythm in the strict sense, according to Vayra, Avesani & Fowler (1984).

5. The older syncopation of word-final vowels (*Santo* → *Sant* → *San*) is not productive any longer.

6. See Pompino-Marschall (1989).

7. Thus it is true that, according to measurements by Bertinetto (1977:86), four-syllable feet in Italian take on an average twice as much time as two-syllable feet to be produced (in an experimental setting)—which should be evidence for syllable-timed instead of stress-timed isochrony. However, the conclusions to be drawn from this finding are relatively modest if one takes into account comparable measurements for English by Faure, Hirst & Chafcouloff (1980), which come to almost the same ratio (two-syllable feet : four-syllable feet = 35.75 : 68.50 cs.; cf. 35.59: 60.35/ 34.08: 68.59 in Bertinetto's results).

8. With the terms 'destressing' and 'stress (or beat) addition', which are found, for instance, in Nespor & Vogel's work on Italian rhythm (see Nespor & Vogel 1989), we use established phonological parlance, although the image of 'underlying' stresses which are adjusted on the phonetic surface by rules of 'euphony' has a touch of determinism in disaccord with our approach to prosody. In particular, generative phonologists have been all too ready to assume that 'underlying' stress can be assigned according to rules that are as strict and watertight as those of syntax (on which they are quite obviously modeled; see Selting 1992a). A less deterministic model would have to take into account that within the limits of grammatically and pragmatically conditioned constraints, strong stress assignment is to a certain degree a matter of the speaker's 'stylistic' choices. It is precisely this liberty that is exploited in the construction of isochronous rhythmic structures in Italian and other languages.

9. Secondary lexical accents are available for the compounds ˌCastrop- ˈRauxel and ˈHeimat ˌort.

10. In the German telephone materials presented in this chapter, F designates a female speaker, M a male speaker.

11. The token *gut*, in addition to preclosing, may be responding to M's announcement in line 5.

12. This exchange should not be considered preclosing because it does not serve as a locus for last-positioned topical material.

13. As noted in an earlier publication by the first author (Auer 1990), this finding casts some doubt on the classification of farewells as being produced with the format of a classic adjacency pair.

14. Although radio phone-in data are not used elsewhere in this chapter, this fragment is reproduced here because the conversation displays little orientation to the overhearing audience (apart from ritual greetings to 'everyone who is listening in') and is in many ways just like a private two-party conversation. (This applies both to sequential development, where the caller plays a decisive role—for instance, in initiating closing, a prerogative of the DJ in institutional radio talk—and to the way in which co-participants construe their mutual relationship; see the use of the *tu* forms by both parties.) In chapter 7 (in this volume) Italian radio phone-in material is discussed which has a very different structure, not as a consequence of being 'on the air' but, rather, as a consequence of the organization of this particular broadcast genre as a social event.

15. A detailed treatment with more material is found in Auer (1990).

16. Longer, usually two-feet phrases occur if address terms are tagged onto the farewells, preclosings or other small tokens used in the closing sequence. They often occasion overlap (see Jefferson 1973).

17. In a northern German corpus, the incidences of *tschüß* would be even higher.

18. Etymologically, *tschüß* (with many local variants such as *schüß, tschü*) is of Romance origin (*addiós*) and is said to have reached the north of Germany through Flanders. In folk etymology it is related to the Italian loan *ciao*.

19. Notation for rhythmic prosody is the same as in the previous chapters. Phonetically stronger and weaker prominences are distinguished in the on-beat and off-beat syllables, in an adaptation of IPA symbols, by ˈ and ˌ. Translations are added below the line in the nonrhythmic parts of the transcript but *en bloc* after the isochronous passages.

20. The fact that it is always the male participant who takes the leading role may be related less to gender differences than to the fact that in each case, M is the caller. There is an old rule of telephone etiquette, which may still be valid to some extent, forbidding the participant who is called to close down the interaction without warrant.

21. The original contains a speech error here (*kufst* instead of *rufst*, most likely a remnant of an earlier sentence plan such as *kannst ja heut abend nochmal anrufen*).

22. Note that in this case M is the caller but F initiates the closing. According to one version of telephone etiquette, this is impolite behavior; see footnote 20.

23. This is not necessarily the case because there is some syllable-internal compensation between consonantal coda and vocalic nucleus, certainly with geminate consonants. It would be wrong for this reason to 'count' heavy syllables as two light syllables (as one might do in a moraic language like Japanese).

CHAPTER 6

1. For the etymolgy of Lat. *scandere*, see Ernout-Meillet (1967). The Latin use of the terms prevails in present-day metrics. See, e.g., for Italian Memmo (1983); for a more general treatment of the history of rhythm terms, see Meschonnic (1982).

2. See the introduction of this notion and the references given in chapter 3.

3. For the indexical nature of 'contextualizing cues', see di Luzio (1992:12), who summarizes work of John Gumperz.

4. For a more detailed discusion of indexicality, see in particular Heritage (1984).

5. I am grateful to Marcello Panese (Lecce) for working through part of the recordings with me. See also Panese (1992).

6. For the notion of 'instantiation', see Tannen (1984). More generally on the role and structure of stories told to serve as examples in everyday argument, see also Müller & di Luzio (1995).

7. See Selting (1989) for a study of the contextualizing value of short versus long intervals between accents (*Akzenteinheiten*). According to this study, the shortness of an accent unit contextualizes 'poignancy':

> Kürzere Akzenteinheiten wirken offenbar "pointierter" und die Äußerung enger fokussiert und "bestimmt," "energisch" oder auch "belehrend" und in den "kommunikativen Vordergrund" gestellt; . . . je kürzere Akzenteinheiten in Äußerungen, umso deutlicher versucht offenbar die Sprecherin oder der Sprecher, dem Rezipienten "offensiv" und "vordergründig" ihre/seine Signale und Mitteilungen "ins Bewußtsein zu hämmern." (223)

As argued below for the present example, this effect may be enhanced by the unusual length ('perseveration') of such a short-cadenced pattern.

8. See the discussion on the preference for isometric patterns in Italian in chapter 5 (in this volume). The preference for isochrony based on isometry is, in fact, well illustrated by the two sequences quoted.

9. For an interactive, rhythm-based notion of what it means 'to know a line', see Erickson (1992).

10. For 'perseveration' as an intonational gesture, see Bolinger (1989:76–77).

11. For the activity of 'formulating the conversation' and the corresponding notion of 'formulations', see Garfinkel & Sacks (1970), Heritage & Watson (1979).

12. For the use and particular qualification of idiomatic expressions as closing elements, see Sacks (1971), Drew & Holt (1990). In our case, given the contents of the preceding list, the idiom might even have a nonmetaphorical, literal reading (*cazzo* = vulg. 'penis').

13. "In 'directly competitive incomings' the incomer has something important to say and . . . he or she is treating the overlap-position as an undesirable or unsuitable place for the saying of it. We hear him or her as wanting the floor to him/ herself not when the current speaker has finished, but now at *this* point in the conversation" (French & Local 1983:18).

14. "We can rate the effectiveness of a sound in a group session by the number of members of the audience who laughed. In the Thunderbird session, there were five members: if one sounded against the other successfully, the other three would laugh; a less successful sound showed only one laughter or none" (Labov 1972:144). As Labov notes (146), members also take definite notice of the final result of a sounding contest.

15. See Uhmann (1992); Barden (1991).

16. See Kiparsky (1975:585–6) on exaggerated and mechanical 'schoolboy's scansions'.

17. The notion of 'itemization' is introduced by Jayyusi (1984: chap. 3), who distinguishes 'lists'—which have gestalt properties and constituent elements displaying that they are 'co-selected to stand together' (78)—from 'itemizations', enumerative paradigms where the items are singled out to stand as individuals. The procedure seems to correspond to a notion in intensification theory (*Stapelung*; see van Os 1989). For example, in an emphatic version of Ger. *ganz besonders herzlichen Dank*, 'very many special thanks', the stresses tend to be aligned on a par in a serial array and are detached from the hierarchical constituency of $((((ganz)(besonders)))(herzlichen))(Dank)$. Seen more generally, 'itemizations' as a prosodic resource would seem to run counter to—or rather create tension with—the stress hierarchies as they are described in metrical trees and grids in phonology.

18. See Jefferson (1990); with particular reference to lists by southern Italian speakers, see Müller (1991).

CHAPTER 7

1. For another discussion of this program and the prosodic cues deployed to contextualize the openings and closings of calls to it, see Panese (1996).

2. For examples of empirical studies which bring together both conversational and rhetorical aspects of radio broadcasts, see the contributions in Scannell (1991a), notably those by Clayman (1991), Hutchby (1991) and the editor (Scannell 1991b).

3. Variations in the openings and the closings can thus also be seen as the result of a conscious 'stylistic' effort by a professional moderator not to become too repetitive.

4. According to Heritage (1984) the application of conversation analysis techniques of description to 'institutional data' (interaction in school and courtroom, therapy, etc.) has shown

> two related phenomena: a selective reduction in the full range of conversational practices available for use in mundane interaction; and (2) a degree of concentration on, and specialization of, particular procedures which have their "home" or base environment in ordinary talk. These findings support the view that not only is mundane conversation the richest available research domain, but also that comparative analysis with mundane interaction is essential if the "special features" of interaction in particular institutional contexts are to receive adequate specification and understanding. (Heritage 1984: 239)

5. For a more detailed description of the 'special features' of radio phone-in interaction, see Hutchby (1991).

6. For the 'two faces' of radio conversation, see also Müller (1995).

7. These numbers are taken from Simonelli & Taggi (1985: 135–136). The authors estimate that the average daily audience of Radiodue 3131 amounts to approximately two million listeners.

8. Other autobiographic topics of the series include: *amicizia* 'friendship'; *vedove* 'widows'; *malinconia* 'melancholy'; *seduzione* 'seduction'; *amore fra i vecchi* 'love among the elderly'.

9. Preparatory orientations enter into and prefigure the observable event in other (nonbroadcast) institutional calls as well. See Zimmerman (1992) for a description.

10. Minimization (of pretopical work) has been found to be a pervasive feature in other phone-in programs as well, see Hutchby (1991): "minimized recipient-designed co-participant identification is preferredly, and overwhelmingly, achieved within the span of the first two turns" (120).

11. For the specific type of topic initiation—topic is initiated anew at the beginning of each call and cannot 'flow' from one which has just been closed down in a previous call—see Pomerantz (1980) and Button & Casey (1985).

12. The notion of 'headline news' is also used in a more technical, conversation-analytic sense by Button & Casey (1985), where it refers to a recipient-designed form of topic generation in mundane conversation: The topic-nominating speaker elicits extended talk from a recipient by announcing 'news' which is recognizably and selectively incomplete. The announcement is therefore not in itself a 'news delivery' but projects that there is more to be told. This notion fits well to the broadcast notion of Clayman (1991) and, taken together, they seem to provide an accurate description of the opening data under analysis. It is argued that 'headline news' should, furthermore, be conceived in a (radio-)rhetorical way—it is designed to work as a 'catchword' for the overhearing audience.

13. This process may again be compared to the initiating structure of broadcast news interviews: Moderators' introductory descriptions of participants portray the identities of interviewees with respect to their relevance for the focal event of the upcoming interview. Descriptive items in initial participant presentation are selected according to (a) a 'topical relevance principle', aligning the participant to the focal event or to a particular point of view concerning this event, and (b) a radio-rhetorical 'recipient-design', that is, "to make the interviewee's alignment to the topic explicit enough so as to be readily graspable by its intended recipient, which in this case, is a typified sample of the American public" (Clayman 1991: 60). The notion of 'discourse identity' or 'situated identity' has also been proposed for the description of the identifying interaction in the openings of institutional, but nonbroadcast calls, see Zimmerman (1992): "Alignment refers to the participant's mutual orientation to the set of articulated identities they have projected or assumed in the local strip of interaction. Procedurally, alignment of situated identities involves the display and coordination of 'who' it is that is calling and 'who' is answering, and hence 'what' these parties are (or might be up to) in the current situation" (45).

14. Obviously, the elicitation of extended talk is not done by its initiation alone but entails a continued state of recipiency for the emerging turn.

15. It has been mentioned previously that there is more evidence documenting that Moderns are the dispreferred category in the moderator's dichotomic program world: Globally, Moderns must argue to make their point; Ancients just reveal and narrate it. For the use of rhythmic patterns in argumentative discourse, see §7 (in this chapter).

16. And, more indirectly, of the moderator's *mise en scène* of the radio show. Varying the well-known maxim *Der Krieg ernährt den Krieg*, 'war feeds war', it can be said of our program—and maybe others—*Die Show ernährt die Show*, 'the show feeds the show'.

17. For a description of this type of intensification in Italian, see Wierzbicka (1986).

18. The proximity of conversational object and its intensified appreciation by a recipient has been described by Goodwin (1986).

19. On the noticeability of micropauses and their role of assuring rhythmic transitions between turns, see Couper-Kuhlen (1990: 130–131). On their potential value as contextualizing cues within turns, see Selting (1995: 85–89).

20. See the 'emphatic spelling' noted in the description of scansions in the previous chapter and corroborative evidence presented by Selting (1994).

21. See Couper-Kuhlen (1990:50) referring to the notion of 'rhythmic landmarks' used by Classe (1939).

22. Contrastive pairs, defined in a looser sense which does not refer to grammatical parallelism, have been found to be used frequently and effectively in present-day public, political and religious rhetorics. See Atkinson (1984a).

23. Contrastive pairing has been related to verse writing by linguists such as Bally (1965), who characterizes the classical French alexandrine as a *moule à antithèses*: "L'alexandrin classique... est un merveilleux recours pour les oppositions de pensée. Avec ses deux hemistiches égaux il est un véritable moule à antithèses" (342).

24. The type of interactive work in excerpt (15) corresponds to what has been described as the 'cooperative recycle' (Heritage 1985: 106–107), a three-turn-sequence of statement—reformulation—confirmation, where the reformulator cooperates with the first speaker 'to get the point across' (Heritage 1985: 197).

25. For 'achieved overlap', in the present instance a converging case of 'recognitional' and 'terminal' overlap, see Jefferson (1984). The overlapping speaker exhibits an understanding of imminent completion and signals the 'substantive adequacy' of the overlapped utterance. Terminal and recognitional overlap of this kind, furthermore, shows a 'principled' (i.e., minimal) 'incursion into the current turn'.

26. This is not the only case in the present data where a speaker adapts the morphology of the verb—cf. *ricordono* instead of the grammatical *ricordano*—to the one prevailing within the paradigm.

27. Features of this overtly stylized and sustained rhetorical style are also present in a less salient and persuasive manner in the 'natural rhetorics' of the callers.

28. These conditions seem to be very similar to those in broadcast news interviews. See Heritage & Greatbatch (1991) for a description.

29. The boundaries of extended turns have been analyzed in studies of 'everyday argument' in conversation, see Schiffrin (1986). Schiffrin (1986) also finds that the answering parts in extended turns "are often placed in boundary positions so that their tie to the prior question can be easily established" (39).

REFERENCES

Abercrombie, David. 1964. Syllable quantity and enclitics in English. In Abercrombie, David, et al., eds. *In Honour of Daniel Jones*. London: Longman, 216–222.
Abercrombie, David. 1967. *Elements of General Phonetics*. Edinburgh: Edinburgh Univ. Press.
Abercrombie, David. 1971. Some functions of silent stress. In Aitken, A. J.; McIntosh, A.; & Pálsson, H., eds. *Edinburgh Studies in English and Scots*. London: Longman, 147–156.
Allen, George D. 1975. Speech rhythm: Its relation to performance universals and articulatory timing. In *Journal of Phonetics* 3, 75–86.
Allen, George D., & Hawkins, S. 1980. Phonological rhythm: Definition and development. In Yeni-Komshian, O. H. (ed.), *Child Phonology*. New York: Academic Press, 227–256.
Atkinson, J. M. 1984a. *Our masters' voices. The language and body language of politics*. London: Methuen.
Atkinson, J. M. 1984b. Public speaking and audience responses: Some techniques for inviting applause. In Atkinson, J. M., & Heritage, John, eds., *Structures of Social Action. Studies in Conversational Analysis*. Cambridge: Cambridge Univ. Press, 370–411.
Atkinson, J. M., & Heritage, John, eds. 1984. *Structures of Social Action. Studies in Conversation Analysis*. Cambridge: Cambridge Univ. Press.
Auer, Peter. 1986. Kontextualisierung. In *Studium Linguistik* 19, 22–47.
Auer, Peter. 1990. Rhythm in telephone closings. In *Human Studies* 13, 361–392.
Auer, Peter. 1991. Zur Phonologie der More. In *Zeitschrift für Sprachwissenschaft* 1, 3–36.
Auer, Peter. 1992. Introduction: John Gumperz's approach to contextualization. In Auer, Peter & di Luzio, Aldo, eds., *Variation and Convergence*. Berlin: de Gruyter, 1–38.

Auer, Peter. 1993. Über ↻. In *Zeitschrift für Literaturwissenschaft und Linguistik* 23, 90–91, 104–138.
Auer, Peter. In press. Silben- und akzentzählende Sprachen als phonologische Typen. In E. König, et al., eds. *Typologie—ein Handbuch*. Berlin: de Gruyter.
Auer, Peter, & di Luzio, Aldo, eds. 1992. *The Contextualization of Language*. Amsterdam: Benjamins.
Auer, Peter; Couper-Kuhlen, Elizabeth; & di Luzio, Aldo. 1990. Isochrony and "uncomfortable moments" in conversation. In Halliday, M. A. K.; Gibbons, J.; & Nicholas, H., eds., *Learning, Keeping and Using Language*. Amsterdam: Benjamins, 269–281.
Auer, Peter, & Uhmann, Susanne. 1988. Silben- und akzentzählende Sprachen. In *Zeitschrift für Sprachwissenschaft* 7(2), 214–259.
Bally, Charles. 1926. Le rythme linguistique et sa signification sociale. In *Compte rendu du Ier congrès du rythme, 16–18 août 1926*. Genève: Inst. Jaques Dalcroze, 253–263.
Bally, Charles. 1965. *Linguistique générale et linguistique française*. 4th ed. Bern: Francke. Orig. pub., 1932.
Barden, Birgit. 1991. Sprechgeschwindigkeit und thematische Struktur. *KontRI Working Paper No. 15*, Univ. of Konstance, Fachgruppe Sprachwissenschaft.
Bauman, Richard, & Briggs, Charles L. 1990. Poetics and performance as critical perspectives on language and social life. In *Annual Review of Anthropology* 19, 59–88.
Bertinetto, Pier Marco. 1977. "Syllabic blood" ovvero l'italiano come lingua ad isocronismo sillabico. In *Studi di Grammatica Italiana* VI, 69–96.
Bertinetto, Pier Marco. 1989. Reflections on the dichotomy "stress" vs. "syllable-timing." In *Revue de phonétique appliquée* 91–93, 99–130.
Bilmes, Jack. 1988. The concept of preference in conversation analysis. In *Language in Society* 17, 161–181.
Bolinger, D. 1989. *Intonation and Its Uses. Melody in Grammar and Discourse*. London: Arnold.
Brazil, D. 1978. *An Investigation of Discourse Intonation*. SSRC Project HR3316, 1, Final Report.
Briggs, Charles L. 1988. *Competence in Performance*. Philadelphia: Univ. of Pennsylvania Press.
Browman, Catherine P., & Goldstein, Louis. 1992. Articulatory phonology: An overview. In *Phonetica* 49, 155–180.
Bühler, Karl. 1934. *Sprachtheorie*. Jena: G. Fischer.
Butterworth, Brian. 1980. Evidence from pauses in speech. In Butterworth, Brian ed., *Language Production*. Vol. I: Speech and Talk. London: Academic Press, 155–176.
Butterworth, Brian, & Goldman-Eisler, Frieda. 1979. Recent studies in cognitive rhythm. In Siegman, A. W., & Feldstein, S., eds. *Of Speech and Time*. Hillsdale, N.J.: Erlbaum, 211–224.
Button, Graham. 1987. Moving out of closings. In Button, Graham, & Lee, J. R. E., eds. *Talk and Social Organisation*. Clevedon (Avon): Multilingual Matters, 101–151.
Button, Graham, & Casey, N. 1985. Topic nomination and topic pursuit. In *Human Studies* 8, 3–55.
Camilli, A. 1965. *Pronuncia e grafia dell'italiano*. Firenze. Orig. pub., 1941.
Chapple, E. D. 1939. Quantitative analysis of the interaction of individuals. In *Proceedings of the National Academy of Science* 25, 58–67.
Chapple, E. D. 1980. The unbounded reaches of anthropology as a research science, and some working hypotheses. Distinguished lecture for 1979. In *American Anthropologist* 82(4), 741–758.

Classe, André. 1939. *The Rhythm of English Prose.* Oxford: Basil Blackwell.
Clayman, S. 1991. News interview openings: Aspects of sequential organization. In Scannell, Paddy, ed. *Broadcast Talk.* Newbury Park, Cal.: Sage, 48–76.
Condon, W. S. 1980. The relation of interactional synchrony to cognitive and emotional processes. In Key, M. R., ed. *The Relationship of Verbal and Nonverbal Communication.* The Hague: Mouton, 49–65.
Cook-Gumperz, Jenny, & Gumperz, John J. 1976. Context in children's speech. In *Papers on Language and Context. Working Paper No. 46*, Language Behavior Research Laboratory, Univ. of California at Berkeley.
Coseriu, Eugenio. 1969. Georg von der Gabelentz et la linguistique synchronique. Preface to reprint of von der Gabelentz 1891. Tübingen: Narr, 5–40.
Couper-Kuhlen, Elizabeth. 1990. Discovering rhythm in conversational English: perceptual and acoustic approaches to the analysis of isochrony. *KontRI Working Paper No. 13*, Univ. of Konstance, Fachgruppe Sprachwissenschaft.
Couper-Kuhlen, Elizabeth. 1992a. Metrical hierarchies and the rhythm of conversational English. *KontRI Working Paper No. 16*, Univ. of Konstance, Fachgruppe Sprachwissenschaft.
Couper-Kuhlen, Elizabeth. 1992b. Contextualizing discourse: The prosody of interactive repair. In Auer, P., & di Luzio, A., eds. *The Contextualization of Language.* Amsterdam: Benjamins, 337–364.
Couper-Kuhlen, Elizabeth. 1993. *English Speech Rhythm. Form and Function in Everyday Verbal Interaction.* Amsterdam: Benjamins.
Couper-Kuhlen, Elizabeth, & Auer, Peter. 1991. On the contextualizing function of speech rhythm in conversation: Question-answer sequences. In Verschueren, J., ed. *Levels of Linguistic Adaptation. Selected Papers of the 1987 International Pragmatics Conference.* Vol. II. Amsterdam: Benjamins, 1–18.
Couper-Kuhlen, Elizabeth, & Selting, Margret. 1996. Introduction. In Couper-Kuhlen, E., & Selting, M., eds. *Prosody in Conversation.* Cambridge: Cambridge Univ. Press, 11–56.
Cruttenden, A. 1986. *Intonation.* Cambridge: Cambridge Univ. Press.
Crystal, David. 1969. *Prosodic Systems and Intonation in English.* Cambridge: Cambridge Univ. Press.
Cutler, Anne, & Foss, Donald. 1977. On the analysis of prosodic turn-taking cues. In Johns-Lewis, C., ed. *Intonation in Discourse.* London: Croom Helm, 139–155.
Davidson, J. 1984. Subsequent versions of invitations, offers, requests, and proposals dealing with potential or actual rejection. In Atkinson, J. M., & Heritage, John, eds. *Structures of Social Action: Studies in Conversation Analysis.* Cambridge: Cambridge Univ. Press, 102–127.
Dauer, R. M. 1983. Stress-timing and syllable-timing reanalysed. In *Journal of Phonetics* 11, 51–62.
de Groot, A. W. 1932. Der Rhythmus. In *Neophilologus* 17, 81–100, 177–197, 241–265.
Delattre, Pierre. 1966. A comparison of syllable length conditioning among languages. In *International Review of Applied Linguistics*, 183–198.
Delattre, Pierre. 1969. An acoustic and articulatory study of vowel reduction in four languages. In *International Review of Applied Linguistics*, 295–325.
den Os, Els. 1988. *Rhythm and Tempo of Dutch and Italian.* Doctoral thesis, University of Utrecht.
de Saussure, Ferdinand. 1972. *Cours de linguistique générale.* Publié par Charles Bally, & Albert Sechehaye. Critical ed. Tullio de Mauro. Paris: Payot. Orig. pub., 1915.
di Luzio, Aldo. 1992. *Laudatio auf Professor John J. Gumperz aus Anlass der Verleihung des philosophischen Ehrendoktorats der Universität Konstanz.* ms. Univ. of Konstanze.

Docherty, G. J. 1992. *The Timing of Voicing in British English.* Berlin: Foris.
Donovan, A., & Darwin, C. J. 1979. The perceived rhythm of speech. In *Proceedings of the 9th International Congress of Phonetic Sciences.* Vol. II. Copenhagen, 268–274.
Drew, Paul, & Holt, Elisabeth. 1990. Complainable matters: the use of idiomatic expressions in making complaints. In Conein, B., et al., eds. *Les formes de la conversation.* Vol. I. Paris: cnet, 109–143.
Edwards, Viv, & Sienkewicz, Thomas J. 1990. *Oral Cultures Past and Present: Rappin' and Homer.* Cambridge: Blackwell.
Ehrenfels, C. 1890. Über Gestaltqualitäten. In *Vierteljahresschrift für wissenschaftliche Philosophie* 14, 249–292.
Erickson, Frederick. 1981. Money tree, lasagna bush, salt and pepper: Social construction of topical cohesion in a conversation among Italian Americans. In Tannen, ed. *Analyzing Discourse: Text and Talk.* Washington, D.C.: Georgetown Univ. Press, 43–70.
Erickson, Frederick. 1992. "They know all the lines": Rhythmic organization and contextualization in a conversational listing routine. In Auer, P., & di Luzio, A., eds. *The Contextualization of Language.* Amsterdam: Benjamins, 365–398.
Erickson, Frederick, & Shultz, Jeffrey. 1982. *The Counselor as Gatekeeper: Social Interaction in Interviews.* New York: Academic Press.
Ernout-Meillet, J. 1967. *Dictionnaire Étymologique de la Langue Latine.* Paris: Klincksieck.
Falk, J. L. 1980. *The Duet as a Conversational Process.* Ann Arbor, MI: Univ. Microfilms International.
Faure, G.; Hirst, D. J.; & Chafcouloff, M. 1980. Rhythm in English: Isochronism, pitch, and perceived stress. In Waugh, Linda R., & van Schooneveld, C. H., eds. *The Melody of Language.* Baltimore: Univ. Park Press, 71–79.
Finnegan, Ruth. 1992. *Oral Poetry.* 2d ed. Bloomington: Indiana Univ. Press. Orig. pub., 1977.
Fleischer, Wolfgang. 1982. *Phraseologie der deutschen Gegenwartssprache,* Leipzig.
Fowler, Carol A. 1979. "Perceptual centers" in speech production and perception. In *Perception and Psychophysics* 25, 375–386.
Fox, James J. 1988. Introduction. In Fox, James J., ed. *To Speak in Pairs.* Cambridge: Cambridge Univ. Press, 1–28.
Fraisse, Paul. 1974. *Psychologie du rythme.* Paris: Presses Universitaires de France.
Fraisse, Paul. 1982. Rhythm and tempo. In Deutsch, D. (ed.), *The Psychology of Music.* New York: Academic Press, 149–180.
French, P., & Local, John K. 1983. Turn-competitive incomings. In *Journal of Pragmatics* 7, 17–38.
Fromkin, Victoria A., & Rodman, Robert. 1988. *An Introduction to Language.* 4th ed. Fort Worth: Holt, Rinehart & Winston. Orig. pub., 1974.
Garfinkel, Harold, & Sacks, Harvey. 1970. On formal structures of practical actions. In McKinney, J. C., & Tiryakian, A., eds. *Theoretical Sociology.* New York: Appleton-Century-Croft, 337–366.
Goffman, Erving. 1955. On face-work. *Psychiatry* 18, 213–31.
Goffman, Erving. 1963. *Behavior in Public Places. Notes on the Social Organization of Gatherings.* New York: Free Press.
Goffman, Erving. 1967. *Interaction Ritual. Essays on Face-to-Face Behavior.* Garden City, N.Y.: Anchor Books, Doubleday.
Goffman, Erving. 1969. On face-work. In Goffman, E. *Where the Action Is. Three Essays.* London: Penguin, 3–36.
Goffman, Erving. 1971. *Relations in Public. Microstudies of the Public Order.* New York: Basic Books.
Goffman, Erving. 1981. *Forms of Talk.* Oxford: Basil Blackwell.

Goldsmith, John A. 1992. *Autosegmental and Metrical Phonology.* Oxford: Basil Blackwell.
Goldman-Eisler, Frieda. 1961. The rate of changes in the rate of articulation. In *Language and Speech* 4, 171–174.
Goodwin, Charles. 1986. Between and within: Alternative sequential treatments of continuers and assessments. In *Human Studies* 9, 205–217.
Goodwin, Charles, & Goodwin, M. Harness. 1987. Concurrent operations on talk: Notes on the interactive organization of assessments. In *IPRA Papers in Pragmatics* 1(1), 1–54.
Goodwin, M. Harness. 1982. Processes of dispute management among urban black children. In *American Ethnologist* 9, 76–96.
Goodwin, M. Harness. 1983. Aggravated correction and disagreement in children's conversations. In *Journal of Pragmatics* 7, 657–677.
Goodwin, Marjorie Harness, & Goodwin, Charles. 1986. Gesture and coparticipation in the activity of searching for a word. In *Semiotica* 62, 51–57.
Gumperz, John J. 1978. Dialect and conversational inference in urban communication. In *Language in Society* 7, 393–409. The role of dialect in urban communication. In *Zeitschrift für Dialektologie und Linguistik* (special issue), 318–335 (1980).
Gumperz, John J. 1982. *Discourse Strategies.* Cambridge: Cambridge Univ. Press.
Gumperz, John J. 1992. Contextualization and understanding. In Duranti, A., & Goodwin, C., eds. *Rethinking Context. Language as an Interpretive Phenomenon.* Cambridge: Cambridge Univ. Press. 229–252.
Gussenhoven, Carlos. 1991. The English Rhythm Rule as an accent deletion rule. In *Phonology* 8, 1–35.
Halliday, M. A. K. 1970. *A Course in Spoken English: Intonation.* Oxford: Oxford Univ. Press.
Hayes, B. P. 1995. *Metrical Stress Theory. Principles and Case Studies.* Chicago: Univ. of Chicago Press.
Heritage, John. 1984. *Garfinkel and Ethnomethodology.* Cambridge: Polity Press.
Heritage, John. 1984. A change-of-state token and aspects of its sequential placement. In Atkinson, J. M., & Heritage, J., eds. *Structures of Social Action. Studies in Conversational Analysis.* Cambridge: Cambridge Univ. Press, 95–119.
Heritage, John. 1985. Analyzing news interviews: Aspects of the production of talk for an "overhearing" audience. In Van Dijk, T., ed. *Handbook of Discourse Analysis.* Vol. 3: Discourse and Dialogue. London: Academic Press, 95–119.
Heritage, John, & Greatbatch, D. 1991. On the institutional character of institutional talk: The case of news interviews. In Boden, D., & Zimmerman, D. H., eds. *Talk and Social Structure. Studies in Ethnomethodology and Conversation Analysis.* Cambridge: Polity Press/ Basil Blackwell, 93–137.
Heritage, John, & Watson, Rodney. 1979. Formulations as conversational objects. In Psathas, George, ed. *Everyday Language: Studies in Ethnomethodology.* New York: Irvington Publishers, 123–162.
Hockett, Charles. 1958. *A Course in Modern Linguistics.* New York: Macmillan.
Hockett, Charles. 1963. The problem of universals in language. In Greenberg, J. H., ed. *Universals of Language.* Cambridge, Mass.: MIT Press, 1–29.
Hoequist, Charles, Jr., Kohler, Klaus J., & Schäfer-Vincent, K. 1986. Speech rate. Final report on a research project. In *Arbeitspapiere des Instituts für Phonetik,* Kiel No. 22, 7–28.
Hutchby, J. 1991. The organization of talk on talk radio. In Scannell, Paddy, ed. *Broadcast Talk.* Newbury Park, Ca.: Sage, 119–137.
Jacobs, S., & Jackson, S. 1981. Argument as a natural category: The routine grounds for arguing in conversation. In *The Western Journal of Speech Communication* 45, 118–132.
Jakobson, Roman. 1966. Grammatical parallelism and its Russian facet. In *Language* 42, 398–429.

Jakobson, Roman. 1971. Two aspects of language and two types of aphasic disturbances. In *Selected Writings*. Vol. II, 239–259. Orig. pub., 1956.
Jakobson, Roman. 1974. Über den tschechischen Vers. In *Postilla Bohemica* 8–10, 1–204. Orig. pub., 1923.
Jayyusi, Lena. 1984. *Categorization and Moral Order*. London: Routledge.
Jefferson, Gail. 1973. A case of precision timing in ordinary conversation: Overlapping tag-positioned address terms in closing sequences. In *Semiotica* 3, 47–96.
Jefferson, Gail. 1981. The abominable "Ne?": A working paper exploring the phenomenon of post-response pursuit of response. Occasional Paper No. 6, Department of Sociology, University of Manchester.
Jefferson, Gail. 1984. Notes on some orderliness of overlap onset. In D'Urso, V., & Leonardi, P., eds. *Discourse Analysis and Natural Rhetorics*. Padova: Cleup editore, 11–38.
Jefferson, Gail. 1986. Notes on "latency" in overlap onset. In *Human Studies* 9, 153–183.
Jefferson, Gail. 1987. On exposed and embedded correction in conversation. In Button, Graham, & Lee, J. R. E., eds. *Talk and Social Organization*. Clevedon: Multilingual Matters, 86–100.
Jefferson, Gail. 1989. Notes on a possible metric which provides for a "standard maximum" silence of approximately one second in conversation. In Roger, D., & Bull, P., eds. *Conversation: An Interdisciplinary Perspective*. Clevedon: Multilingual Matters, 166–196.
Jefferson, Gail. 1990. List-construction as a task and resource. In Psathas, G., ed. *Interaction Competence*. Latham, Md.: University Press of America, 63–92.
Jones, Mari Riess. 1986. Attentional rhythmicity in human perception. In Evans, J. R., & Clynes, M., eds. *Rhythm in Psychological, Linguistic and Musical Processes*. Springfield, Ill.: Charles C. Thomas, 13–40.
Kallmeyer, Werner, ed. 1996. *Gesprächsrhetorik. Rhetorische Verfahren im Gesprächsprozess*. Tübingen: Narr.
Kallmeyer, Werner, & Keim, Inken. 1994. Formelhaftes Sprechen in der "Filsbachwelt." In Kallmeyer, Werner, ed. *Kommunikation in der Stadt*. Berlin: de Gruyter, 250–317.
Kallmeyer, Werner, & Schmitt, R. 1996. Forcieren oder: Die verschärfte Gangart. In Kallmeyer, Werner, ed. *Gesprächsrhetorik: Rhetorische Verfahren im Gesprächsprozess*. Tübingen: Narr, 19–118.
Keim, Inken. 1996. Verfahren der Perspektiven abschottung und ihre Auswirkung auf dic Dynamik des Argumentierens. In Kallmeyer, Werner, ed. *Gesprächsrhetorik. Rhetorische Verfahren im Gesprächsprozess*. Tübingen: Narr, 198–278.
Kempton, Willett. 1980. The rhythmic basis of interactional micro-synchrony. In Key, Mary Ritchie, ed. *The Relationship of Verbal and Non-Verbal Communication*. The Hague: Mouton, 67–75.
Kendon, Adam. 1988. Goffman's approach to face-to-face interaction. In Drew, P., & Wootton, Antony, eds. *Erving Goffman. Exploring the Interaction Order*. Oxford: Polity Press, 14–40.
Kendon, Adam. 1990. Movement coordination in social interaction. In Kendon, A., ed. *Conducting Interaction*. Cambridge: Cambridge Univ. Press, 91–116. Orig. pub., 1970.
Kiparsky, Paul. 1975. Stress, syntax, and meter. In *Language* 51, 576–616.
Kiparsky, Paul, et al., eds. 1989. *Rhythm and Meter*. San Diego: Academic Press.
Klages, Ludwig. 1934. *Vom Wesen des Rhythmus*. Kampen auf Sylt: Kampmann.
Kohler, Klaus J. 1982. Rhythmus im Deutschen. In *Arbeitsberichte des Instituts für Phonetik der Universität*, Kiel (AIPUK) No. 19, 89–106.
Kohler, Klaus J. 1983. Stress-timing and speech rate in German. In *Arbeitsberichte des Instituts für Phonetik der Universität*, Kiel (AIPUK) No. 20, 55–97.

Komter, Martha. 1983. *A case of rhythm in coordinated simultaneous conversations*. ms. Amsterdam: Instituut voor Algemen Taalwetenschap, Univ. of Amsterdam.
Kotthoff, Helga. 1993. Disagreement and concession in disputes: On the context sensitivity of preference structures. In *Language in Society* 22, 193–216.
Kuiper, K., & Haggo, Douglas. 1984. Livestock auctions, oral poetry and ordinary language. In *Language in Society* 13(2), 205–234.
Labov, William. 1972. Rules for ritual insults. In Sudnow, D., ed. *Studies in Social Interaction*. New York: Free Press, London: Collier-MacMillan, 120–169.
Labov, William, & Waletzky, J. 1967. Narrative analysis: Oral versions of personal experience. In Helm, J., ed. *Essays on the Verbal and Visual Arts*. Seattle: Univ. of Washington Press, 12–44.
Lausberg, Heinrich. 1967. *Elemente der literarischen Rhetorik*. München: Hueber.
Lehiste, Ilse. 1970. *Suprasegmentals*. Cambridge, Mass.: MIT Press.
Lehiste, Ilse. 1973. Rhythmic units and syntactic units in production and perception. In *Journal of the Acoustic Society of America* 54, 1228–1234.
Lehiste, Ilse. 1977. Isochrony reconsidered. In *Journal of Phonetics* 5, 253–263.
Lerdahl, Fred, & Jackendoff, Ray. 1982. A grammatical parallel between music and language. In Clynes, M., ed. *Music, Mind and Brain. The Neuropsychology of Music*. New York, London: Plenum Press, 83–117.
Lerdahl, Fred, & Jackendoff, Ray. 1983. *A Generative Theory of Tonal Music*. Cambridge, Mass.: MIT Press
Lerner, Gene. 1987. *Collaborative Turn Sequences: Sentence construction and social action*. Unpublished doctoral dissertation. Univ. of California, Irvine.
Lerner, Gene. 1991. On the syntax of sentences-in-progress. In *Language in Society* 20, 441–458.
Levinson, Stephen C. 1983. *Pragmatics*. Cambridge: Cambridge Univ. Press.
Lord, Albert Bates. 1960. *The Singer of Tales*. Cambridge, Mass.: Harvard Univ. Press.
Lyons, John. 1968. *Linguistics*. Cambridge: Cambridge Univ. Press.
Marotta, Giovanna. 1985. *Modelli e misure ritmiche: la durata vocalica in italiano*. Bologna: Zanichelli.
Martin, J. G. 1972. Rhythmic (hierarchical) versus serial structure in speech and other behavior. In *Psychological Review* 79, 487–509.
Maynard, Douglas W. 1980. Placement of topic changes in conversation. In *Semiotica* 30(3–4), 262–290.
Meschonnic, H. 1982. Qu'entendez-vous par oralité? In *Langue française* 56 (Special Issue), 6–23.
Moritz, Karl Ph. 1973. *Versuch einer deutschen Prosodie*. Darmstadt. Orig. pub. 1776.
Morton, J.; Marcus, S.; & Frankish, C. 1976. Perceptual centers. In *Psychological Review* 83, 405–409.
Müller, Frank E. 1988. Uncodified code: A look at some properties of the dialects of Sicily and a presentation of one speaker. In Auer, P., & di Luzio, A., eds. *Variation and Convergence*. Berlin: de Gruyter, 175–193.
Müller, Frank E. 1989a. Rhythmische Alternation im Italienischen. *KontRI Working Paper No. 10*, Univ. of Konstance, Fachgruppe Sprachwissenschaft.
Müller, Frank E. 1991. Metrical emphasis—Rhythmic scansions in Italian conversation. *KontRI Working Paper No. 14*, Univ. of Konstance, Fachgruppe Sprachwissenschaft.
Müller, Frank E. 1993. Rhythmus in formulaischen Paradigmen der Alltagssprache. In *Zeitschrift für Literaturwissenschaft und Linguistik* 24/96, 53–77.
Müller, Frank E., 1995, Trilogue et 'double articulation' de la conversation radiophonique. In Kerbrat-Orecchioni, Ch., & Plantin, Ch., eds. *Le trilogue*. Lyon: Presses Universitaires de Lyon, 201–224.

Müller, Frank E., & di Luzio, Aldo. 1995. Stories as examples in everyday argument. In *Versus* 70/71, 115–145.
Müller, Klaus, 1992, Theatrical moments: On contextualizing funny and dramatic moods in the course of telling a story in conversation. In Auer, P., & Di Luzio, A., eds. *The Contextualization of Language*. Amsterdam: Benjamins, 199–222.
Nespor, Marina, & Vogel, Irene. 1989. On clashes and lapses. In *Phonology* 6, 69–116.
Nooteboom, Lieb. 1997. The prosody of speech: Melody and Rhythm. In Hardcastel, W. J. & Laver, J., eds. *The Handbook of Phonetic Science*. London: Bradewell, 640–673.
Owen, M. 1983. *Apologies and Remedial Interchanges: A Study of Language Use in Social Interaction*. Berlin: Mouton.
Panese, Marcello. 1992. Calling in sequential and prosodic aspects of openings in radio-talk. *KontRI Working Paper No. 20*, Univ. of Konstance, Fachgruppe Sprachwissenschaft.
Panese, Marcello. 1996. Calling in prosody and conversation in radio-talk. In *Pragmatics* 6, 19–87.
Parry, Milman. 1930. Studies in the epic technique of oral verse-making. I: Homer and Homeric style. In *Harvard Studies in Classical Philology* 41, 73–147.
Parry, Milman. 1932. Studies in the epic technique of oral verse-making. II: The Homeric language as the langauge of an oral poetry. In *Harvard Studies in Classical Philology* 43, 1–50.
Paul, Otto, & Glier, Ingeborg. 1970. *Deutsche Metrik*. 8th ed. München: Hueber. Orig. pub., 1961.
Payne, M. C., Jr., & Holzmann, Th. G. 1986. Rhythm as a factor in memory. In Evans, J. R., & Clynes, M. (eds.), *Rhythm in Psychological, Linguistic and Musical Processes*. Springfield, Ill.: Charles C. Thomas, 41–54.
Pelose, Gina C. 1987. The functions of behavioral synchrony and speech rhythm in conversation. In Sigman, S. J., ed. *Multichannel Communication Codes*. Part I: Research on Language and Social Interaction, No. 20, 171–220.
Pike, Kenneth. 1945. *The Intonation of American English*. Ann Arbor: Univ. of Michigan Press.
Pomerantz, Anita. 1978. Compliment responses: Notes on the cooperation of multiple constraints. In Schenkein, J., ed. *Studies in the Organization of Conversational Interaction*. New York: Academic Press, 79–112.
Pomerantz, Anita. 1980. Telling my side: "Limited access" as a "fishing" device. In *Sociological Inquiry* 50, 186–198.
Pomerantz, Anita. 1984. Agreeing and disagreeing with assessments: Some features of preferred/dispreferred turn shapes. In Atkinson, J. M., & Heritage, J., eds. *Structures of Social Action. Studies in Conversational Analysis*. Cambridge: Cambridge Univ. Press, 57–101.
Pomerantz, Anita. 1986. Extreme case formulations: A way of legitimizing claims. In *Human Studies* 9, 219–229.
Pompino-Marschall, Bernd. 1989. On the psychoacoustic nature of the P-center phenomenon. In *Journal of Phonetics* 17, 175–192.
Rosenfeld, Howard M. 1981. Whither interactional synchrony? In Bloom, K., ed. *Prospective Issues in Infancy Research*. Hillsdale, N.J.: Erlbaum, 71–97.
Sacks, Harvey. 1971. *Lectures on Storytelling in Conversation*. Mimeo. Univ. of California at Irvine.
Sacks, Harvey; Schegloff, Emanuel; & Jefferson, Gail. 1974. A simplest systematics for the organization of turn-taking for conversation. In *Language* 50, 696–735.
Saran, Franz. 1907. *Deutsche Verslehre*. München: Beck.
Scannell, Paddy, ed. 1991a. *Broadcast Talk*. Newbury Park, Ca.: Sage.

Scannell, Paddy. 1991b. Introduction to Scannell, P. ed. *Broadcast Talk*. Newbury Park, Ca.: Sage, 1–13.
Schegloff, Emanuel A. 1972. Sequencing in conversational openings. In Gumperz, J. J., & Hymes, D., eds. *Directions in Sociolinguistics. The Ethnography of Communication*. New York: Holt, Rinehart & Winston, 346–380.
Schegloff, Emanuel A. 1980. Preliminaries to preliminaries: "Can I ask you a question?". In *Sociological Inquiry*, 104–152.
Schegloff, Emanuel A. 1982. Discourse as an interactional achievement: Some uses of "uh huh" and other things that come between sentences. In Tannen, D., ed. *Analyzing Discourse: Text and Talk*. Washington, D.C.: Georgetown Univ. Press, 71–93.
Schegloff, Emanuel A. 1984. On some gestures' relation to talk. In Atkinson, J. M., & Heritage, J., eds. *Structures of Social Action. Studies in Conversational Analysis*. Cambridge: Cambridge Univ. Press, 266–296.
Schegloff, Emanuel A. 1988. On an actual virtual servo-mechanism for guessing bad news: A single case conjecture. In *Social Problems* 35, 442–457.
Schegloff, Emanuel A. 1996. Turn organization. One intersection of grammar and interaction. In Ochs, E.; Schegloff, E.; & Thompson, S., eds. *Interaction and Grammar*. Cambridge: Cambridge Univ. Press, 52–133.
Schegloff, Emanuel A.; Jefferson, Gail; & Sacks, Harvey. 1977. The preference for self-correction in the organization of repair in conversation. In *Language* 53, 361–382.
Schegloff, Emanuel A., & Sacks, Harvey. 1973. Opening up closings. *Semiotica* 8, 289–327.
Schiffrin, D. 1986. Everyday argument: The organization of diversity in talk. In Van Dijk, T., ed. *Handbook of Discourse Analysis*. Vol. 3: Discourse and Dialogue. London: Academic Press, 35–46.
Scollon, Ron. 1981. *Tempo, density, and silence: Rhythms in ordinary talk*. ms. Univ. of Alaska at Fairbanks.
Scollon, Ron. 1982. The rhythmic integration of ordinary talk. In Tannen, D., ed. *Analyzing Discourse: Text and Talk*. Washington, D.C.: Georgetown Univ. Press, 335–349.
Séguinot, Candace. 1979. A phonostylistic study of rhythm in English. In Léon, P., & Rossi, M., eds. *Problèmes de prosodie*. Ottawa: Didier, 149–157.
Selkirk, Elizabeth O. 1984. *Phonology and Syntax: The Relation between Sound and Structure*. Cambridge, Mass.: MIT Press.
Selting, Margret. 1987. Reparaturen und lokale Verstehensprobleme, oder: Zur Binnenstruktur von Reparatursequenzen. In *Linguistische Berichte* 108, 128–149.
Selting, Margret. 1988. The role of intonation in the organization of repair and problem handling sequences in conversation. In *Journal of Pragmatics* 12, 293–322.
Selting, Margret. 1989. Konstitution und Veränderung von Sprechstilen als Kontextualisierungsverfahren. Die Rolle von Sprachvariation und Prosodie. In Hinnenkamp, V., & Selting, M., eds. *Stil und Stilisierung. Arbeiten zur interpretativen Soziolinguistik*. Tübingen: Niemeyer, 203–225.
Selting, Margret. 1992a. Phonologie der Intonation. Probleme bisheriger Modelle und Konsequenzen einer neuen interpretativ-phonologischen Analyse. In *Zeitschrift für Sprachwissenschaft* 1, 99–138.
Selting, Margret. 1992b. Intonation as a contextualization device: Case studies on the role of prosody, especially intonation, in contextualizing story telling in conversation. In Auer, P., & di Luzio, A., eds. *The Contextualization of Language*. Amsterdam: Benjamins, 233–258.
Selting, Margret. 1994. Emphatic (speech) style—with special focus on the prosodic signalling of heightened emotive involvement in conversation. In *Journal of Pragmatics* 22, 375–468.

Selting, Margret. 1995. *Prosodie im Gespräch. Aspekte einer interpretativen Phonologie der Konversation.* Tübingen: Niemeyer.

Silverstein, Michael. 1976. Shifters, linguistic categories and cultural description. In Basso, K. (ed.), *Meaning in Anthropology.* Albuquerque: Univ. of New Mexico Press, 11–56.

Silverstein, Michael. 1992. The indeterminacy of contextualization: when is enough enough? In Auer, P., & di Luzio, A., eds. *The Contextualization of Language.* Amsterdam: Benjamins, 55–76.

Simonelli, Giorgio, & Taggi, Paolo. 1985. *Il fantasmi del dialogo: Il telefono nella radio e nella televisione.* Roma: Bulzoni.

Sonnenschein, E. A. 1925. *What Is Rhythm?* Oxford: Basil Blackwell.

Steele, Joshua. 1775. *An Essay Towards Establishing the Melody and Measure of Speech.* Reprint: Menston: The Scholar Press, 1969.

Stern, William L. 1900. Das psychische Tempo. In *Über Psychologie der individuellen Differenzen.* Leipzig: Barth.

Tannen, Deborah. 1984. *Conversational Style,* Norwood, N.J.: Ablex.

Tedlock, Dennis. 1981. Phonography and the problem of time in oral narrative events. *Working Paper No. 107,* Centro Internazionale di Semiotica e di Linguistica, Urbino.

Trubetzkoy, Nikolaus. 1956. *Grundzüge der Phonologie.* Göttingen: Vandenhoeck & Ruprecht. Orig. pub., 1939.

Tuller, B., & Fowler, C. A. 1980. Some articulatory correlates of perceptual isochrony. In *Perception and Psychophysics* 24, 277–283.

Uhmann, Susanne. 1992. Contextualizing relevance: On some forms and functions of speech rate changes in everyday conversation. In Auer, P., & di Luzio, A., eds. *The Contextualization of Language.* Amsterdam: Benjamins, 297–336.

Urban, Greg. 1986. Semiotic functions of macro-parallelism in the Shokleng Origin Myth. In Sherzer, J., & Urban, G., eds. *Native South American Discourse.* Berlin: Mouton de Gruyter, 15–58.

van Os, Charles. 1989. *Aspekte der Intensivierung im Deutschen.* Tübingen: Narr.

Vayra, M.; Avesani, C.; & Fowler, C. A. 1984. Patterns of temporal compression in spoken Italian. In van den Broecke, M. P. R., & Cohen, Anthony, eds. *Proceedings of the 10th International Congress of the Phonetic Sciences.* Dordrecht: Foris, 541–546.

Visch, E. 1989. *A Metrical Theory of Rhythmic Stress Phenomena.* Dordrecht: Foris.

Vogel, Irene, & Scalise, Sergio. 1982. Secondary stress in Italian. In *Lingua* 58, 213–242.

Voloshinov, V. N. 1926. Slovo v žizni i slovo v poèzii: k voprosom sociologičeskoj poètiki. In *Zvezda* 6, 244–267. English translation: Discourse in life and discourse in art (concerning sociological poetics). Appendix I of: V. N. Voloshinov, *Freudianism—A Marxist Critique.* New York: Academic Press, 93–116.

Voßler, Karl. 1904. *Positivismus und Idealismus in der Sprachwissenschaft.* Heidelberg: K. Winter.

von der Gabelentz, Georg. 1901. *Die Sprachwissenschaft, ihre Aufgaben, Methoden und bisherigen Ergebnisse.* 2d ed. Leipzig: Weigel. Orig. pub., 1891.

von Humboldt, Wilhelm. 1836. *Über die Kawi-Sprache auf der Insel Java, nebst einer Einleitung über die Verschiedenheit des menschlichen Sprachbaus und ihren Einfluß auf die geistige Entwicklung des Menschengeschlechts.* Abhandlungen der königlichen Akademie der Wissenschaften zu Berlin. Aus dem Jahre 1832. Part II. Berlin.

Vuchinich, S. 1984. Sequencing and social structure in family conflict. In *Social Psychology Quarterly* 47(3), 217–234.

Vuchinich, S. 1990. The sequential organization of closing in verbal family conflict. In Grimshaw, A. D., ed. *Conflict Talk: Sociolinguistic Investigations of Arguments in Conversations,* Cambridge: Cambridge Univ. Press, 118–138.

Wegener, Philipp. 1885. *Untersuchungen über die Grundfragen des Sprachlebens.* Halle, Niemeyer.
Wierzbicka, Anna. 1986. Italian reduplication: Cross-cultural pragmatics and illocutionary semantics. In *Linguistics* 24, 287–315.
Woodbury, Anthony C. 1987. Rhetorical structure in a Central Alaskan Yupik Eskimo traditional narrative. In Sherzer, J., & Woodbury, Anthony C., eds. *Native American Discourse.* Cambridge: Cambridge Univ. Press, 176–239.
Woodrow, H. 1951. Time perception. In Stevens, S. S., ed. *Handbook of Experimental Psychology.* New York: Wiley, 1224–1236.
Wunderlich, Hermann. 1894. *Unsere Umgangsprache in der Eigenart ihrer Satzfügung.* Weimar/Berlin: E. Felber.
Wundt, Wilhelm. 1912. *Probleme der Völkerpsychologie.* Leipzig: Engelmann.
Zollna, Isabel. 1994. Der Rhythmus in der geisteswissenschaftlichen Forschung. Ein Überblick. In *Zeitschrift für Literaturwissenschaft und Linguistik* 24/96, 12–52.
Zimmerman, Don H. 1992. Achieving context: Openings in emergency calls. In Watson, Graham, & Seiler, Robert M., eds. 1992. *Text in Context. Contributions to Ethnomethodology.* Newbury Park, Ca.: Sage, 35–51.

INDEX

accelerandos, 204
accent
   secondary, 122–123
   strong, 39
   weak, 39
actions
   dispreferred, 112
   preferred, 108
activity
   report, 177
   sequences, 60–61
   type, 83
adjacency pair, 124, 129
afterthought, 162
agreement, 93
alliteration, 158, 169
anisochrony, 141–143, 148. *Also see* arrhythmicity; rythmic nonintegration
anticipated, 75
   onsets, 82, 99, 203. *Also see* beats, early
   timing, 50, 115
aphoristic formulation, 167
argumentation, 78, 91, 103, 206

argumentative
   assertions, 78
   discourse, 181
   questioning, 83
arrhythmicity, 21, 74. *Also see* anisochrony; rhythmic nonintegration
arsis, 153
assessments, 70, 93, 108, 112

beats, 25, 27, 31, 40
   clash, 157, 160
   early, 50, 56, 75–76, 80, 203. *Also see* anticipated onsets
   late, 50, 56, 83. *Also see* delayed onsets
   silent, 11, 12, 18, 48, 83, 87, 203
   syncopated, 25, 49–50, 75–76, 80, 99, 109, 137

chronography, 15
closings, 33, 67, 70, 116, 124, 137, 173, 185, 202, 204, 207
   canonical, 124–126
   contextualization of, 133–143
   extended, 126, 129–133, 135, 143
   foreshortening of, 125, 138, 148

closings (*continued*)
    German, 127, 133–143
    Italian, 128, 143–150
    moving out of, 141–143
    out-of-phase, 141
comparatio, 166
competence, 9
complaint, 160, 169, 170
compression, 118–121, 123
contextualization, 23, 27–28, 33, 55, 139, 153, 158, 160, 206
    cue, 57, 91, 108, 134, 136, 153, 160, 165, 202
contrastive
    pairs, 187–188, 190, 200
    structure, 199
conversation analysis, 22
conversational involvement, 18
conversational language, 123
counting terms, 169
credibility work, 160

decontextualization, 5
deixis, 5–6
delayed
    onsets, 71, 83, 86, 89, 91, 106–107, 111–112. *Also see* beats, delayed
    timing, 50, 115
denials, 81
density, 28–31
detemporalization, 3, 4–9
disagreement, 93, 95
dispreferred, 203
    actions, 112
    responses, 93, 98, 100, 113, 115
    seconds, 92
dueling, 163

emphasis, metrical, 153, 160
emphatic
    speech, 165, 171, 196, 205
    spelling, 168, 183, 218
ethnopoetics, 16, 170. *Also see* poetics
euphony, 11, 27, 31
extreme case formulation, 157, 158, 160, 162–163, 166–167, 170, 205

face, 88, 92, 102, 109, 113, 203
    preserving, 103
    threat, 85, 103, 115, 203, 206
    work, 151

farewells, 60, 129, 132–134, 138
focused encounters, 57–58
formulaic
    expressions, 167
    paradigms, 172, 186–195, 200, 206
    speech, 186
formulation, 175, 179, 183, 185, 190, 199, 205, 207

generic
    sentences, 198, 206
    statement, 196
genres, 152, 172
German, 118–120, 122–123
gestalt psychology, 7, 13–14
gestalts, rhythmic, 23–27, 31, 45, 48–49, 51, 54, 157f., 187, 195, 202, 204
Gestaltschluss, 187, 189, 191
gestures, 153
gradation, 166, 169
greeting, 65, 82, 185

hyperbole, 160, 167

idiomatic expressions, 160, 162
imperative, 168
indexicality, 153, 206
inferencing, 70, 87, 203
information processing, 15–16
informings, 104
    hot news, 104, 105, 107
    news, 203
instantiating, 154
instrumental measurement, 51
intonation, 156, 170
    boundary, 180
    calling, 176
    phrase, 45, 156, 160, 162, 168
isochrony, 12, 15f., 22, 24, 26, 39, 42, 56, 117–119, 121–123, 134–136, 138, 151
    perception of, 39, 46
    threshold of perception of, 14, 51, 53, 121, 123
isometrical pattern, 24, 40, 42, 52, 122–123, 147, 157, 162, 164, 204
Italian, 118–120, 122–123
itemization, 168, 217

kinaesthetics, 153

INDEX

language
  decontextualized, 10
  ideology, 4–6, 13
  as a tool, 5, 6
last word, 167
lexicon, 9
linearization, 7
line structures, 189
lists, 41, 58, 169–170, 191, 193, 199–200, 206
loudness, 160, 163f., 165, 180, 197

meter, 7, 12, 17, 25–26, 157
Metrical Phonology, 9–12, 44
micropauses, 43, 64, 182–183, 189, 203, 218
multiparty constellations, 154
music, 55
musical notation, 18–20

news inquiry, 177

onsets, 20. *Also see* anticipated onsets; delayed onsets
openings, 65, 70, 82, 175, 177, 185
oral display, 187
orality, 16–17
overlap, 160, 162, 191, 203
  nontransitional, 65
  transitional, 65
  See also simultaneous talk

pair-part formulas, 187
parallelism, 17f., 27, 206
  grammatical, 172, 191–192
  poetic, 189, 195
  same token, 187
pauses, 28, 48, 50, 63, 180, 197
P-center, 14, 53
performance, 152, 154, 158, 170, 172, 191, 205–206
  studies, 16–17, 33
poetics, 34, 175, 195, 206. *Also see* ethnopoetics
precision timing, 64
preclosing, 69, 124, 129–130, 132–134, 136, 139–140
preference, 92, 102, 202–203
  reversal, 96, 97
  structure, 33

preferred, 203
  actions, 108
  responses, 93, 97, 99, 115
problem
  of hearing, 109, 111, 112
  of understanding, 109
prominence, 37. *Also see* beat
prosody, 7, 59, 186, 192

questioning, 113
  argumentative, 83
  nonargumentative, 86, 91
questions, 72

rapid fading, 4
reflexivity, 153
relevance, 10, 29, 31
reluctance markers, 107, 112
repair, 57, 67, 192
  initiation, 89, 91, 109, 112
  interactive, 75
  other-, 77
  self-, 75, 90
responses. *See* preferred responses; dispreferred responses
rhetoric, 205
  Afro-American, 17
  of complaining, 168
  of everyday language, 152, 158
  radio, 172–174, 177, 180, 218
  and rhythmic well-formedness, 167, 190
rhythm
  abstract, 9–13
  as an affirmative gesture, 158–160
  in anthropology, 16–22
  coordination, 61
  interactional, 57, 61
  intersequential, 59
  intrasequential, 59
  kinaesthetic origin of, 153
  marked, 97, 108
  optimal, 14
  perception of, 13–14, 23, 48, 121, 123
  in psychology, 13–16
  as a survival strategy, 154, 163
  as a turn-exit technique, 195–200
  at turn transitions, 58
  units, 117
  unmarked, 97, 108, 112, 115

rhythmic
  analysis, 36, 50
  attending, 15–16
  coordination, 59
  follower, 61, 63
  grouping, 14
  integration, 58, 70, 74, 91, 97, 100, 102, 106, 107, 110, 111, 115, 151, 182, 186, 193, 200, 202, 203–204
  intervals, 25, 40–41, 48, 117, 121, 157, 162, 216
  leader, 61, 63, 186, 200
  markedness, 163
  nonintegration, 58, 74, 91, 97, 99, 115, 141–143, 148–151. *Also see* arrhythmicity; anisochrony
  pattern, 40
  perseveration, 158–159, 160
  tours de force, 156–158
rhythmicity, 36, 180, 185, 202, 204, 206
routine formulae, 151

scanning, 105
  a verse, 153
scansion, 16, 34, 152–171, 196, 205
simultaneous talk, dispreference, 151
sounding, 163
Spanish, 118–120
speech rate, 28–29, 153, 157, 162, 167. *Also see* tempo
staccato, 157
story-telling, 154–156, 158, 160–163
stress, 27, 31
  clashes, 11
  lexical, 37, 44
  main, 44
  maximalist use of, 157, 171
  secondary, 44
  sentence, 10
  shifts, 11–12, 44
  -timing, 117–118, 120–121, 123, 150
summons, 176, 185

syllable, 120–122
  anacrustic, 63–64
  post-tonic, 64
  stressed, 36
  -timing, 117–118, 120, 123
  unstressed, 63
synchrony, interactional, 14–15
syncopation. *Also see* beat, syncopated
syntagme, 8–9, 11

"telling my side," 177
tempo, 28–32, 45–46, 54, 63, 76, 150, 202, 204
  acceleration, 136–140. *Also see* accelerandos
  shifts, 47–48
thesis, 153
thetic acts, 158
topic, 30, 175–176
  nomination, 175–178, 185, 200
topical talk, 180, 182, 185
transcription, 35–36
transition relevance place, 56–57, 62, 195, 202. *Also see* turn transitions
trochaic, 158, 164
  mode, 157
  words, 157
turn
  construction, 152–171
  exit technique, 196
  extended, 153, 195–197, 200, 205–206
  onsets, 75
turn-taking, 33, 56, 202, 205
turn transitions, 21, 65
  integrated, 183
  marked, 203
  nonintegrated, 74

verse, 158, 189–191, 219
vowels, reduced, 120

withholding, 180
writing, 5